# Investigative Interviewing

# Investigative Interviewing
## Adopting a Forensic Mindset

John E. Grimes III, CFE, CFI

CRC Press
Taylor & Francis Group
Boca Raton London New York

CRC Press is an imprint of the
Taylor & Francis Group, an **informa** business

First edition published 2022
by CRC Press
2 Park Square, Milton Park, Abingdon, Oxon, OX14 4RN

and by CRC Press
6000 Broken Sound Parkway NW, Suite 300, Boca Raton, FL 33487-2742



CRC Press is an imprint of Informa UK Limited



*British Library Cataloguing-in-Publication Data*
A catalogue record for this book is available from the British Library

*Library of Congress Cataloging-in-Publication Data*
Names: Grimes, John E., III author.
Title: Investigative interviewing : adopting a forensic mindset / John E. Grimes III, CFE, CFI.
Description: First edition. | Milton Park, Abingdon, Oxon ; Boca Raton, FL : CRC Press, 2021. |
Includes bibliographical references and index. |
Summary: "Investigative Interviewing: Adopting a Forensic Mindset aims to promote legal and ethical investigative interview methods. Accordingly, possessing a forensic mindset should be the foundation that governs every aspect of an investigative interviewer's actions. Being a forensic professional-which includes the field of forensic interviewing-infers that one applies the highest standards in collecting, analyzing, preserving, and presenting evidence to a court of law or other tribunals. The term "investigative interview" with an interviewer's forensic mindset can be used to achieve all interview objectives, even obtaining truthful confessions that stand up to the scrutiny of the courts and public opinion. Key to this, the author contends, is eliminating the term "interrogation" and the confession-obtaining mindset it creates. In its place, the term "investigative interview" is used, promoting a forensic mindset to achieve desired interview objectives. What transpires during the interview must stand up to the scrutiny of the courts and public opinion. In this regard, due process, documenting the procedure, and practicing proven, effective techniques is paramount to getting to the truth-the ultimate goal of any investigation. The book includes a chapter dedicated to false confessions, due to is criticality and frequent occurrences of this. It continues with a discussion on the desired qualities of an investigative interviewer and strategies to break down barriers and gain trust with reluctant, uncooperative, and hostile interviewees. Proper report writing, an underrated key to any interview and investigation, is addressed in detail. Lastly. the book provides training on best practice interview steps and strategies to lead the interviewee to the truth that will stand up to the scrutiny of the courts and public opinion. Investigative Interviewing: Adopting a Forensic Mindset is well-suited as a textbook-outlining techniques and detailing all relevant case law concerning confessions- in addition to providing an Instructor's Manual with Test Bank and PowerPoint slides for professors to utilize in classroom instruction"—Provided by publisher.
Identifiers: LCCN 2021004768 (print) | LCCN 2021004769 (ebook) | ISBN 9780367771461 (hardback) |
ISBN 9780367771911 (paperback) | ISBN 9781003170150 (ebook)
Subjects: LCSH: Interviewing in law enforcement. | Forensic sciences.
Classification: LCC HV8073.3 .G66 2021 (print) | LCC HV8073.3 (ebook) | DDC 363.25/4—dc23
LC record available at https://lccn.loc.gov/2021004768
LC ebook record available at https://lccn.loc.gov/2021004769

ISBN: 978-0-367-77146-1 (hbk)
ISBN: 978-0-367-77191-1 (pbk)
ISBN: 978-1-003-17015-0 (ebk)

Typeset in Palatino
by codeMantra

*Dedication*

*To my wife and children who have indulged my passions with love and support*

# CONTENTS

## PART 2 The Human Factor

# PREFACE

Investigations, and therefore investigative interviews, should be conducted to find the truth and nothing but the truth. It is the ultimate objective of any legitimate investigation. An investigation should not be tainted by inaccuracy, bias, or coercive methods. A factually accurate and complete investigation is in society's best interest to ascertain the truth of the matter that is under investigation. Getting to the truth requires the investigation be conducted legally and ethically. The ends should not justify the means. The consequence of not finding the truth can be a setback. However, reaching a false conclusion based on incomplete, or more importantly, bias, or inaccurate information can be dire. An innocent person's livelihood, social standing, freedom, and life could be in jeopardy.

This book is well suited as it explores interviewee due process considerations and case law concerning confessions. Due to its criticality, there is a chapter dedicated to false confession hazards. In this regard, this book promotes the discontinuance of the word "interrogation" due to its negative connotation and its "confession obtaining mindset." In its place, the term "investigative interview" is used to achieve all interview objectives, including obtaining legal, ethical, and truthful confessions that stand up to the scrutiny of the courts and public opinion. This book stresses adopting a forensic mindset when conducting investigative interviews. Possessing a forensic mindset indicates that one applies the highest standards in collecting, analyzing, preserving, and presenting evidence in a court of law or other tribunals. Accordingly, possessing a forensic mindset should be the foundation that governs every aspect of an investigative interviewer's actions.

In addition to the due process section, this book provides insight into the "Human Factor," including the desired qualities an investigative interviewer should possess, understanding interviewees and offenders, and breaking down barriers and gaining trust with uncooperative, reluctant, and hostile interviewees. Additionally, this book provides instruction on the interview process, which begins when an investigator realizes that an individual needs to be interviewed and ends with preparing a Report of Interview. The interview instruction includes methods to lead an interviewee to the truth and persuasive strategies to seek legal, ethical, and truthful confessions.

To add context to the investigative interview instruction, this book includes a microexamination of a fictitious procurement fraud case, somewhat paralleling an actual case involving bid manipulation and kickbacks. The case study includes investigative activity, and six interviews captured in interviews notes or interview transcripts.

An Instructor's Manual with Test Bank and PowerPoint slides is available to qualified adopting professors for use in classroom instruction.

John E. Grimes III, MS, CFI, CFE

# AUTHOR

**John E Grimes III, MS CFE, CFI,** has over 45 years of law enforcement, criminal investigation, fraud examination, and teaching experience. John began his law enforcement career with the Baltimore City Police Department where he became a Detective in the Criminal Investigation Division (CID). Later, John joined the Amtrak Police Department (APD) and was appointed as a Special Agent with the Fraud and Organized Crime Unit. He was then promoted to Captain of the CID. In 1993, John joined the Amtrak Office of Inspector General/Office of Investigations. He held the positions of Special Agent, Supervisory Special Agent, and Regional Supervisory Special Agent. In 1999, John was appointed Chief Inspector. He retired from service in 2016.

John is a member of the Association of Certified Fraud Examiners (ACFE) and has been recognized as a Certified Fraud Examiner (CFE) since 1997. He is a Past President of the Maryland Chapter-ACFE (July 2013 to June 2015). During his term as President, the Maryland Chapter was the honored recipient of the 2015 ACFE Chapter of the Year Award. John was also the recipient of the Maryland Chapter-ACFE 2020 Fraud Fighter of the Year Award. Furthermore, John is recognized as a Certified Forensic Interviewer (CFI) by the Center for Interview Standards and Assessments, Ltd.

Since 2013, John has been an Adjunct Faculty member of the Forensic Studies and Forensic Investigation programs at Stevenson University located in Owings Mills, Maryland. There he developed and still teaches a graduate-level course on Investigative Interviewing. Additionally, John provides training and speaks on a variety of fraud topics, including Procurement Fraud and Fraud Prevention Strategies. Moreover, he provides investigative interviewing training to government, private, and professional organizations.

John holds an AA in Criminal Justice from The Community Colleges of Baltimore County, a BA in Business with an emphasis in Accounting from the Notre Dame of Maryland University, and an MS in Forensic Studies from Stevenson University. John is also a 1987 graduate of the New England Institute of Law Enforcement Management Command Training Center at Babson College.

John also served as a Division Staff Officer with the United States Coast Guard Auxiliary where he was recognized as an Instructor Specialist and a Marine Safety and Environmental Protection Specialist.

John has received numerous awards and commendations throughout his career, including the 2006 Amtrak President's Award for Valor due to his unit's effort in the Gulf Region in the aftermath of Hurricane Katrina, assisting with the Federal Law Enforcement response. He received the 2008 United States Coast Guard Flotilla 13-01 Auxiliarist of the Year and the 2011 United States Coast Guard Division 22 Marine Safety and Environmental Protection Award.

# Part 1

# *Due Process, The Foundation of Investigative Interviewing*

In the 13th century, English barons sought to limit King John's authority, petitioning him to grant certain liberties to be enjoyed by his subjects. The early agreements, and annulments of those agreements, eventually led to the historic Magna Carta, which bestowed rights on Englishmen. Among those rights was the concept of due process, a principle that protects individual life and liberty from a powerful and potentially abusive government. Simply put, due process equals fairness.

Six hundred years later and an ocean away, the Founding Fathers of the United States of America included the model of due process in the Bill of Rights to the United States Constitution, making it a foundation of American liberty. The intent, as in 13th-century England, was to protect individuals from an abusive government. The Fifth, Sixth, and Fourteenth Amendments provide individuals certain rights during a custodial questioning by government law enforcement agencies.

The concept of due process has made its way into other areas of society through union agreements and employment contracts. Due process is the foundation of the book *Investigative Interviewing*. Part 1 of this book includes the following chapters:

1. Due Process and Case Law
2. Interviewing Union Employees
3. Confessions
4. False Confessions

# 1

# *Due Process and Case Law*

## LEARNING OBJECTIVES

- To understand the concept of due process as included in the Bill of Rights of the United States Constitution.
- To identify and discuss the constitutional amendments that address an individual's due process rights.
- To explain the Supreme Court's reasoning behind the landmark *Miranda v. Arizona* case.
- To discuss government law enforcement's responsibility as it pertains to *Miranda.*
- To explain the ramifications if the *Miranda* ruling is violated.
- To identify what could cause an individual to believe they are in custody.
- To summarize the exceptions to *Miranda.*
- To explain the reasoning behind the rulings in *Garrity v. New Jersey* and *Kalkines v. United States.*
- To explain a government agency's options per *Garrity.*
- To identify the *Garrity* warnings.
- To explain a government agency's options per *Kalkines.*
- To identify the *Kalkines* warnings.

## INTRODUCTION

In the United States, due process is based on guarantees found in the Constitution's Bill of Rights, specifically, the Fifth, Sixth, and Fourteenth

Amendments. This chapter reviews case law that has shaped the conduct of investigative interviews by providing interviewees certain rights and establishing interviewer obligations.

## THE FIFTH, SIXTH, AND FOURTEENTH AMENDMENTS

The Fifth Amendment provides that no person should be compelled to be a witness against themselves. The Fifth Amendment reads:

> No person shall be held to answer for a capital, or otherwise infamous crime, unless on a presentment or indictment of a Grand Jury, except in cases arising in the land or naval forces, or in the Militia, when in actual service in time of War or public danger; nor shall any person be subject for the same offence to be twice put in jeopardy of life or limb; nor shall be compelled in any criminal case to be a witness against himself.

The right that, "no person shall be compelled in any criminal case to be a witness against himself," has been held by the U.S. Supreme Court to apply not just to a criminal trial, but also to questioning by the government. The Fifth Amendment privilege against self-incrimination is such a fundamental inherent right that its application has surfaced in certain workplace rules.

The Sixth Amendment guarantees the rights of the accused to have the assistance of counsel. The Sixth Amendment reads:

> In all criminal prosecutions, the accused shall enjoy the right to a speedy and public trial, by an impartial jury of the state and district wherein the crime shall have been committed, which district shall have been previously ascertained by law, and to be informed of the nature and cause of the accusation; to be confronted with the witnesses against him; to have compulsory process for obtaining witnesses in his favor, and to have the assistance of counsel for his defense.

The U.S. Supreme Court ruled in *Escobedo v. Illinois*, 378 U.S. 478 (1964), that per the Sixth Amendment, criminal suspects have a right to counsel during police interrogations. The Supreme Court has applied the protections of the Fifth and Sixth Amendments to the states through Section 1 of the Fourteenth Amendment known as the Due Process Clause. The Fourteenth Amendment was adopted in 1868. Section 1 reads:

> No state shall make or enforce any law which shall abridge the privileges or immunities of citizens of the United States; nor shall any state deprive any person of life, liberty, or property, without due process of law; nor deny to any person within its jurisdiction the equal protection of the laws.

Until the adoption of the Fourteenth Amendment in 1868, the federal courts were unable to dictate the evidentiary rules for the states. Most criminal cases were held in state courts. Each state developed its own rules and opinions regarding custodial questioning. Since the late 1800s, the U.S. Supreme Court has ruled and opined on various tactics utilized by law enforcement and due process rights of individuals subject to custodial questioning. The Court focused on the admissibility of a petitioner's statement or confession and if there were violations of due process rights.

The Fifth Amendment right against self-incrimination and the Sixth Amendment right to have the assistance of counsel during custodial questioning were established. However, the Court realized that some individuals might not be aware of or exercise these rights on their own volition. In 1966, the U.S. Supreme Court addressed this in the landmark case of *Miranda v. Arizona*, 384 U.S. 436 (1966).

## *MIRANDA*

In *Miranda*, the U.S. Supreme Court ruled that law enforcement must inform an individual that they are questioning of his or her constitutional right against self-incrimination per the Fifth Amendment. Also, as in *Escobedo*, the Court held that per the Sixth Amendment, an individual must be told of their right to have an attorney present during questioning. The case details and the Supreme Court ruling are as follows.

In 1963, Ernesto Miranda was arrested by the Phoenix, Arizona police and charged with rape, kidnapping, and murder. The police did not inform Miranda of his constitutional rights before being interrogated. During the 2-hour interrogation without an attorney present, Miranda confessed to committing the crimes. The prosecution's case was based entirely on Miranda's confession. Miranda was convicted of rape and kidnapping and sentenced to 20–30 years in prison. Miranda appealed to the Arizona Supreme Court, claiming that the police violated his constitutional rights in obtaining the confession. The Court disagreed and upheld the conviction.

Miranda appealed to the U.S. Supreme Court. In a 5-to-4 decision, the Court reversed the conviction. It ruled that the prosecution could not introduce Miranda's confessions as evidence due to the police not informing Miranda of his constitutional rights against self-incrimination and to have an attorney present during questioning. Ernesto Miranda was retried and convicted without the use of his confession.

The Court held that the Fifth Amendment privilege against self-incrimination is available outside of criminal court proceedings and serves to protect persons in all settings in which their freedom of action is curtailed in any significant way. The Court concluded that:

> Without proper safeguards, the process of in-custody interrogation of persons suspected or accused of crimes contains inherently compelling pressures which work to undermine the individual's will to resist and to compel him to speak where he would not otherwise do so freely. In order to combat these pressures and to permit a full opportunity to exercise the privilege against self-incrimination, the accused must be adequately and effectively apprised of his rights and the exercise of those rights must be fully honored.

The Sixth Amendment right to have an attorney present during custodial police questioning is also a fundamental right. Chief Justice Earl Warren wrote, the presence of an attorney during such questioning permits "the defendant under otherwise compelling circumstances to tell his story without fear, effectively, and in a way that eliminates the evils in the interrogation process."

The Court instructed that if the individual being questioned indicates in any manner and at any stage of the process that he or she wishes to consult with an attorney before speaking, there can be no questioning. In addition, if the individual indicates in any manner that he or she does not wish to be "interrogated," the police may not question him. The Court held that:

> The mere fact that he may have answered some questions or volunteered some statements on his own does not deprive him of the right to refrain from answering any further inquiries until he has consulted with an attorney and thereafter consents to be questioned.

The Court's ruling led to the formulation of what is known as the *Miranda* warnings, which must be recited to an individual in law enforcement custody prior to questioning:

- You have the right to remain silent.
- Anything said can be used against you in the court.
- You have the right to have an attorney present.
- If you cannot afford an attorney, one will be appointed by the court.

The Court offered that the defendant may waive these rights, provided that the waiver is made voluntarily, knowingly, and intelligently.

## Violations of *Miranda*

If a violation of *Miranda* occurs, any incriminating statement will be subject to suppression if the defendant files a motion. The Court held that the prosecution may not use statements, whether exculpatory or inculpatory, stemming from custodial interrogation of the defendant unless it demonstrates the use of procedural safeguards to secure the privilege against self-incrimination. However, the suppressed statement can be used to impeach the defendant's testimony. The rationale for this sanction stems from the "exclusionary rule," which applies to evidence obtained in violation of due process protections both in federal and state courts. Two exclusionary rule landmark cases are briefly discussed below.

In 1914, the U.S. Supreme Court heard the landmark case of *Weeks v. United States,* 232 U.S. 383 (1914), which dealt with a warrantless seizure of property. The Court held that the property was seized in violation of the Fourth Amendment right against unreasonable search and seizure. This set forth the exclusionary rule, which prohibits the admission of illegally obtained evidence in the federal court system.

The U.S. Supreme Court case, *Mapp v. Ohio,* 367 U.S. 643 (1961), was another landmark case in which the Court expanded the exclusionary rule to the state courts. The Court accomplished this by use of a principle known as "selective incorporation." This involved the incorporation of the provisions, as interpreted by the Court, of the Fourth Amendment which are applicable only to actions of the federal government into the Fourteenth Amendment's Due Process Clause, which is applicable to actions of the states.

The exclusionary rule is extended by The Fruit of the Poisonous Tree doctrine that makes evidence inadmissible if it was derived from evidence that was illegally obtained. As the metaphor suggests, if the evidential "tree" is tainted, so is its "fruit." The doctrine was established in 1920 in the U.S. Supreme Court case, *Silverthorne Lumber Co., Inc. v. United States*, 251 U.S. 385 (1920). The phrase "fruit of the poisonous tree" was coined by Justice Frankfurter in his 1939 opinion in the U.S. Supreme Court case, *Nardone v. United States*, 308 U.S. 338 (1939). Like the exclusionary rule itself, this doctrine is subject to three important exceptions. The evidence will not be excluded:

1. If it was discovered from a source independent of the illegal activity.
2. If its discovery was inevitable.
3. If there is attenuation between the illegal activity and the discovery of the evidence.

Unlike other illegally obtained evidence, the Fruit of the Poisonous Tree doctrine does not apply to *Miranda* violations. Therefore, other evidence obtained from a suppressed statement would be fully admissible.

## Custodial Questioning

The intention of *Miranda* is to protect individuals who are in custody and to equalize the vulnerabilities inherent in being detained. To determine if an individual is in custody, a reasonableness rule is applied. Some determining factors are obvious:

- If a law enforcement officer tells an individual that he or she is "under arrest."
- If freedom of movement was restrained to an extent associated with a formal arrest.
- If physical force is used to make an arrest.
- If the individual is handcuffed.

Other circumstances might not be so obvious:

- The individual is kept in a locked room.
- The interview room door is blocked preventing exit.
- Certain words spoken by the interviewer that could indicate the individual cannot leave.
- The interviewer's demeanor.
- Length of the questioning (based on circumstances and a reasonableness standard).
- Failure to tell the interviewee that he or she is not in custody and is free to leave at anytime.

If any of the above scenarios existed, then an individual may be able to articulate that they were in custody. In the private sector, an interviewer and organization can face serious consequences if an individual can successfully argue that they were in custody when questioned.

In contrast, the U.S. Supreme Court ruled what would not be considered custody. In *Oregon v. Mathiason*, 429 U.S. 492 (1977), the Court ruled that:

> If a suspect voluntarily comes to the station for questioning, is advised that he is not under arrest, and allowed to leave after the interview, he is not in custody or otherwise deprived of his freedom. The Miranda warning is not required. Miranda warnings are required only where there has been such a restriction on a person's freedom as to render him "in custody".

## Exceptions to *Miranda*

The Court ruled in several instances wherein the absence of the *Miranda* warnings being offered, statements to law enforcement could be admitted as evidence. One being exception is a spontaneous statement made by a defendant while in custody. Even though the defendant has not been provided the *Miranda* warnings or invoked the right to counsel and a lawyer is not yet present, the statement is admissible as evidence as long as the statement was not given in response to police questioning or other conduct by law enforcement likely to produce an incriminating response.

There is also a "public safety" exception to the requirement that the *Miranda* warnings be given before questioning: for example, if the defendant possesses information regarding the location of an unattended gun or there are other similar exigent circumstances that require protection of the public, the defendant may be questioned without warning, and any incriminating response will be admissible in evidence, *New York v. Quarles*, 467 U.S. 649 (1984).

In *Berkemer v. McCarty*, 468 U.S. 420 (1984), the Court held that routine traffic stops do not rise to the level of custody for the purpose of the *Miranda* ruling. In addition, the "curbside" questioning of a person can be conducted without the *Miranda* warning as long as the person is not subjected to "in-custody" treatment.

In addition, routine booking questions of an arrestee do not fall under *Miranda*. The booking officer is allowed to ask questions to obtain name, date of birth, and address without reciting the warnings.

## *Miranda* Application

When *Miranda* was first decided and became law, much of law enforcement complained the decision tied their hands when questioning suspects. However, law enforcement adapted. The impact of *Miranda* was not lost on Hollywood. Many police television shows or movies had an officer reciting the *Miranda* warnings, often as they were wrestling with a suspect and putting on handcuffs. Of course, since reality mimicked fantasy, actual police officers would do the same. It made no difference if the arrestee was being questioned or not.

In the early 1970s, officers were taught that once a person became the focus of an investigation, the *Miranda* warnings must be offered before questioning, even if the individual was not in custody or detained. It later became clear that *Miranda* applied to individuals who were arrested, in custody, or otherwise not free to leave in a significant way. Law enforcement agencies had *Miranda* warning cards and forms printed. Officers would read the warnings from the card so they could articulate to a court that they were correctly read. Forms were used so the person in custody could read the *Miranda* warnings and sign the form indicating they voluntarily, knowingly, and intelligently waived their rights and agreed to be questioned without an attorney present.

## Challenges to *Miranda*

In 1968, Congress passed a law that overruled *Miranda* as part of the Omnibus Crime Control and Safe Streets Act of 1968. This statute directed federal judges to admit voluntary statements of criminal defendants without regard to whether the *Miranda* warnings were issued. The law only applied to federal criminal proceedings and criminal proceedings in the District of Columbia. The law was tested with the U.S. Supreme Court case, *Dickerson v. United States*, 530 U.S. 428 (2000).

Charles Dickerson had been arrested for bank robbery and for using a firearm during a crime of violence, both of which were federal crimes. He moved to suppress statements he made to the FBI because he had not received the *Miranda* warnings before being questioned. The District Court suppressed the statements, and so the government appealed. The Fourth Circuit reversed the District Court, reasoning that the 1968 Congressional law supplanted the requirement that the police give the *Miranda* warnings because *Miranda* was not a constitutional requirement. The Supreme Court held in a 7-to-2 split that the *Miranda* warnings have become part of the "national culture." The Court held that *Miranda* was constitutional, and that Congress cannot overrule it, because the Court alone is the final arbiter of what the Constitution requires.

## PUBLIC EMPLOYEE DUE PROCESS

The Supreme Court case, *Garrity v. New Jersey*, 385 U.S. 493 (1967), and the United States Court of Claims case, *Kalkines v. United States*, 473 F.2d 1391 (Fed. Cir. 1973), safeguard the Fifth Amendment rights of government employees involved in internal investigations.

### *Garrity*

*Garrity* involved a group of New Jersey police officers who were being investigated by the State Attorney General for ticket fixing. Edward Garrity, the Police Chief, and other officers were interviewed by a Deputy Attorney General who warned them that anything they said might be used against them in a criminal proceeding. He also warned the officers that they could refuse to answer questions if their statements would be incriminating; however, the refusal to answer questions would automatically lead to termination pursuant to state law. Garrity signed a "waiver of immunity." In doing so, he agreed that any statements he made could in fact be used against him in a criminal prosecution. Subsequently, Garrity did make incriminating statements, which led to his conviction in the state court.

A Supreme Court majority reversed the conviction. In delivering the majority opinion, Justice Douglas wrote that:

> The choice imposed on petitioners was one between self-incrimination or job forfeiture. We think the statements were infected by the coercion inherent in this scheme of questioning and cannot be sustained as voluntary.

In this decision, the Court held that public employees are not required to forfeit their privilege not to incriminate themselves granted under the Fifth and Fourteenth Amendments of the Bill of Rights.

In establishing the public sector due process nexus, the Supreme Court majority in Garrity referred to the previous case of *Slochower v. Board of Education*, 350 U.S. 551 (1956), wherein the Court ruled that a public-school teacher could not be terminated for invoking his Fifth Amendment privilege against self-incrimination when questioned by a Congressional committee. The Court concluded that police officers, like teachers and lawyers, are not "relegated to a watered-down version of constitutional rights." Two similar-issue Supreme Court decisions followed: *Gardner v. Broderick*, 392 U.S. 273 (1968), and *Uniformed Sanitation Men Association, Inc. v. Commissioner of Sanitation of the City of New York*, 426 F.2d 619 (2d Cir. 1970), both of which reaffirmed *Garrity*.

As a result of the Court's decision, it is recommended that local, state, and federal law enforcement officers cite a variation of the following warnings to protect the employee's constitutional right against self-incrimination:

- You are being asked to provide information as part of an internal and/or administrative investigation.
- This is a voluntary interview and you do not have to answer questions if your answers would tend to implicate you in a crime.
- No disciplinary action will be taken against you solely for refusing to answer questions. However, the evidentiary value of your silence may be considered in administrative proceedings as part of the facts surrounding your case.
- Any statement you do choose to provide may be used as evidence in criminal and/or administrative proceedings.

The above warnings are provided to an employee or a contractor when the agency does not want to forgo the option to seek criminal prosecution, if warranted. The agency is not obligated to provide this warning if the interviewee is voluntarily providing information. However, the burden is on the agency to show that the interview was in fact voluntary if information provided by the interviewee later leads to a criminal prosecution. If an agency policy requires an individual to cooperate with agency investigators and appear for an interview, then by default any statement can be considered not voluntary but compelled.

## *Kalkines*

George Kalkines, a U.S. Bureau of Customs employee, was the subject of an internal investigation for accepting a bribe in the performance of his duties. Concurrently, Kalkines was the subject of a criminal investigation by the U.S. Attorney's office for the same bribery allegation. The Customs investigators did not inform Kalkines that he had a constitutional right to remain silent. He was advised of the Department's regulation, which required him to cooperate and truthfully answer questions. However, the investigators did not advise Kalkines that if he did make incriminating statements, the statements and fruits would not be used against him in a criminal proceeding.

Kalkines became aware of the parallel U.S. Attorney criminal investigation, and so during one interview, he requested a delay to obtain the services of an attorney. The Bureau of Customs cited this delay in its determination that Kalkines was not cooperating with the internal investigation. It became one of the counts that led to his termination. The Court ruled that Kalkines' termination was not valid, and he was entitled to recover lost wages. In reaching its opinion, the Court cited *Sanitation Men*, *Gardner*, and *Garrity*. If an agency wants to compel a federal employee to provide information in an administrative investigation and close off any criminal prosecutorial avenue, the employee must be advised of their rights. The *American Federation of Government Employees Local 704* (American Federation) identified the warnings as follows:

- You are being questioned as part of an internal and/or administrative investigation.
- You will be asked a number of specific questions concerning your official duties, and you must answer these questions to the best of your ability.
- Failure to answer completely and truthfully may result in disciplinary action, including dismissal.
- Your answers and any information derived from them may be used against you in administrative proceedings. However, neither your answers nor any information derived from them may be used against you in criminal proceedings, except if you knowingly and willfully make false statements.

The wording of these warnings may vary between federal agencies. As an investigator with the Amtrak Office of Inspector General, the author was involved in many investigations where *Kalkines* applied. Investigators usually determined the decision to relinquish prosecution and seek administrative remedies in consultation with investigative counsel and supervision. In addition, before proceeding with the use of the *Kalkines* warnings, the investigator would normally discuss the case with the Assistant United States Attorney (AUSA) and seek a formal declination of prosecution. At this point, the AUSA would strategize with the investigators to ensure that the decision is the right one. Once the *Kalkines* warnings are provided, the compelled statement or any fruits of the compelled statement cannot be used in a criminal trial. Any independent evidence used in a criminal proceeding creates a "heavy burden" for the prosecution to prove that this evidence was not the result of the compelled statement.

## SUMMARY

Case law protecting interviewee rights guaranteed by the Fifth, Sixth, and Fourteenth Amendments of the U.S. Constitution governs the conduct of investigative interviews. The landmark *Miranda v. Arizona* case resulted in law enforcement's obligation to inform an individual in custody of their right against self-incrimination prior to questioning. In this regard, it is important for interviewers to identify what constitutes custody. Additionally, two pertinent cases, *Garrity* and *Kalkines*, resulted in public employees' and government contractors' rights against self-incrimination during investigative interviews, as well as requirements and guidelines for investigators conducting the interviews.

## EXERCISE 1.1. MULTIPLE CHOICE AND TRUE AND FALSE

1. The U.S. constitutional amendment that guarantees the rights of the accused to have the assistance of counsel is:

   _____ Fifth
   _____ Sixth
   _____ Fourteenth
   _____ Sixteenth

2. The U.S. constitutional amendment that provides that no person should be compelled to be a witness against themselves is:

   _____ Fifth
   _____ Sixth
   _____ Fourteenth
   _____ Sixteenth

3. The U.S. constitutional amendment that applies the protections of the Fifth and Sixth Amendments to the states is:

   _____ Fourth
   _____ Sixth
   _____ Fourteenth
   _____ Sixteenth

4. The length of questioning could be a factor in determining if an interviewee is in custody.

   _____ True
   _____ False

5. If an interviewer is situated between the interviewee and the only door in the room, an interviewee could argue that they were in custody.

   _____ True
   _____ False

6. *Miranda, Garrity,* and *Kalkines* involve an individual's rights against self-incrimination.

   ____ True
   ____ False

7. The *Miranda* warnings must be provided to custodial and noncustodial interviewees before questioning.

   ____ True
   ____ False

8. *Miranda* applies to both government and private sector interviewers.

   ____ True
   ____ False

9. If an individual in custody waives his rights under *Miranda,* they cannot later change their mind and invoke their rights.

   ____ True
   ____ False

10. Besides government employees, *Garrity* affects private contractors doing business with the government.

    ____ True
    ____ False

## EXERCISE 1.2. ESSAY TOPICS

1. Discuss the reasoning behind the Supreme Court ruling in *Miranda v. Arizona.*
2. Discuss the reasoning behind the Supreme Court ruling in *Garrity v. New Jersey.*
3. Identify a government agency's responsibility if it does not want to forgo an option to seek criminal prosecution of an employee that is interviewed.
4. Provide what is required of a government agency if it wants to compel an employee to provide information in an administrative investigation per *Kalkines.*
5. Identify the factors that could cause a reasonable person to believe that they are in custody.
6. Relate what steps an interviewer can take to create a noncustodial interview environment.

## REFERENCES

*Berkemer v. McCarty,* 468 U.S. 420 (1984).
*Dickerson v. United States,* 530 U.S. 428 (2000).
*Escobedo v. Illinois,* 378 U.S. 478 (1964).
*Gardner v. Broderick,* 392 U.S. 273 (1968).
*Garrity v. New Jersey,* 385 U.S. 493 (1967).
*Kalkines v. United States,* 473 F.2d 1391 (Fed. Cir. 1973).
*Mapp v. Ohio,* 367 U.S. 643 (1961).
*Miranda v. Arizona,* 384 U.S. 436 (1966).
*Nardone v. United States,* 308 U.S. 338 (1939).
*New York v. Quarles,* 467 U.S. 649 (1984).
*Oregon v. Mathiason,* 429 U.S. 492 (1977).
*Silverthorne Lumber Co., Inc. v. United States,* 251 U.S. 385 (1920).
*Slochower v. Board of Education,* 350 U.S. 551 (1956).
The American Federation of Government Employees Local 704, afgelocal704.org/your-rights/kalkines-warning. Federal Labor Relations Authority, Web, 19 October 2020, www.flra.gov.
*Uniformed Sanitation Men Association, Inc. v. Commissioner of Sanitation of the City of New York,* 426 F.2d 619 (2d Cir. 1970).
*Weeks v. United States,* 232 U.S. 383 (1914).

# 2

# *Interviewing Union Employees*

## LEARNING OBJECTIVES

- To understand and identify the relevant federal acts and agencies that safeguard union employee's rights.
- To explain the issues that led to the *Weingarten* Ruling.
- To identify the factors that must exist for *Weingarten* to apply.
- To identify the situations where *Weingarten* is applicable.
- To identify the situations where *Weingarten* does not apply.
- To explain management's responsibility when interviewing union employees.
- To explain the union employee's responsibility per *Weingarten.*
- To explain the union representative's rights and roles.
- To identify employer prohibited acts per *Weingarten.*

## INTRODUCTION

The federal government has created several acts and agencies that safeguard employees belonging to a qualified labor organization, or union. The groundbreaking case of *National Labor Relations Board v. J. Weingarten, Inc.,* created guidelines that employers and employees must follow when an employer or its agents interview a union employee who is suspected of wrongdoing. This chapter discusses a brief history of the labor movement beginning with the Railway Labor Act of 1926 to present. In addition, this chapter discusses in detail the *Weingarten* case and the resultant *Weingarten* ruling application.

## BACKGROUND

In 1926, Congress passed the Railway Labor Act to promote bargaining, arbitration, and mediation to settle labor disputes (Railway Labor Act). The Act was amended in 1934, and in 1936 it was expanded to include airlines. Following the Railway Labor Act, Congress passed the National Labor Relations Act (NLRA) in 1935. The NLRA's mission is to protect the rights of employees and employers, encourage collective bargaining, and curtail certain private sector labor and management practices that can harm the general welfare of workers, businesses, and the U.S. economy. The NLRA created the National Labor Relations Board (NLRB) as an independent federal agency vested with the power to safeguard employees' rights to organize and to determine whether to have unions as their bargaining representative (National Labor Relations Board). The Civil Service Reform Act of 1978 created the Federal Labor Relations Authority (Federal Labor Relations Authority). This independent federal agency administers labor relations between the federal government and its employees.

Union membership reached a peak in the 1950s, with 33% of all workers in the United States belonging to a union. Since that time, union membership has dwindled. As of 2019, only a little over 10% of American workers belonged to a union (U.S. Bureau of Labor Statistics, 2020). Interestingly, the public sector has a high percentage of union membership, with almost 34% or 7.1 million employees. These union members include police officers, firefighters, teachers, and many other public sector professions. Private sector union membership is around 6.2%, or 7.6 million union workers of a total private sector workforce of 114 million. Industries, such as automobile manufacturing, railroads, steel, and electrical, continue to have high union membership levels.

Even though union membership has dwindled since the 1950s, many investigations undertaken by public and private sector investigators have involved union employees. Union members are entitled to due process protections involving employee discipline and internal investigations for misconduct. The 1975 U.S. Supreme Court case, *NLRB v. J. Weingarten, Inc.*, 420 U.S. 251 (1975), governs management and investigators' conduct when interviewing a union employee. The ruling involves a union employee's right to have a union representative present during an investigatory interview if the response to questioning can lead to discipline.

## *WEINGARTEN*

Weingarten's was a supermarket chain in the southern United States until Safeway acquired it in 1983. A store employee, Leura Collins, who was represented by The Retail Store Clerk's Union Local 455, was interviewed by a loss prevention specialist and a store manager for suspicion of theft. Several times during the interview, Collins requested that the store manager contact a union representative to be present; however, the manager denied her requests. Subsequently, Weingarten's cleared Collins of the theft allegation.

Collins informed her shop steward of the incident, including the store manager's refusal to contact a union representative. As a result, The Retail Store Clerks Union filed an unfair labor practice violation with the NLRB against Weingarten. The NLRB sought enforcement for an unfair labor practice against Weingarten; however, the Fifth Circuit Court of Appeals denied the action. The Court argued that no union presence was necessary during Collins' questioning because the company was not attempting to bargain with her in any way. Additionally, the Court argued that requiring a union representative any time the threat of discipline was present would extend the scope of the NLRA far too broadly.

In response to a grant of certiorari, the Supreme Court majority ruled that the store manager's denial of Collins' request for a union representative to be present during the investigatory interview, while she reasonably believed that the meeting could lead to discipline, violated her right to engage in concerted activities for mutual aid or protection and constituted an unfair labor practice. The Court stated that having a representative present will help the employee who may be too "fearful or inarticulate" to meaningfully participate in the investigation. Also, the Court claimed that a union representative present could assist the employer by eliciting facts and helping find other sources for the investigation. The Court explained that the NLRB is entrusted with the responsibility to adapt the NLRA to changing times. As a result, courts reviewing its decisions only have the authority to reject its interpretations of the NLRA if those decisions are impermissible under it. The Court also observed that the NLRB could change its interpretation of the NLRA over time and is not required to comply with its earlier decisions.

Since the 1975 *Weingarten* decision, the NLRB has changed its mind several times regarding nonunion workers being entitled to a representative of their choice to participate in an investigatory interview. As of 2007, only unionized employees are the beneficiary of the *Weingarten* Ruling.

## *Weingarten* Ruling Application

**For *Weingarten* to apply, the following factors must exist:**

- Management or a representative (such as an investigator) must be meeting or interviewing an employee.
- The employee must belong to a recognized labor organization.
- The employee must have a reasonable expectation that discipline may occur as a result of the meeting.
- Management must believe that discipline could occur as a result of the meeting.
- The employee must ask for a union representative to be present.

**Following are situations where *Weingarten* is applicable:**

- The meeting or interview is to investigate an employee's inadequate work or other misconduct where discipline of any kind is a possible result.
- The purpose of the interview or meeting is to obtain admissions or other evidence to determine whether discipline is warranted or to support a disciplinary decision already made.
- The purpose of the meeting or interview is to obtain the employee's statement regarding an allegation of wrongdoing.
- The employee must explain or defend his or her conduct when the employee reasonably fears his or her working conditions or job security could be affected.
- The employee takes a polygraph examination.
- The employee takes a sobriety test.
- The employee takes a drug test.
- The employee is questioned about other employees' illegal activities. (An employee is usually required to volunteer this information without being asked. If the employee does have knowledge of wrongdoing and does not report it, then that is a violation of policy, and the employee is subject to discipline.)

A union employee's reasonable expectation that discipline might occur can include knowing that they have been involved in misconduct. Also, the employee can be aware of an investigation in which they are under scrutiny, or others have been disciplined. Furthermore, if the employee has been the subject of progressive discipline, they could articulate a reasonable belief that further punishment can occur as a result of the meeting. The mere fact that an employee is asked to appear for an interview with an internal investigative unit could trigger their belief of possible discipline.

## Non-*Weingarten* situations

- The interview or meeting is to convey instructions or training.
- The meeting is to inform an employee of a disciplinary decision. Management does not seek information.
- Management believes that the employee is not subject to discipline as a result of the interview.
- Management is seeking information from witnesses, possible witness, or information providers.
- Management might not want a union representative present to hear sensitive information.
- If the employee asks for union representation, management must inform the employee that no discipline will result from the interview.

If it becomes evident during the interview that the employee might face discipline based on the discussion, management should inform the employee of the possibility. The employee must then either waive or assert *Weingarten* Rights. (The employee continuing to talk is an implied waiver.) If the union employee asserts his or her *Weingarten* Rights at that time or any time during the interview, management has several options:

- Grant the request and delay the interview until the representative arrives and allow the union representative to confer privately with the employee.
- Discontinue the interview.
- Give the employee a choice to continue without representation or forego the interview altogether.

## Union Employee's Responsibility

- Most entities have a policy that requires all employees to cooperate with management investigations, including participation in interviews.
- Employees are required to be truthful in their responses and to volunteer information regarding known wrongdoing.
- If *Weingarten* is asserted and management allows the delay to obtain a representative, then the employee must act to obtain a representative.

Occasionally, the request for a representative and the coordination of having one appear is a delay tactic. Generally, the employee can have a representative of his or her choosing; however, management does not have to accept an unreasonable delay. The reasonableness is on a case-by-case situation. A representative does not have to be a union official. The representative could be another union employee.

### Union Representative Rights and Roles

- Inquire of management the nature of the interview. (Management must provide the information.)
- Consult in private with the employee before the interview.
- To be proactive during the interview, as long as there is no interference.
- To counsel the employee during the interview.
- To provide information to management to assist.
- The union representative cannot advise an employee not to answer questions.
- The union representative cannot advise the employee not to be truthful.

### Employer Prohibited Acts

**An employer commits a prohibited act if:**

- Refuses an employee's request for a representative during an investigatory interview or meeting when *Weingarten* Right's apply.
- Disciplines an employee for asserting *Weingarten* Rights.
- Threatens or coerces an employee exercising *Weingarten* Rights.
- Threatens a union representative for assisting in a *Weingarten* meeting.

If an employer violation occurs, a remedy could be a Cease-and-Desist order. An employer can also be ordered to rescind discipline and reinstate a terminated employee with back wages.

## PERSONAL APPLICATION OF INTERVIEWING UNION EMPLOYEES

The National Railroad Passenger Corporation, better known as Amtrak, employs approximately 23,000 workers. Of those, around 20,000 are members of one of 15 separate crafts represented by 15 independent labor unions. As an investigator with the Amtrak Office of Inspector General (OIG), the author was involved in many cases that required interviews of union employees. The fact that the OIG requested an interview with a union employee usually triggered the request for a union representative present per the *Weingarten* Ruling.

The author's approach to interviewing union employees was the same as nonunion employees, treating every interviewee with dignity and respect and providing them the opportunity to have their say. Additionally, the author made an effort to build rapport with the representatives, appreciating their role in the investigative and interview process. This approach generally diminished the contention that could arise in an interview with a union representative present. Often, the union representative assisted in the process by explaining to the employee the consequences of not cooperating and being truthful. By treating everybody fairly, investigators who work in an industry that employs union workers will earn a good reputation, which will assist in reaching investigative and interview objectives.

## SUMMARY

Even though union membership has dwindled since the 1950s, many private and public unions exist with over close to 15 million private and public sector members. Union members are afforded certain due process considerations when they are suspected of wrongdoing and the subject of an investigation. The *NLRB v. J. Weingarten, inc.,* case and its subsequent ruling enacted guidelines that employers and union employees must follow during the course of an investigative interview.

## EXERCISE 2.1. MULTIPLE CHOICE AND TRUE AND FALSE QUESTIONS

1. Union membership has increased since the 1950s.

   _____ True
   _____ False

2. The National Labor Relations Act's (NLRA) missions to protect the rights of employees, encourage collective bargaining, and curtail private sector labor management practices that can harm the general welfare of workers.

   _____ True
   _____ False

3. The National Labor Relations Board was created by the NLRA.

_____ True
_____ False

4. As of 2007, both union and nonunion employees are beneficiaries of the *Weingarten* Ruling.

_____ True
_____ False

5. Management must inform a union employee of their *Weingarten* Rights prior to an interview.

____ True
____ False

6. Choose one. *Weingarten* does not apply to:

_____ A union employee taking a drug test.
_____ A union employee taking a polygraph test.
_____ A union employee believes they might receive discipline as a result of the meeting.
_____ A union employee meets with management to learn of a disciplinary decision.

7. If during a non-*Weingarten* interview, management realizes that discipline might result, they must inform the union employee of that possibility

____ True
____ False

8. If a union employee arrives for an interview, then asserts their *Weingarten* Rights and *Weingarten* is applicable, management must delay the interview to afford the employee time to obtain a union representative.

____ True
____ False

9. Per *Weingarten,* a union representative can advise a union employee not to answer questions.

____ True
____ False

10. Per *Weingarten*, a union representative is not allowed to counsel a union employee during the interview.

    ____ True
    ____ False

## EXERCISE 2.2. ESSAY TOPICS

1. Discuss the Supreme Court's rationale with the *Weingarten* Ruling.
2. Discuss what factors must exist for *Weingarten* to be applicable.
3. Explain the situations that would trigger *Weingarten*.
4. Discuss what may constitute a union employee's reasonable expectation that discipline might occur as a result of meeting with management.
5. Discuss management and union employees' meetings that do not trigger *Weingarten*.
6. Explain the union representative's rights and roles per *Weingarten*.

## REFERENCES

Federal Labor Relations Authority, Web, 19 October 2020, https://www.flra.gov.
National Labor Relations Act, 29 U.S.C. §§ 151–169.
National Labor Relations Board, Web, 19 October 2020, https://www.nlrb.gov.
*National Labor Relations Board v. J. Weingarten, Inc.*, 420 U.S. 251 (1975).
Railway Labor Act, 45 U.S.C. §§ 151–164 and 45 U.S.C. §§ 181–188.
U.S. Bureau of Labor Statistics, Web, 20 October 2020, https://www.bls.gov/news.release/union2.nr0.htm.

# 3

# Confessions

## LEARNING OBJECTIVES

- To identify the importance of receiving confessions.
- To identify interrogation tactics that critics determine are nefarious.
- To identify an unambiguous definition of "investigative interview" that can be used for all interview objectives.
- To explain what is meant that confessions must be voluntarily given.
- To discuss what interviewer actions could invalidate a confession.
- To identify interviewer actions that could be perceived as physical pressure.
- To discuss interviewer actions that could be perceived as psychological pressure.
- To identify what deceptive tactics are allowed when seeking a confession.
- To identify what deceptive tactics are not allowed when seeking a confession.
- To identify other prohibited tactics when seeking a confession.
- To discuss the standard of "clear and convincing evidence."
- To identify the difference between an "investigative interview" and an "interrogation."
- To discuss the various descriptions of the term "investigative interview."
- To discuss the issues with the term "interrogation."
- To identify the problems with having an "interrogation mindset."

## INTRODUCTION

A question many people ponder is, if you have evidence to show that an individual is responsible, why would you need a confession? Good question. Contrary to belief, many cases would not be successfully resolved and prosecuted without a confession. A confession is often the most compelling evidence in a case. The Supreme Court acknowledged in *Haynes v. Washington,* 373U.S. 503, 515 (1963) that custodial interrogation has long been recognized as "undoubtedly an essential tool in effective law enforcement." Of course, the confession should be obtained legally and ethically, and must be truthful. This chapter discusses confession case law and what tactics the courts allow and do not allow and other prohibited tactics when seeking a confession. Also, this chapter incudes a discussion on the term "interrogation" and suggests eliminating its use.

Truthful confessions are important for society to have certainty of guilt before judgment and punishment is rendered. Usually, a confession indicates remorse and accountability for one's actions and often leads to quick adjudication and resolution with a guilty plea. In the private sector, some agencies and companies hesitate to take disciplinary action against an employee unless the individual acknowledged responsibility. This is especially true if the employee is a member of a union with several layers of disciplinary review. Following is a case in point:

———

Several years ago, the author investigated a $40,000 embezzlement that occurred over a four-year period. Overwhelming evidence revealed that the person responsible was a union employee/supervisor responsible for the operation. The individual was interviewed several times; however, he stoically denied being the perpetrator. He had no other explanation for the missing funds. The United States Attorney's Office accepted the case. The Assistant United States Attorney (AUSA) convened a Grand Jury, who issued subpoenas for bank accounts and other external documents. The author, along with another agent, spent many weeks out of town issuing subpoenas, conducting interviews, and performing a forensic examination of the records.

Concurrently, the organization removed the employee from service. Per the union contract, the employee was entitled to a company hearing. Evidence was presented that clearly showed that the employee was responsible. At the hearing, the employee testified that the investigation could not show that he had possession of the money. The company found him responsible, and the employee was terminated. Even so, many of the employee's co-workers, including his management supervisor, doubted his guilt. They did not base their doubt on factual evidence. Their doubt was based on the suspect's long-term "good" employment record, and that he would always do what was asked. He even would come in on his days off to handle the cash and the deposits. (A Red Flag!)

The author presented testimony and delivered subpoena returns to the Grand Jury. The Grand Jury returned a True Bill for indictment. The employee was arrested and arraigned, and a trial was scheduled. For several months prior to trial, members of my office copied and Bates Stamped thousands of documents, including daily cash reports, deposit slips, and bank statements for the defense on discovery. During this process, the AUSA and the author met with the defendant and his attorney. The AUSA offered the defendant a plea deal, which would keep him out of prison. The defendant declined the offer. Despite the overwhelming evidence, the AUSA began doubting the defendant's guilt because he would not confess and accept the plea deal. A trial took place.

The prosecution took two days to present its case. The defense called several character witnesses, including the defendant's former management supervisor. The defendant testified that the investigation could not show that he had the cash in his possession. The jury took two hours to deliberate and came back with a guilty verdict. The defendant was sentenced to one year in prison, probation upon release, and ordered to pay restitution. The AUSA still had doubts about the individual's guilt. The defendant appealed because the federal government did not pay for the defense to hire a CPA to conduct a parallel forensic examination of the documents. Despite the defense argument, the Appeals Court upheld the conviction.

A terminated union employee is entitled to a review by the Labor Relations Department to ensure no violations of union due process per the labor agreement took place during the investigation. Often this review process takes two to three years. One year after the employee's conviction and two years after his termination, a Labor Relations official performing the final review contacted the author. Despite the conviction, the official expressed concern in upholding the subject's dismissal because he did not confess. However, since the defendant was found guilty and the appeal upheld the conviction, he remained terminated.

It is difficult to calculate the monetary cost of not obtaining a confession and reaching a quick resolution. Of course, the confession must be true and obtained legally and ethically. Even though the loss was only $40,000, relatively small compared to other thefts, the expenditure was worth the effort to remove a dishonest employee from employment and strengthen internal controls.

## CONFESSION CASE LAW

Investigative interviews are conducted pursuant to an investigation to find the truth. In Chapter 1, we explored the due process rights of interviewees and rules that law enforcement and investigators must follow when questioning an individual under certain circumstances. If, based on evidence, an investigator has determined to a reasonable degree of certainty based on clear and convincing evidence that an individual is responsible for the matter under investigation, an objective of an investigative interview would be to obtain a truthful acknowledgment of responsibility, a confession.

### Confessions Must Be Voluntary

Due process requires that a statement or a confession be obtained voluntarily by the interviewee's free will. The requirement that a statement must be voluntary stems from the Fifth Amendment right against self-incrimination and the Fourteenth Amendment right to due process applied to the states.

In 1896, a mention of a confession's voluntariness was found in the U.S. Supreme Court case, *Wilson v. United States*, 162 U.S. 613 (1896). Wilson was convicted of murder on Creek Indian land. Wilson brought forth several "exceptions" to his conviction, one being his statement, which he claimed was made involuntarily. The Court wrote:

> This brings us to consider the exception taken to the admission of defendant's statement in evidence. The ground of the objection was that it was not voluntary. Although his answers to the questions did not constitute a confession of guilt, yet he thereby made disclosures which furnished the basis of attack, and whose admissibility may be properly passed on in the light of the rules applicable to confessions. Of course, all verbal admissions must be received with caution, though free, deliberate, and voluntary confessions of guilt are entitled to great weight. But they are inadmissible if made under any threat, promise, or encouragement of any hope or favor.

The court affirmed Wilson's conviction.

Another early Supreme Court Case, *Bram v. United States*, 168 U.S. 532 (1897), addresses voluntariness:

> In the federal courts, the requisite of voluntariness is not satisfied by establishing merely that the confession was not induced by a promise or a threat. A confession is voluntary in law if, and only if, it was, in fact, voluntarily made. A confession may have been

> given voluntarily, although it was made to police officers, while in custody, and in answer to an examination conducted by them. But a confession obtained by compulsion must be excluded whatever may have been the character of the compulsion, and whether the compulsion was applied in a judicial proceeding or otherwise.

In determining voluntariness, courts look at the *totality of circumstances* surrounding the interview. In *State of Maine v. Dodge*, 2011 ME 47, the Supreme Judicial Court of Maine wrote:

> To determine whether a statement was voluntary, we assess the totality of the circumstances, including both external and internal factors, such as: the details of the interrogation; duration of the interrogation; location of the interrogation; whether the interrogation was custodial; the recitation of Miranda warnings; the number of officers involved; the persistence of the officers; police trickery; threats, promises or inducements made to the defendant; and the defendant's age, physical and mental health, emotional stability, and conduct.

An involuntarily made statement is made against the individual's free will by either physical or undue psychological pressure. Physical pressure seems to be an easily identifiable occurrence and is indisputably prohibited. It is indeed illegal to commit assault or battery against an individual, including interviewees. An assault or a threat of an assault would almost certainly cause any statement made to be against one's free will and ruled as involuntary.

Below is a discussion on both physical and psychological pressure.

**Physical Pressure, Assault, and Battery**

It is widely accepted that in the past, law enforcement sometimes resorted to physical abuse to obtain confessions. In *Miranda,* the United States Supreme Court cited the high incidence of police violence designed to compel a suspect to confess. According to Cornell Law School, the definition of assault varies by jurisdiction, but is generally defined as intentionally putting another person in reasonable apprehension of an imminent harmful or offensive contact. Physical injury is not required. In the interview room, an assault could occur if the interviewer threatens bodily harm by words, actions, or demeanor. An assault could include:

- Raising one's voice in a threatening way
- Slamming the table with the palm of hand
- Losing one's temper

- Shaking fist at the interviewee
- Standing up quickly in an aggressive manner
- Standing too close to the interviewee in a threatening pose

If an interviewee can articulate that they were in fear of bodily harm due to the interviewer's words, actions, or demeanor, then any statement made could invalidate an otherwise truthful confession. Also, according to Cornell Law School, a prima facie case of battery contains the following elements:

- The defendant acts.
- The defendant intends to cause contact with the victim.
- The defendant's contact with the victim is harmful or offensive.

The subjective word in the elements is "offensive." What might be offensive to one person might not be to another. Also, what might be a normal touching in a social situation could be offensive in the interview room.

Some techniques teach when the interrogation has reached a step where the suspect is emotional, and on the verge of confessing, it could be appropriate to move closer to the suspect and place a calming hand on the suspect's arm or shoulder. Due to issues surrounding offensive touching, this text does not support that tactic.

**Psychological Pressure**

Critics of interrogation techniques complain that individuals will not confess to a crime against their self-interest without the use of nefarious psychological tactics. That is not necessarily the case. Most interviewees responsible for the matter under investigation experience some sort of internal psychological pressure when interviewed.

Critics use words such as manipulation, coercion, and deception to make the point. These words have negative connotations and fuel the perception of questionable interview practices. Manipulation in the interview room indicates attempting to change the behavior of the interviewee by using underhanded tactics. Coercion is related to manipulation and implies using threats, force, or undue psychological pressure to obtain suspect compliance.

## DECEPTION

Deception can be described as giving an appearance or impression different from the true one. Critics of interrogation tactics believe that the use of deception is unethical in most situations. They argue that if an investigator/interviewer will lie in the interview room to obtain a confession, why wouldn't they lie regarding other aspects of the investigation, such as a false affidavit for a search warrant or testifying under oath. The argument is an "apples and oranges" comparison. The fact is that the vast majority of police officers do not lie when providing sworn testimony or preparing an affidavit. However, they believe that the strategic use of deception is often necessary to obtain a truthful confession.

The courts understand that eliciting a confession often requires a level of deception or cleverness on the interviewer's part. Most suspects will not confess just because an interviewer asked them, "did you do it?" Some offenders will confess early in the interview process. However, interviewers often need to use deception to obtain the truth. With that said, there is undoubtedly a "line of deception" that interviewers should not cross. Crossing that line can invalidate an otherwise truthful confession. The courts have ruled on the use of deception in obtaining a confession.

## Case Law That Allows Deception

**Falsely Stating That a Confederate Confessed**: U.S. Supreme Court case, *Frazier v. Cupp*, 394 U.S. 731 (1969). In response to a tip, the police picked up and interrogated Martin Frazier about his possible involvement in the murder of Russell Anton Marleau. Frazier and his cousin, Jerry Lee Rawls, were seen at a bar with Marleau before the murder. During the interrogation, the police falsely told Frazier that Rawls confessed. Frazier then confessed, and the confession was used against him at trial. Frazier was convicted. Rawls pled guilty.

Later case law has interpreted *Frazier as* the case permitting police deception during interrogations. The Court opined:

> The fact that the police misrepresented the statements that Rawls had made is, while relevant, insufficient, in our view, to make this otherwise voluntary confession inadmissible. These cases must be decided by viewing the totality of the circumstances.

**Falsely Stating That Evidence Exists**: U.S. Supreme Court case, *Oregon v. Mathiason*, 429 U.S. 492 (1977). The police suspected Carl Mathiason of burglary. They looked for him for 25 days and finally put a business card on his door requesting him to call. Mathiason called, and the officer asked him to come to the station. Mathiason complied, and once there, the officer told him that he was not under arrest. The officer falsely informed Mathiason his fingerprints were found at the scene. Mathiason confessed. The officer then read Mathiason his *Miranda* warnings and recorded the confession. Mathiason was then allowed to leave and return home.

This case centered on whether the confession was admissible, due to the initial confession being made pre-*Miranda*. The confession was allowed in the trial court, and Mathiason was found guilty. The Appellate Court upheld the conviction stating *Miranda* did not apply. The Oregon Supreme Court reversed the conviction claiming that even though Mathiason was not in custody, he confessed due to a "coercive environment," including the false statement of finding his fingerprints. The United States Supreme Court reversed the Oregon Supreme Court and remanded.

**Another Case That Refers to Falsely Stating That Evidence Exists**: Supreme Judicial Court of Maine case, *State of Maine v. Nightingale,* ME 132 (2012). Nathaniel Nightingale was suspected of murdering two people at their home. A noncustodial polygraph examination took place in stages over 9 hours. The police falsely told Nightingale that aerial satellite surveillance and DNA evidence existed that put him compromisingly at the crime scene. Nightingale did not confess, and he went home. The police learned that Nightingale then confessed to his mother and his girlfriend. The police went to the home and obtained a confession. In addition to *Miranda* issues, the Court ruled that falsely stating that evidence exists was not coercive. The Court ruled that "a confession must be the free choice of a rational mind, fundamentally fair, and not a product of coercive police conduct."

## Deception That Is Generally Allowed

- Telling the suspect that the purpose of the interview is to determine "why" the suspect committed the crime when the real goal is to obtain a confession.
- Telling the suspect that he or she is a good person who made a mistake when the interviewer does not believe that all.
- Telling the suspect that the interviewer believes the crime was committed for some mitigating, morally acceptable reason (stealing money to buy food for a hungry baby) when the interviewer does not believe that all.

- Showing false sympathy or concern for the suspect.
- Projecting the blame on some other factor (poor internal controls, or being influenced by another person)

Also, an investigator can use visual props. For instance, carrying a large file in the interview room to provide the appearance of substantial incriminating evidence.

**Note**: Using allowed deception should be carefully considered and used only if necessary. If the interviewee uncovers a deceptive statement or practice, the interviewer will lose credibility with the interviewee. Furthermore, with the "totality of circumstances" test, a deception that is allowed in one case might be disallowed in another. Additionally, what the courts have ruled as being acceptable in the past, might not be acceptable in the future.

## Deception Not Allowed

Unlike the cases detailed above that allow certain deceptive practices based on the totality of circumstances, there are other deceptive practices that the courts find intolerable in every circumstance.

**Misleading Statements Regarding the Individual's Due Process Rights**: Massachusetts Supreme Judicial Court case, *Commonwealth v. Baye*, SJC-11044 (2012). Anthony Baye was suspected of a series of arsons that destroyed several homes and buildings and resulted in two deaths. Baye voluntarily participated in three interviews with the police over a month. During the third interview, Baye confessed. The police informed Baye he was not under arrest, but nonetheless, read him his *Miranda* warnings. Throughout the interview, the police made several misrepresentations: (1) misleading statements regarding the strength of the case; (2) assurances that the district attorney would follow their charging recommendations; and (3) mischaracterizations of an "accident" and "felony murder."

**Baye Asked for an Attorney**: The police stated they could "clear this up" if Baye would talk to them without an attorney present. With that false assurance, Baye confessed and was convicted. On appeal, the Massachusetts Supreme Judicial Court held that the troopers' misrepresentations, combined with their attempts to persuade the defendant not to obtain the advice of counsel, constituted an affirmative interference with the defendant's understanding of his fundamental constitutional rights. On the record before the Court, "the Commonwealth had not shown beyond a reasonable doubt that defendant's statements were nevertheless freely and voluntarily made." Accordingly, the Court vacated the judgment and remanded for further proceedings.

**Fabricating Evidence**: Florida District Court of Appeal case, *State v. Cayward*, 552 So2d 971 (1989). The police suspected Paul Cayward of sexually assaulting and smothering his 5-year-old niece. The police conducted an extensive interview of the defendant in three stages. Although they suspected the defendant, they did not think they had sufficient evidence to charge him. With the knowledge of the state attorney's office, the police fabricated two scientific reports used as ploys in interrogating the defendant. One false report was prepared on stationery of the Florida Department of Criminal Law Enforcement; another was prepared on stationery of Life Codes, Inc., a testing organization. These false reports indicated that a scientific test established that the semen stains on the victim's underwear came from the defendant. The police showed the reports to the defendant as a device to induce a confession. Cayward confessed. The trial Court held that fabricating laboratory reports violated the interviewee's due process rights and suppressed Cayward's statement from the point after the police showed him the false reports. The state appealed; however, the District Court of Appeal of Florida upheld the suppression. The Court held that "the manufacturing of false documents by police officials offends our traditional notions of due process of law under both the federal and state constitutions..." "Unlike oral misrepresentations, manufactured documents have the potential of indefinite life and the facial appearance of authenticity. A report falsified for interrogation purposes might well be retained and filed in police paperwork. Such reports have the potential of finding their way into the courtroom."

## OTHER PROHIBITED TACTICS

In addition to misrepresenting an interviewee's due process rights and fabricating evidence, interviewers are not permitted to provide false promises or implied leniency in return for a confession. A false promise is when an interviewer offers lenient treatment if the interviewee confesses.

Implied leniency occurs if an interviewer makes a statement indicating that if the interviewee confesses, they will receive favorable treatment. Examples would include an interviewer saying:

- "You know the judge will probably give you a break if you confess."
- "If you tell us the truth, everything will work out for you."
- "I am sure that if you acknowledge your involvement, the company will look favorably upon your employment status."

Other nonallowed statements include threats of dire circumstances unless a confession is obtained, such as:

- "You will never see your children again unless you tell me what I want to know."
- "If you want to go home tonight, I need you to tell me the truth."

The courts also frown upon interviewer tactics if they involve threats against a suspect's family member, such as "You need to tell me what I want to hear, or I will arrest your wife." Additionally, offering leniency for a family member to obtain a confession can also be considered coercive and can cause an otherwise truthful confession to be invalidated. In addition to probably invalidating a truthful confession, there is a risk of obtaining a false confession with these tactics.

Moreover, interviewers must be mindful that juveniles, distraught individuals, and people with emotional or mental impairments are impressionable, and the use of deception could be considered coercive. (Chapter 4 discusses issues with interviewing juveniles.)

## PRIVATE SECTOR CONFESSIONS

A common perception is that confession seeking interrogations take place when an individual is in custody by government law enforcement. In the United States, the Supreme Court and lower courts use the term "interrogation" when making rulings on law enforcement requirements and restrictions during the questioning of an individual in custody. However, seeking confessions is not limited to law enforcement. Investigators, loss prevention personnel, or others working for a nonpublic entity can conduct an interview or interrogation in a noncustodial situation seeking a confession to a crime or violation.

Many large retailers use aggressive loss prevention interviewing and interrogation to curtail employee theft, the most significant factor in store losses. Often, tactics involve indicating that there is evidence such as videotape of theft activity that does not exist. Additionally, loss prevention investigators might attempt to obtain a confession or an admission for a minor transgression if a confession to a more significant crime is not forthcoming.

AutoZone, the largest auto parts retailer in the United States, has been sued by terminated employees who were the subject of loss prevention interrogation tactics. The tactics included offering false promises of not losing their job if they confess, and not being allowed to leave the interview. A case of note is *Robles v. AutoZone, Inc.*, Court of Appeals of California Fourth Appellate District, Division One, D049259, July 22, 2008.

Joaquin Robles, an AutoZone employee in San Diego, CA., was accused of stealing an $820.00 deposit that did not make it to the bank. According to Robles, the loss prevention investigator questioned him for 3 hours and promised him he could keep his job if he confessed. If not, the police would be notified. Robles eventually confessed and AutoZone fired him. Two weeks later, the bank found the misplaced deposit. Robles sued AutoZone for false imprisonment. In addition to compensatory damage of over $70,000, the Court awarded Robles punitive damages of $7.5 million. AutoZone appealed and the damages were reduced to $700,000.

Without a doubt, companies have the right to protect their assets and conduct internal investigations. With that said, companies should afford employees due process in the workplace.

## CLEAR AND CONVINCING EVIDENCE

There is a difference between accusing an interviewee of an offense and seeking a confession, and asking an interviewee if they are responsible. An interviewer has to understand the distinction. Accusing an individual of an offense should be reserved for an interviewee who has been classified as a suspect. A common approach has been to classify an individual as a suspect if they had opportunity and/or motive to commit the offense. With this mindset, many innocent people could be accused. An innocent interviewee's worst fear is being accused of something they did not do. Contrary to this approach, an interviewer with a forensic mindset should only classify an individual as a suspect if there is clear and convincing evidence to do so.

According to the U.S. Supreme Court Case, *Colorado v. New Mexico*, 467 U.S. 310 (1984), "clear and convincing means that the evidence is highly and substantially more likely to be true than untrue; the fact finder must be convinced that the contention is highly probable." Clear and convincing evidence is a medium-level burden of proof, which is a more rigorous standard to meet than the preponderance of evidence standard, but a less rigorous standard to meet than proving evidence beyond a reasonable doubt. Even though the Court's standard applies to cases presented to a trier of fact, the standard is a recommended one for interviewers to adopt when seeking a legal, ethical, and truthful confession.

## INVESTIGATIVE INTERVIEW INSTEAD OF INTERROGATION

Interviewing individuals to obtain a confession is arguably the most delicate and reviewed aspect of an investigation. As discussed in Chapter 1, individuals being questioned have due process rights that must be considered. Issues surrounding coerced and false confessions usually are attributed to the investigator's "confession obtaining" mindset. In this regard, adopting a forensic mindset will be helpful in alleviating these issues.

Traditionally, investigative interviews and interrogations are considered two different processes. However, many people including seasoned investigators, incorrectly use the two terms interchangeably. Even some court opinions use both terms when describing police obtaining confessions from suspects. In the forensic world, it is problematic to use the two terms interchangeably.

Historically, interview books define or describe an "investigative interview" in a variety of inconsistent ways. Some of the definitions refer to the process as being nonaccusatory. Some definitions differentiate interviews into informal and informal. Some refer to an interview as being free-flowing and nonstructured. At the same time, other interpretations refer to an interview as a structured question and answer session. Another description of an investigative interview refers to a conversation with a purpose between two people.

Furthermore, one definition limits the interviewee categories to victims, witnesses, and suspects; however, it correctly includes the objective of discovering the truth. Inappropriately, some definitions include the skills required to interpret the interviewee's responses. These definitions and description variations of the term "investigative interview" are confusing and problematic.

Today, the word "interrogation" is out of favor due to its negative connotation and the mindset that it creates. As a result, some organizations and countries no longer use the term "interrogation." Having an "interrogation mindset" affects the way the police and other investigators approach an interviewee. Many seasoned investigators will tell you that an interrogation's purpose or objective is to obtain a confession. That mindset implies it makes no difference how investigators obtained the confession, or if the confession is even true. Herein lies the problematic negative perception of what happens during an interrogation.

Words are powerful and can stimulate emotions, either positive or negative. Words also paint mental pictures. The term "interrogation" provokes an image of police aggressiveness, intimidation, and physical or psychological abuse. The "third degree" is a famous phrase for interrogation tactics that imply using brute force to obtain confessions.

Critics of interrogation techniques believe that individuals will not confess to a crime against their self-interest unless the interrogator used nefarious tactics. In the landmark U.S. Supreme Court case, *Miranda v. Arizona* 384 U.S. 436, (1966), Chief Justice of the United States Supreme Court Earl Warren referred to the "evils in the interrogation process." The "evil" tactics include manipulating the suspect by using deception, providing false promises of leniency, implying leniency, using other coercive tactics, or physical threats to obtain a confession.

A major criticism is that harsh interrogation techniques can lead to false confessions. It is valid with police, as well as corporate investigators or loss prevention agents conducting interrogations. Documented cases of wrongful convictions reveal that some people under certain circumstances will falsely confess to something they did not do. (Chapter 4 discusses false confessions.) Critics of interrogation tactics and defense counsel can exploit this perception. Imagine a jury trial where a defense counsel cross-examines an investigator regarding the tactics used to elicit a confession. Adopting a forensic mindset implies that the main objective of an investigative interview is to discover the truth in a legal and ethical manner.

A forensic approach requires an articulable standardized definition for an investigative interview that encompasses all interview objectives, including obtaining a truthful confession if warranted. The definition should not create opportunities for critics to challenge the process. The definition should not be too restrictive or too broad. With that said, the following definition of "investigative interview" is offered:

> The questioning of an individual to gather truthful information pursuant to a matter under investigation, including the individual's knowledge of or involvement in the matter, and

to receive a truthful acknowledgement of responsibility if warranted.

The above definition is unambiguous. Interviewers can easily substitute the word "interrogation" with the term "investigative interview." With this definition, an investigative interview can be a free-flowing field interview or an arranged interview with structure. Also, the above definition allows an investigative interview to include an accusation and seek a truthful acknowledgment of responsibility. Professional interviewers with a forensic mindset must use the proper terms when articulating to a court or others how they elicited truthful information from an interviewee.

When an investigator is cross-examined by defense counsel regarding interrogation methods that led to their client's confession, a response can be, "I did not conduct an interrogation, I conducted an investigative interview."

## SUMMARY

Truthful confessions are important to society to alleviate doubt and lead to a quick resolution. Of course, confessions must be obtained legally and ethically. The courts recognize that it is often necessary to use deception to obtain a confession. The courts have ruled on what deception is allowed and what deception is not allowed. Interviewers seeking a truthful confession must be aware of case law and other prohibited tactics. Accusing an individual of an offense and seeking a confession is serious. A clear and convincing evidence standard should govern that decision. This chapter identified the difference between an investigative interview and interrogation and the benefits of eliminating the term "interrogation" due to its negative connotation and confession seeking mindset. In this regard, a definition of "investigative interview" is offered that is appropriate for all interview objectives, including seeking a truthful confession.

## EXERCISE 3.1. MULTIPLE CHOICE AND TRUE AND FALSE QUESTIONS

1. One of the aspects a court will look at to determine the voluntariness of a confession is the weakness of the suspect.

   _____ True
   _____ False

2. In determining the voluntariness of a confession, the courts will examine the totality of circumstances of the interview.

   _____ True
   _____ False

3. If an interviewer falsely tells an interviewee that evidence exists, the courts will automatically invalidate a confession.

   _____ True
   _____ False

4. Fabricating a laboratory report that indicates the suspect's DNA was found at a crime scene to obtain a truthful confession is accepted by the courts.

   _____ True
   _____ False

5. Which one of the following tactics is generally allowed to obtain a confession?

   ____ Telling the suspect that if they tell the truth and confess, everything will work out.
   _____ Showing false sympathy and concern for the suspect's situation.
   _____ Telling the suspect that the courts look favorably on an individual who confesses.
   _____ Telling the suspect that without a confession, there is no choice but to charge the crime that calls for the most severe punishment (i.e., first-degree murder versus manslaughter).

6. It is acceptable to use the terms "investigative interview" and "interrogation" interchangeably.

   _____ True
   _____ False

7. Having an "interrogation mindset" affects the way some interviewers approach an interviewee.

   _____ True
   _____ False

8. The term "investigative interview" can be used instead of the term "interrogation" for an objective to achieve a truthful confession.

    ____ True
    ____ False

9. Critics of interrogation techniques believe that individuals will not confess against their self-interest unless nefarious tactics are used.

    _____ True
    _____ False

10. A forensic approach requires an articulable standardized definition for an investigative interview that encompasses all interview objectives.

    ____ True
    ____ False

## EXERCISE 3.2. ESSAY TOPICS

1. Discuss the importance of obtaining confessions.
2. Discuss the issues with the term "interrogation."
3. Discuss why it is problematic to have various descriptions of the term "investigative interview."
4. Discuss the interrogation tactics that critics identify as nefarious.
5. Discuss the benefit of a having single definition for the term "investigative interview."
6. Explain what is meant by the voluntary confession standard.
7. Discuss what interviewer actions could invalidate a confession.
8. Discuss allowed and not allowed deception when seeking a confession.
9. Explain the "clear and convincing evidence" standard when making an accusation.

## REFERENCES

*Bram v. United States*, 168 U.S. 532 (1897).
*Colorado v. New Mexico*, 467 U.S. 310 (1984).
*Commonwealth v. Baye*, SJC-11044 (2012).

Cornell Law School, Web, 22 October 2020, https://www.law.cornell.edu/wex/assault.
Cornell Law School, Web, 22 October 2020, https://www.law.cornell.edu/wex/battery.
*Frazier v. Cupp*, 394 U.S. 731 (1969).
*Haynes v. Washington*, 373 U.S. 503, 515 (1963).
*Miranda v. Arizona*, 384 U.S. 436, (1966).
*Oregon v. Mathiason*, 429 U.S. 492 (1977).
*Robles v. AutoZone, Inc.*, Court of Appeals of California Fourth Appellate District, Division One, D049259, July 22, 2008.
*State v. Cayward*, 552 So2d 971 (1989).
*State of Maine v. Dodge*, 2011 ME 47.
*State of Maine v. Nightingale*, ME 132 (2012)
*Wilson v. United States*, 162 U.S. 613 (1896).

# 4

# False Confessions

**LEARNING OBJECTIVES**

- To discuss false confession hazards.
- To discuss coerced and false confession hazards when interviewing juveniles.
- To identify the International Association of Chiefs of Police recommendations when interviewing juveniles.
- To identify potential solutions to prevent false confessions.

## INTRODUCTION

Many people believe that individuals will not confess to a crime they did not commit. However, this is not the case. It can be difficult to understand why a person would wrongly confess to a crime they did not commit. In recent years, highly publicized cases have come to light where an individual convicted of a crime is later exonerated because of new DNA testing technology. The Innocence Project, founded in 1992, by Peter Neufeld and Barry Scheck at Cardozo School of Law, exonerates the wrongly convicted through DNA testing and reforms the criminal justice system to prevent future injustice. According to the Innocence Project, many of the nation's more than 360 wrongful convictions overturned by DNA evidence, over 25%, involved some form of a false confession (Innocence Project, 2020).

Without supporting data, it is plausible to believe that false confessions are rare. Most law enforcement officers and others who conduct investigations set a high standard and would not condone a false confession to be introduced as evidence or a cause for an administrative adverse action. However, it is unconscionable if even one individual is wrongly convicted or is terminated from employment due in whole or in part to a false confession. Because of the potential dire consequences of a false confession the subject is critical to explore.

Interviewers have a moral responsibility to understand that some individuals will confess to a crime they did not commit. Furthermore, interviewers must be aware of their attitudes, behavior, and shortcomings that may create a false confession risk. Following is a discussion from the author's perspective and experience as to why false confessions occur both in the private and in the public sectors.

## FALSE CONFESSION HAZARDS

**Bias**: An interviewer seeking a confession might have a bias against a particular individual or class of individuals and prejudge their guilt.

**Relying on Instinct**: Many investigators are intuitive and have great instincts. However, that characteristic alone is not adequate to accuse someone and seek a confession. An interviewer should be able to articulate to a court why they sought a confession from an individual. Interviewees should be placed in the suspect category only after clear and convincing evidence leads to a reasonable certainty of guilt.

**External Pressure**: An interviewer seeking a confession could be the recipient of pressure from prosecutors, supervisors, the public, and others to find the offender and obtain a confession.

**Internal Pressure**: Interviewers often create their own internalized pressure to obtain a confession. This pressure could be to protect a perfect "confession obtaining record," to maintain a reputation, or satisfy external pressure sources. Some retailers evaluate loss prevention agents by the number of employee theft confessions they receive.

**Not Having a Forensic Mindset**: Many practitioners believe that the objective of an interrogation is to obtain a confession. This mindset implies that it makes no difference if the confession is true, or what methods the interviewer used to obtain it.

**Misclassification of Suspects**: It is common to classify any person who might have had an opportunity or motive to commit the crime as a suspect. This mindset can cause a confession-seeking approach where the interviewee is accused and placed in a position of trying to prove their innocence. As discussed in the previous chapter, an individual should be accused only if there is clear and convincing evidence to support the accusation.

**Not Recognizing Suggestible Interviewees**: Juveniles, individual from different cultures, and others with intellectual disabilities could be suggestible and easily provide a false confession to please the interviewer, not understanding their rights and the gravity of the situation.

**Stubbornness**: In combination with the above reasons, interviewer stubbornness is a factor. Stubbornness occurs when an interviewer determines that an individual is guilty, seeks a confession, and fails to retreat from the accusation when the interviewee's responsibility or involvement becomes questionable. This relentless pursuit can wear down an interviewee who might falsely confess to end the process. These individuals might not be aware of their rights. Often, these individuals will recant their confession soon after.

**Interrogation Duration**: A national study by Steven A. Dirzin of the Center on Wrongful Convictions and Richard A Leo of the University of California-Irvine found that 84% of false confessions occurred after intgerrogations of 6 hours or longer and that the average duration was more than 16 hours. (The Problem of False Confessions in the Post DNA World,2004)

## JUVENILE COERCED AND FALSE CONFESSION HAZARDS

Juveniles are especially vulnerable to the pressures of being interviewed. The United States Supreme Court in *JDB v. North Carolina.* 131 s. CT. 2394 (2011) *(JDB)* asserted that juveniles under the age of 18 need to be treated differently than adults during questioning. In *JDB,* a 13-year old juvenile suspected of two burglaries was interrogated in a school conference room by police and school officials. He was not Mirandized because officers believed he was not in custody, which would allow him to leave at any time. The Court opined that when police take a person into custody, they must consider age. The Court wrote:

> "It is beyond dispute that children will often feel bound to submit to police questioning when an adult in the same circumstances would feel free to leave." The Court also opined that the risk of a juvenile false confession is all the more troubling.

To address the issue, the International Association of Chiefs of Police (IACP) published "Reducing Risk: An Executive's Guide to Effective Juvenile Interview and Interrogation" (IACP, 2020). In the guide, the IACP quoted a study that reveals that the prefrontal cortex of a person's brain does not fully develop until the end of adolescence. This condition results in a juvenile having difficulty assessing risks and focusing on immediate rewards rather than long-term consequences, which can lead to making poor choices. These characteristics make juveniles vulnerable to interrogation tactics, making them susceptible to provide coerced and false statements. Police, investigators, and others interviewing juveniles need to be aware of these issues.

Another consideration is an interviewer's misinterpretation of a juvenile's nonverbal behavior. As detailed in Chapter 9, an interviewee's nonverbal behavior can indicate truth, deception, or lies when they are answering sensitive questions. Nonverbal behavior indicating deception by adults is not necessarily applicable to juveniles. It could be normal for young people not to make eye contact, slouch, fidget, or mumble, even if they are telling the truth.

When interviewing a juvenile, it is vital to involve a friendly adult and allow him or her to consult throughout the interview. The adult could be a parent or guardian, a youth officer, a social worker, a teacher, or an attorney. Involving an adult is particularly essential if the juvenile is a potential suspect or suspect and the purpose of the interview is to determine involvement in the matter under investigation or to receive a confession.

As discussed above, prolonged questioning of 6 hours or more is a significant factor leading to false statements and false confessions. A juvenile is more susceptible to a lengthy examination. The IACP recommends that a juvenile be interviewed not longer than 4 hours, with breaks every hour. They also recommend, as with every interviewee, to offer refreshments and restroom breaks.

If the juvenile is in custody, the Miranda Warning should be provided. However, courts may invalidate a juvenile's confession because they did not comprehend the consequences of waiving their rights. This factor emphasizes the criticality of having an adult present during the interview. The questioning of juveniles should take place during the day, not late or during the night. Sleep deprivation and the stress of the interview can increase the risk of false confessions.

As discussed in Chapter 3, interviewers are allowed to use some deception to obtain a confession. However, due to the issues of suggestible interviewees, any deception should be carefully considered before use. For instance, if an interviewer falsely implies or suggests there is evidence that incriminates the juvenile, he or she might believe it is futile to try to persuade the interviewer of their innocence. The use of deception can also cause a young person to mistrust their memory and accept the evidence offered and falsely confess.

An interviewer must avoid promises or indications of leniency with all interviewees. Stated or implied leniency offered to a juvenile can more easily cause a coerced or false confession. An implied promise of leniency could include an interviewer's statement that they can "help" if they confess. In the District Court of Appeals of Florida case, *Ramirez v. State*, 15 So.3d 852 (Fla. APP Ct. 2009), the Court invalidated a juvenile's confession as being involuntary because the interviewer told the juvenile suspect that he would help him if he confessed but failed to explain the limits of his ability to help.

The juvenile must understand the consequences of confessing. In the Superior Court of Massachusetts case, *Commonwealth v. Truong*, 2011 Mass. Super LEXIS 61, the Court invalidated a 16-year-old's confession for murder. The interviewer continually led the juvenile to believe that she would get help and be placed in foster care as opposed to prison if she admitted her guilt.

Juveniles are particularly susceptible to leading questions. Interviewers should not provide leading questions that provide details or hints as to what they want the juvenile to say. For instance, when questioning a juvenile about a burglary, the interviewer should not provide details, such as the entry point or items taken. A suggestible interviewee will often agree with what the interviewer is saying. The interviewer would not know if the juvenile is speaking from first-hand experience or just repeating the interviewer's words.

## SOLUTIONS

### Standardized Training

Public and private practitioners should receive standardized training in the legal and ethical methods to seek a confession and how to prevent false confessions. At this time, there are approximately 18,000 federal, state, county, and municipal law enforcement agencies employing approximately 800,000 sworn officers. In addition, private sector entities employ thousands of loss prevention agents, investigators, and others that conduct investigations and are in a position to seek confessions for criminal activity and administrative offenses. The training should include recognizing and handling suggestible interviewees.

## Record All Critical Interviews

The author is a proponent of recording all critical interviews. According to the Innocence Project, half of the states in the country and the District of Columbia require recording of certain custodial interrogations either through statute or through court action. Federal law enforcement agencies, including the FBI, DEA, and ATF, are required to record all custodial interrogations of individuals suspected of any federal crime (Innocence Project, 2020).

As discussed later in this book, critical interviews are best conducted in a dedicated interview room with audio and video capabilities. Critical interviews are not limited to custodial questioning. It happens that an interviewee might not be in custody during the interview and by the end of the interview, he or she is taken into custody. Also, as discussed in the previous chapter, many noncustodial confession seeking interviews/interrogations are conducted by loss prevention investigators and others who do not have the authority to take an individual into custody. Most of these interviews do not take place in a dedicated interview room. Many are conducted in the back storage rooms of retail establishments or other makeshift spaces. However, with today's availability of relatively inexpensive digital recorders, at a minimum, interviews should be audio recorded.

Recording interviews benefits both the interviewer and the interviewee. Interviewees are presumably protected from coercive tactics that could lead to false confessions. Interviewers can concentrate on the interviewee without the need to take copious notes. The recording can be reviewed for details that might have been missed at the time of the interview. The interviewer has documentation of the conduct of the interview if there is an interviewee claim of poor treatment.

## Peer, Supervisory, and Legal Review

All confessions should be reviewed by a peer, supervisors, and government or entity counsel to ensure they were elicited legally and ethically.

## Investigate Confession Recants

Most individuals who made a false confession, recant it soon afterward. Therefore, the recants should be taken seriously. Facts should be reviewed to ensure that the confession was obtained legally and ethically. In addition, the clear and convincing evidence that was the basis for the confession seeking accusation should be reviewed.

Recording critical interviews in the public and private sectors is good policy to help prevent false confession. As previously discussed, interviewers should also possess a forensic mindset knowing that what takes place during an interview should pass the scrutiny of the courts and public opinion.

## SUMMARY

Interviewer false confession hazards are bias, relying on instinct, external pressure, internal pressure, not having a forensic mindset, misclassification of suspects, not recognizing suggestible interviewees, stubbornness, and interviews lasting 6 or more hours. Juveniles are particularly vulnerable to providing false confessions due to their suggestibility. The International Association of Chiefs of Police (IACP) addressed the issue and recommendations in a publication. Some solutions offered to assist in the prevention of false confessions include standardized training; recording all critical interviews; confession review by peers, supervisors, and counsel; and investigating all confession recants.

## EXERCISE 4.1. MULTIPLE CHOICE AND TRUE AND FALSE QUESTIONS

1. 10% of DNA-related conviction exonerations involved a false confession.

   _____ True
   _____ False

2. Investigative interviewers have a moral responsibility to prevent false confession from occurring.

   _____ True
   _____ False

3. Investigative interviewers should be aware of their behavior and shortcomings that may lead to a false confession hazard.

   _____ True
   _____ False

4. Misclassification of suspects involves identifying individuals as suspect if they had the opportunity or motive to commit the offense.

_____ True
_____ False

5. It is recommended that an individual should be classified as a suspect only if there is clear and convincing evidence to support it.

_____ True
_____ False

6. Select all that apply. False confessions occur both in the public and in the private sector because of:

______ Interviewer bias.
______ Possessing a confession mindset.
______ External pressure to obtain a confession.
______ Interviewer stubbornness.

7. False confessions by suggestible individuals can occur because they lack understanding of their Fifth Amendment right against self-incrimination.

____ True
____ False

8. When interviewing a juvenile, it is best not to have a parent or friendly adult present so the juvenile will talk freely.

____ True
____ False

9. A juvenile false confession factor is that they might have difficulty assessing the risk of the confession and focus on the immediate rewards.

____ True
____ False

10. A recommended solution to false confessions is that only public sector law enforcement officers should record all critical interview. It is not necessary for private sector investigators to do so.

_____ True
_____ False

## EXERCISE 4.2. ESSAY TOPICS

1. Discuss the issue of an interviewer relying on instinct to identify an individual as a suspect and seek a confession.
2. Discuss the issue of an interviewer classifying anyone who had an opportunity or motive to commit the offense as a suspect.
3. Explain why juveniles are susceptible to offering a false confession.
4. Discuss interviewer considerations when interviewing juveniles.
5. Discuss the various recommended solutions to prevent false confession.

## REFERENCES

*Commonwealth v. Truong*, 2011 Mass. Super LEXIS 61.

IACP, Web, 9 September 2020, https://www.theiacp.org/resources/document/juvenile-interview-and-interrogation.

Innocence Project, Web,9 September 2020, https://innocenceproject.org/false-confessions-recording-interrogations.

*JDB v. North Carolina*, 131 S. CT. 2394 (2011).

*Ramirez v. State*, 15 So.3d 852 (Fla. APP Ct. 2009).

"The Problem of False Confessions in the Post DNA World." North Carolina Law Review, March 2004.

# Part 2

# The Human Factor

Investigations involve the collecting, analyzing, preserving, and presenting of evidence. Evidence is collected from various sources, such as crime scenes, computers, and documents. Often, the collection of evidence is performed by specialist in crime scene investigations, digital forensics, and forensic accounting. Evidence can also be collected from humans by conducting investigative interviews, usually performed by investigators or auditors. Conducting investigative interviews should not be considered a peripheral task. It is an essential part of an investigation. Obtaining information from humans is the most delicate and sensitive area of an investigation. An investigator who conducts investigative interviews should have a fundamental understanding of human behavior. In addition, investigative interviewers should strive to possess desired qualities that are beneficial for human interaction and professional success. The Human Factor is discussed in the following chapters:

1. Investigative Interviewer Desired Qualities
2. Understanding the Interviewee
3. Understanding the Offender
4. Breakdown in Internal Controls
5. Breaking Down Barriers and Gaining Trust
6. Evaluating Nonverbal Response Behavior

# 5

# Investigative Interviewer Desired Qualities

## LEARNING OBJECTIVES

- To explain the importance for an investigator to earn a good reputation.
- To identify and discuss the seven qualities that an investigative interviewer should strive to possess.
- To identify how an investigative interviewer can master the Art of Human Interaction.

## INTRODUCTION

Investigative interview training can teach the requisite steps, methods, and skills that must be mastered to be an effective interviewer. However, much of an interviewer's effectiveness stems from their mindset in addition to their skill set. Successful professional investigative interviewers possess certain qualities that cannot be taught in training sessions. Mindsets are a result of your life's experiences and beliefs. They become who you are, your personality, your inner core.

With that said, an investigative interviewer can realize desired qualities that will assist with their profession. A goal would be to earn a good reputation, not just with among colleagues, but with the population served. This can be accomplished by treating people fairly, with dignity and respect. Individuals who are involved in an investigation may be distraught, reluctant, uncooperative, and even hostile. Whether the interviewer works as an investigator for a government agency, a corporation, or another organization, a good reputation is often the first step in breaking down barriers and gaining trust. The same is true for police officers and how the community perceives them. If the officer treats people fairly, they will be successful and earn a good reputation. A negative reputation is difficult to overcome and will lead to failure.

## DESIRED QUALITIES

Below are the seven desired qualities the author believes interviewers should endeavor to possess in order to earn a good reputation and be successful:

1. The Art of Human Interaction

   Investigative interviewing is all about dealing with people. Most people do not want to be involved in an investigation and do not wish to be interviewed. An interviewer must understand and relate with people. Building rapport with interviewees is a critical aspect when conducting interviews. Many interviewees are at their worst when they are involved one way or another in an investigation. Finding some common ground can assist in gaining trust and breaking down barriers.

   Some people are naturally talented in the art of human interaction. If you are not, you can develop this quality. First and foremost, treat everybody with dignity and respect. You will be a better person for it. One of the most harmful things that one human being can do to another, other than physical harm, is to make a person feel insignificant. Allow everyone to have their voice. Do not denigrate what others say. The following are tips on how to master the Art of Human Interaction:

   - Be Empathetic

     Being empathetic allows you to understand the motivations and emotions of individuals involved in an investigation. An empathetic interviewer understands why people make the decisions they do, both good and bad. Importantly, a professional interviewer understands what motivates interviewees to lie or be less than forthcoming. It is equally important to understand what motivates an interviewee to be truthful.

Empathy is the quality that assists in breaking down barriers and gaining trust with distraught, reluctant, uncooperative, and hostile interviewees. Interviewees usually respond to genuine empathy.

- Be Cordial and Polite

  Most people respond favorably to someone who is cordial and polite. A friendly demeanor must be genuine. A disingenuous approach will have the opposite outcome. Since interviews are all about people, it is valuable to be a "people person."

- Be a Good Listener

  Having a conversation with an individual and realizing that they are not listening to what you are saying is unnerving. In a social context, it is rude. In an interview context, it is disastrous. An interviewer who thinks ahead to other questions and is not focused on what the interviewee is saying could miss important details. Also, if the interviewee goes off topic, some interviewers will not listen because they are mentally trying to re-direct the interview to the topic at hand. An astute interviewee who does not want to be forthcoming will detect the lack of attention and take advantage of it.

  Being a good listener means not interrupting, unless necessary. Again, in a social context, interrupting is rude. In an interview context, interrupting is counterproductive. Let the interviewee talk. It is their opportunity to tell their story. When an interviewee stops responding to a question, do not be quick to ask the next question. Listening puts an interviewee at ease and assists with gaining trust. Listening also allows the interviewer to detect truthfulness, deception, and lies. Only interrupt if necessary and after giving the interviewee leeway.

- Do not Impress with Authority

  Some interviewers flaunt their authority to satisfy their ego, which often results in further alienating an already uncooperative interviewee. Inform the interviewee they may call you by your first name. Seek permission to refer to the interviewee by his or her first name. With that said, it sometimes becomes necessary to educate the interviewee of your authority to conduct the interview.

- Do not Lecture

  Lecturing should be left to teachers in the classroom, parents with their children, or judges in the courtroom. Lecturing does not belong in the interview room. As an adult, being on the receiving end of a lecture can be a humiliating experience. Unless the interview objective is to humiliate the interviewee (and of course, it should never be), do not lecture.
- Be Conversational

  An interview should be considered a conversation between two people. An interviewer should speak in even conversational tones. Be natural. Do not sound bureaucratic or officious. Do not talk as if you are reading from a script. Talk to the interviewee like you would talk to an acquaintance in a social situation. It is beneficial if an interviewer adapts to the language that is used and understood by the interviewee. A professional investigative interviewer should be able to effectively communicate with individuals from all social strata and educational levels. Conversational language often includes incorrect grammar, short phrases, and slang; however, the Report of Interview should be grammatically correct (see Chapter 17, Writing a Report of Interview).
- Be Objective

  Professional interviewers should approach interviews with objectivity and not be influenced by personal feelings or prejudice. An interviewer might have evidence that reveals the interviewee is responsible for the matter under investigation (the guilty party). However, this conclusion should be based on clear and convincing evidence, not bias.
- Be Even Tempered

  Losing one's temper is unhealthy. We all get angry at times; however, losing your temper means you have lost control. Outside the interview room, this can destroy relationships. Inside the interview room, it can ruin the interview and is inexcusable. If that happens, discontinue the interview because it will not be productive. A professional interviewer should not take anything that is said personally. Some interviewees will try to make the interviewer lose their temper. If the interviewee succeeds, then they have the advantage.

Imagine a psychiatrist or psychologist speaking with a patient and losing their temper. It just should not happen. That is the mindset that a professional investigative interviewer should possess. Many television shows and movies depict a police interviewer standing up, slamming their hand or a file on the table, and yelling at the interviewee. Besides losing control of the interview, the courts look disfavorably on interviewer behavior that could be considered threatening or coercive.

2. Be Passionate

   Strive for excellence. Abraham Lincoln said, "Whatever you are, be a good one." Being passionate leads to success. Passion is the energy that fuels the desire to excel and continually hone your skills as a professional.

3. Be Positive

   Be positive. Do not allow negativity to creep into your life. A negative attitude can be changed to a positive one. Embrace life as a momentous event. Embrace other people's lives and celebrate their accomplishments. Choose to be happy. Again, Abraham Lincoln said, "Most folks are as happy as they make up their minds to be."

   There is a battle between negative and positive attitudes. Win the attitude battle. Attitudes are infectious. Try to influence negative people, and if that does not work, avoid them. Throughout the interview, an interviewee will be assessing the interviewer's attitude. A positive attitude and demeanor can assist in breaking down barriers and gaining trust and achieving interview objectives. Conversely, a negative attitude seldom leads to success.

4. Exercise Mental Agility

   To be mentally agile or flexible means that one can quickly adjust. Mental agility is a crucial trait for an interviewer to possess because an interview can be fluid and change at any second. Depending on the interviewee's information, the interviewer may have to adjust and deviate from prepared interview topics and questions. Some interviewers can become flustered when the interview does not proceed as planned.

5. Be Confident in Your Ability

   A lack of confidence is usually a result of inexperience and poor preparation. Confidence can be gained by thoroughly preparing for the interview. An interviewer must know the subject matter and prepare well-thought-out topics and questions to ask. The interviewer should also learn as much as they can about the interviewee before the interview. Experience and practicing the Art of Human Interaction will lead to confidence.

6. Live by a Code of Integrity

   A professional interviewer should have unimpeachable integrity. In today's environment, law enforcement officers and other investigators are subject to intense scrutiny. An integrity issue could jeopardize the results of an investigation and a successful interview, as well as damage the interviewer's reputation.

7. Be a Life-Long Learner

   Being a life-long learner is essential to be successful in life and is coupled with passion. A professional interviewer should keep abreast of laws, regulations, and trends that impact their job. Interviewers should embrace their profession and continually hone their skills. Investigative interviewing has changed dramatically in the past 50 years, and the profession will continue to evolve. This book is relevant today, and many of the concepts and teachings will remain appropriate for some time to come. However, expect that a new issue will arise at some point in the future that will warrant a change in interview methods. Stay tuned!

## SUMMARY

Successful investigative interview should strive for the desired qualities to assist them in their profession. Interview training can teach requisite skills; however, qualities cannot be taught. The seven desired qualities that will assist in realizing the goal of earning a good reputation among colleagues and the population served are identified as follows: (1) the Art of Human Interaction, which includes being empathetic, being cordial and polite, being a good listener, not impressing with authority, being conversational, not lecturing, being objective, and being even tempered; (2) being positive; (3) being passionate; (4) able to exercise mental agility; (5) being confident in ability; (6) living by a code of integrity; and (7) being a life-long learner.

## EXERCISE 5.1. MULTIPLE CHOICE AND TRUE AND FALSE QUESTIONS

1. Much of an interviewer's effectiveness stems from their mindset as well as their skill set.

_____ True
_____ False

2. A successful interviewer only needs to possess the requisite skills to achieve interview objectives.

_____ True
_____ False

3. Investigative interviewers should strive to earn a good reputation.

_____ True
_____ False

4. A good reputation can assist in breaking down barriers and gaining trust.

_____ True
_____ False

5. Pick all that apply. To be a master in the Art of Human Interaction, an interviewer should:

_____ Be empathetic.
_____ Impress with authority.
_____ Be a good listener.
_____ Be conversational.

6. Being passionate fuels the desire to excel, a quality an investigative interviewer should possess.

_____ True
_____ False

7. A professional interviewer should not allow the interview to go off topic.

_____ True
_____ False

8. It is important that an investigative interviewer have unimpeachable integrity.

   _____ True
   _____ False

9. Preparing for the interview leads to confidence.

   _____ True
   _____ False

10. Investigative interviewing concepts and practices have not changed in the past 50 years.

   _____ True
   _____ False

## EXERCISE 5.2. ESSAY TOPICS

1. Discuss the importance of a professional interviewer earning a good reputation.
2. Discuss how an interviewer can practice the Art of Human Interaction.
3. Explain how an interviewer can gain confidence in their ability.
4. Discuss the importance of an interviewer living by a code of integrity.

# 6

# Understanding the Interviewee

## LEARNING OBJECTIVES

- To identify the various attitudes an interviewee might possess.
- To discuss the reasons an interviewee might possess a negative attitude.
- To discuss the reasons an interviewee might not be truthful.
- To discuss what motivates an interviewee to be truthful.

## INTRODUCTION

Most people do not want to be involved in an investigation, and they do not wish to be interviewed, even if they are not responsible for the matter being investigated. The prospect of appearing for an interview can cause anxiety, even panic. Some interviewees will be cooperative; however, many will not. A person's degree of cooperativeness is related to their attitude. People develop a general attitude, either positive or negative, based on their life experience. With that said, an individual may possess a specific attitude in a particular situation. An interviewee's attitude could be due to the reason they are being interviewed or the mere fact that they are being interviewed. In that regard, it is important to recognize and understand interviewees attitudes. In addition, it is beneficial to understand what motivates an interviewee to be untruthful or truthful.

## INTERVIEWEE NEGATIVE ATTITUDES

Some common noncooperative attitudes displayed by interviewees are:

- Reluctance
- Reticence
- Indifference
- Cageyness
- Resentfulness
- Hostility
- Wariness
- Evasiveness
- Superiority

Assessing an interviewee's attitude begins with the first contact. The first contact with an interviewee is often when the interview is arranged by phone. (Chapter 11 discusses arranging the interview.) An individual's reaction to being asked to appear and their questions can provide a clue to their attitude. Further indications of an interviewee's attitude are revealed when they appear for the interview, during the introduction, and during the preliminary questioning.

The interviewee's demeanor, body language, and tone of voice can also provide clues. For instance, an interviewee with a reluctant or an indifferent attitude might not make eye contact and can have poor posture when seated. An interviewee who is resentful or hostile might show anger, either real or feigned. They might respond to questions with clipped, short answers and not volunteer information. An interviewee who is evasive might not be forthright when asked simple preliminary questions (Figure 6.1).

Understanding why an interviewee might possess a particular negative uncooperative attitude is valuable. Following are some reasons:

- Previous bad experience with law enforcement agencies or investigators.
- General lack of trust of authority.
- Belief they are being singled out.
- Fear that they will be wrongly accused.
- Fear of retaliation.
- Does not want to be perceived as a "snitch."
- Does not want to become involved due to inconvenience.
- Does not feel they should be subject to an interview due to their position or status.

**Figure 6.1** This interviewee's body language portrays an attitude of indifference or resentment.

There are other attitudes that interviewees might possess. The ones listed above are the most common. As discussed in Chapter 9, an interviewer should attempt to break down barriers and gain trust with an uncooperative interviewee.

## INTERVIEWEE UNTRUTHFULNESS/TRUTHFULNESS

In addition to understanding interviewee attitudes, it is also essential to understand what motivates an interviewee to not be truthful or forthcoming. It is not only the person responsible for the matter under investigation (the guilty party) who will lie. Others will lie even if they seemingly have no reason to do so. The guilty party is motivated to not be truthful to escape consequences. Other interviewees will lie or not be forthcoming for a variety of reasons as follows:

- Seeking revenge against an individual.
- Seeking attention.
- To conceal their knowledge of the matter being investigated.
- To conceal their involvement in another crime.
- To conceal a compromising or an embarrassing situation unrelated to the matter being investigated.
- Protecting another individual.
- Not wanting to become involved.
- Fearful of retaliation or repercussions.
- Solidarity with the wrongdoer.
- Protecting the reputation of their organization.
- Prefers to handle the situation without the involvement of investigators.
- They do not trust the interviewer.

As discussed in Chapter 15, "Leading the Interviewee to the Truth," an interviewer who understands the reasons an interviewee might not be truthful can present this knowledge in an attempt to persuade the interviewee to be truthful. It is equally important for an interviewer to understand what motivates an interviewee to be truthful. Motivations to be truthful include:

- Some people are just honest and will tell the truth, no matter what.
- A belief that there is no alternative.
- A belief that the interviewer knows the answers, so why lie.
- The evidence is overwhelming.
- Some guilty persons look for consideration in exchange for being truthful.
- Some guilty persons cannot bear the guilt.
- They trust the interviewer.

Notice that listed in the reasons as to what motivates interviewees to lie is that they do not trust the interviewer. Also, notice that a motivation for interviewees to be truthful is because they trust the interviewer. If the interviewer has gained trust, many interviewees will tell the truth, either readily or eventually.

## SUMMARY

An interviewee may possess various attitudes, either positive or negative. Some attitudes are a result of their personality. Some negative attitudes are a result of the reason they are being interviewed or the mere fact they are being interviewed. Attitudes include reluctance, reticence, indifference, cageyness, resentfulness, hostility, wariness, evasiveness, and superiority. An interviewer assesses an interviewee's attitude with the first contact. An interviewee's body language and demeanor will provide clues. There are various reasons interviewees may possess a negative attitude. It is beneficial for the interviewer to understand this. It is also beneficial for an interviewer to understand what motivates an interviewee to be untruthful and truthful.

## EXERCISE 6.1. MULTIPLE CHOICE AND TRUE AND FALSE QUESTIONS

1. An investigative interviewer does not need to understand why an interviewee might have a particular attitude.

   _____ True
   _____ False

2. The prospect of appearing for an investigative interview can cause the interviewee anxiety.

   _____ True
   _____ False

3. An interviewee might possess a certain attitude due to the reason they are being interviewed.

   _____ True
   _____ False

4. Assessing an interviewee's attitude begins with the first contact.

   _____ True
   _____ False

5. An interviewee will provide a clue to their attitude through their:

   _____ Body language.
   _____ Tone of voice.
   _____ Demeanor.
   _____ All of the above.

6. An investigative interviewer should only concern themselves with why an interviewee might be untruthful. It is not important to understand why an interviewee might be truthful.

_____ True
_____ False

7. The reasons an interviewee might possess a negative attitude include:

_____ Past bad experience with you or your profession.
_____ Fear of retaliation.
_____ Belief they are being singled out.
_____ All of the above.

8. An investigator should understand that only an interviewee who is responsible for or involved in the matter under investigation might not be truthful.

_____ True
_____ False

9. A reason an interviewee might not be truthful is that they do not trust the interviewer.

_____ True
_____ False

10. A reason an interviewee might be truthful is that they trust the interviewer.

_____ True
_____ False

## EXERCISE 6.2. ESSAY TOPICS

1. Discuss the reasons an interviewee might possess a negative, non-cooperative attitude.
2. Discuss how an interviewer might determine an interviewee's attitude.
3. Discuss the reasons an interviewee might have a particular negative attitude.
4. Discuss the reasons an interviewee may not be truthful.
5. Discuss the reasons an interviewee might be truthful.

# 7

# Understanding the Offender

## LEARNING OBJECTIVES

- To discuss the importance for an investigator to understand what motivates an individual to commit an offense.
- To identify the three sides of the Fraud Triangle.
- To explain each side of the Fraud Triangle.
- To discuss the 10-10-80 rule and its relationship to the Fraud Triangle.
- To discuss the reasons an offender might confess.

## INTRODUCTION

Many investigations are initiated as a result of an allegation that someone committed a crime or violation. Other investigations stem from a proactive inquiry or audit that determined a violation occurred. As we have learned, the purpose of an investigation is to discover the truth. That includes identifying the offender(s). To achieve the objective of finding the truth and identifying the offender, investigators should understand what motivates an individual to commit an offense.

## THE FRAUD TRIANGLE

The Association of Certified Fraud Examiners (ACFE) is the world's premier fraud fighting organization. The ACFE's "Fraud 101" training discusses the question, "Why does Fraud Occur?" The training discusses

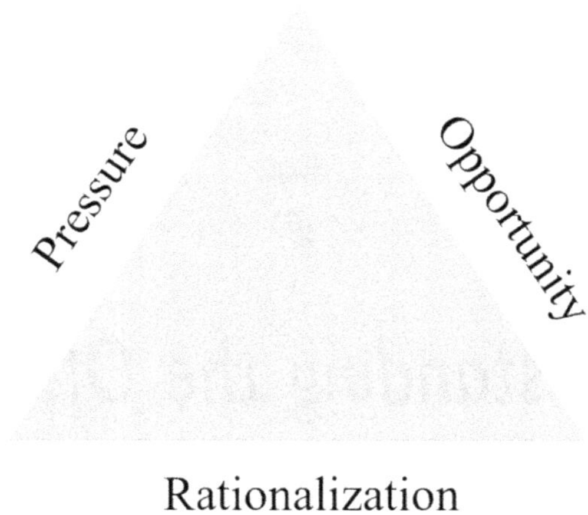


**Figure 7.1** The Fraud Triangle.

criminologist Doctor Donald Cressey, who in the 1950s, created the Fraud Triangle Theory, which explains why a trusted individual will commit fraud against their employer, identified as occupational fraud. The Fraud Triangle Theory is that the three sides of the triangle, that is, financial pressure, opportunity, and rationalization, must come together for an occupational fraud to take place (The Perfect Storm). Below is a discussion of the theory (Figure 7.1).

## Pressure

The first side of the triangle involves an employee feeling some level of personal financial pressure. Financial pressure could be triggered by any number of situations, including:

- Insurmountable bills.
- Habits or addictions.
- Spouse loses job.
- Helping a relative.
- Lack of discretionary income for vacations, luxury items, or other nonessential goods.
- Greed.
- Keeping up with the Joneses.

## Opportunity

The second side of the triangle represents the employee's belief that there is an opportunity to alleviate the financial pressure by committing fraud against the employer (theft, embezzlement, accepting kickbacks, or bribes). The opportunity, actual or perceived, usually presents itself as a result of an internal control issue:

- Lack of internal controls.
- Ineffective internal controls.
- Internal control procedures are not followed.
- Internal controls are manipulated and create opportunity.

## Rationalization

The third side of the triangle involves the employee rationalizing their behavior. Rationalization is similar, but not the same as justification. Justification indicates that one's actions are morally and legally correct, such as justifiable homicide. Rationalization is when an individual concludes that their unethical or illegal behavior is morally acceptable for some reason. For instance, a person who has no means is not justified in shoplifting food from a store to feed his or her family. However, they may rationalize the act as "the store can afford it." Motivation is also different than rationalization. The pressure and opportunity side of the Fraud Triangle would be the motivation to cause somebody to act. They could then rationalize their wrong decision in a number of ways, including:

- Contempt for their employer or supervisor.
- Poor supervisory role models.
- Sense of entitlement. ("I did not receive the pay increase or promotion I deserved.")
- Getting back at the company for some real or perceived injustice that took place.
- The company is wealthy. They will not miss the little amount taken.
- I am just borrowing the money. I will pay it back.

The Fraud Triangle Theory can be adapted to many other nonoccupational criminal acts and violations. Many people who commit theft, shoplifting, burglary, or robbery have an actual need. It could be to support a drug habit, buy necessities, or possess something they usually could not afford.

These violators perceive the opportunity, which could be a lack of security or another actual or perceived vulnerability. And of course, they can rationalize their behavior in many ways.

## THE 10-10-80 RULE

In addition to the Fraud Triangle Theory, a popular fraud fighting concept is the 10-10-80 rule. The 10-10-80 rule suggests that 10% of people will not commit any offenses no matter what pressure they are experiencing and what opportunities are present. Another 10% of people will look for and create opportunities to commit crimes. These people are considered hardened or deviant offenders. The remaining 80% of people are on the fence. Depending on pressure, they might fall on the wrong side of the fence if an opportunity is present, rationalizing their offensive behavior. These 80% could be considered soft. If a soft offender continues with the same dishonest activity without detection, they often become hardened offenders. As with the Fraud Triangle, the 10-10-80 rule can be applied to other offenses against society.

## WHAT CAUSES AN OFFENDER TO CONFESS?

It is useful to understand what motivates an interviewee to confess. A professional interviewer who understands the Fraud Triangle and the 10-10-80 rule can use these concepts to seek a truthful, legal, and ethical confession.

Based on information and an evaluation of the interviewee, a determination can be made if the interviewee is a soft or hardened offender. In an occupational fraud setting, it is safe to say that many offenders are soft, or at least they begin that way.

If trust has been gained and rapport has been built, some soft offenders will easily confess when they are asked if they are responsible or if they are accused of wrongdoing. Many soft offenders feel guilty and experience remorse for what they have done. The illegal act goes against their value system. Many cannot stand the internal pressure and are relieved to get it off their chest. However, not all soft offenders will easily confess. Many offenders will initially deny their guilt. A quick denial is a fight or flight reflex. Many will contemplate their action and the fact that their worst nightmare of being caught has arrived. An interviewer can use information they have learned about the interviewee and persuade a soft offender to truthfully confess. (Chapter 15, "Leading the Interviewee to the Truth," discusses persuading an offender to truthfully confess.)

When seeking a confession from a hardened or deviant offender, the interviewer often has to reveal some evidence to encourage a confession. The offender might consider the evidence and believe it is overwhelming. They might decide it is best to admit responsibility, seeking a way to minimize their consequences.

## SUMMARY

It is important for an investigator to understand what motivates an individual to commit an offense. The Fraud Triangle Theory explains that it takes three sides of the triangle to come together for a trusted individual to commit an offense against their employer. Those sides are financial pressure, opportunity, and rationalization. The Fraud Triangle can be applied to other offenses. The 10-10-80 rule indicates that 10% of individuals will not commit a crime no matter what financial pressure they are experiencing and what opportunities might present itself. Another 10% will look for opportunities to commit an offense. The other 80% are on the fence and might commit an offense if they are experiencing financial pressure and an opportunity presents itself. Soft offenders will often confess because they feel remorse for what they did. Often, hardened or deviant offenders will confess if evidence is revealed.

## EXERCISE 7.1. MULTIPLE CHOICE AND TRUE AND FALSE QUESTIONS

1. The three sides of the Fraud Triangle are pressure, opportunity, and justification.

   _____ True
   _____ False

2. Pick all that apply. Pressure to commit an occupational fraud can come from:

   _____ Addictions.
   _____ Greed.
   _____ Insurmountable bills.
   _____ Lack of discretionary income.

3. Opportunity to commit fraud usually presents itself by a breakdown or lack of internal controls.

_____ True
_____ False

4. Opportunity can be actual or perceived.

_____ True
_____False

5. Rationalization is the same as justification.

_____ True
_____ False

6. Rationalization involves an individual concluding their immoral, unethical, or illegal act, and is morally acceptable for some reason.

_____ True
_____ False

7. Employees might rationalize their wrongful behavior in a variety of ways, such as:

_____ Poor supervisory role model.
_____ Sense of entitlement.
_____ Getting back at their employer for some real or perceived injustice.
_____ All of the above.

8. The 10-10-80 rule suggests that 80% of people will commit an offense if internal controls are lacking.

_____ True
_____ False

9. Some soft offenders will easily confess if they trust the interviewer.

_____ True
_____ False

10. An interviewer might have to reveal some evidence to persuade a hardened offender to truthfully confess.

_____ True
_____ False

## EXERCISE 7.2. ESSAY TOPICS

1. Discuss the "perfect storm" as it relates to the Fraud Triangle.
2. Discuss difference between rationalization and justification.
3. Explain the 10-10-80 rule.
4. Discuss what might cause a soft offender to confess.
5. Discuss what might cause a hardened offender to confess.

## REFERENCE

Association of Certified Fraud Examiners, Web, 17 December 2020, https://www.acfe.com/fraud-triangle.aspx.

# 8

# Breakdown in Internal Controls

## LEARNING OBJECTIVES

- To identify the purpose of internal controls.
- To identify the Four Ps of fraud prevention.
- To discuss why employees do not follow internal controls.
- To discuss why an interviewer should understand why employees do not follow internal controls.

## INTRODUCTION

The purpose of internal controls is to minimize an organization's risks; protect assets; ensure accuracy of records; promote operational efficiency; and encourage adherence to policies, rules, regulations, and laws (Michigan Tech). With regard to fraud risks, internal controls should be designed to deter and prevent fraud and losses, and if that fails, to detect fraud or losses early.

Remember, according to the 10-10-80 rule, 10% of employees might attempt to manipulate or exploit internal control lapses or breakdowns to commit an offense against their employer. Another 10% of employees will not take advantage of internal control failures. However, effective internal controls could prevent some of the 80% of employees from making a wrong decision. If any of the 80% are experiencing financial pressure, then effective internal controls may cause them to alleviate the pressure in some legitimate way. A breakdown in internal controls is usually the cause when an organization suffers an asset loss. Therefore, it is beneficial for an investigator to understand why employees do not follow internal controls.

## THE FOUR Ps OF INTERNAL CONTROLS

An organization that is serious about protecting its assets will institute strong internal controls. Their effectiveness relies on the Four Ps of internal controls: Philosophy, Policies, Procedures, and Practices (See Figure 8.1).

- **Philosophy**: An organization should embrace a philosophy that leads to success, including a strong code of ethics and a zero tolerance for fraud and asset losses.
- **Policies**: Overarching published policies incorporate general goals and fortify corporate philosophy. For example, mandating separation of duties, and planned or random audits to prevent fraud and losses or to detect them early.
- **Procedures**: Established procedures are detailed step-by-step measures that implement internal control policies, such as instructions on how a store manager goes about performing a cash register audit.
- **Practices**: Practices are what employees actually do. Practices should conform to established procedures. When practices do not conform to procedures, a breakdown occurs, and fraud hazards exist.

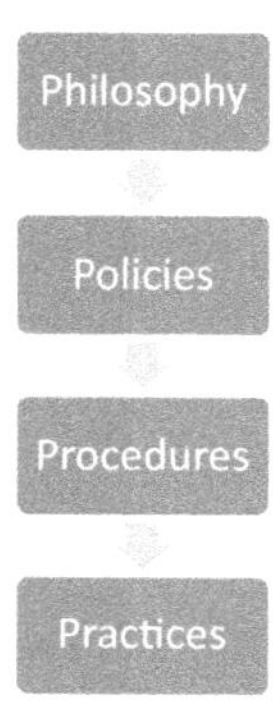


**Figure 8.1** The four Ps of internal controls.

## INTERNAL CONTROL REVIEWS AND AUDITS

Internal control practices should be regularly reviewed and audited. The frequency is dependent on the risk. The organization's size, structure, and core business purpose will dictate the internal control review and audit policies and procedures. For instance, a retail chain might have several tiers of reviewers. In the retail chain example, a store manager might be required to perform a cash register audit on each cashier once per week, documenting the action and the result. The district manager might be required to review the store manager's documented cash register audit action once per week and randomly perform a cash register audit on each cashier once per month. And the District Loss Prevention Manager might be required to review the district manager and store manager's documented cash register audit action once per month and conduct random cashier audits.

## WHY EMPLOYEES DO NOT FOLLOW INTERNAL CONTROLS

When interviewing employees responsible for practicing internal controls, be aware of the human factor. Humans might not follow internal control procedures for many reasons. The author has identified eight prevalent reasons why internal controls are not followed. They are as follows:

- Lack of procedural training.
- Awkwardness.
- Other pressing duties.
- Circumventing controls is the best way to "get the job done."
- Lack of internal control audits.
- Contempt for their employer.
- Apathy.
- Dishonesty.

Following is a brief discussion on the above reasons.

**Lack of Procedural Training**: Employees must be trained to effectively perform internal control procedures. Internal control training should be incorporated with operational training. The purpose of internal controls and the importance of the procedures should be emphasized. All employees must understand that they have a role to play in the organization's success and that following internal control procedures is expected.

**Awkwardness**: Internal controls are designed to prevent or deter employees from making mistakes or committing fraud that is detrimental to the organization. Many internal control procedures involve co-workers double checking each other. Some controls involve supervisors who work with the employees on a daily basis performing first-tier audits or security checks. In addition to a desire to trust co-workers, familiarity can cause awkwardness in carrying out internal controls.

**Other Pressing Duties**: Some procedures can be time-consuming and distracting. In a tiered structure, most first-, second-, and third-tier internal control responsibilities are the responsibility of operational employees. These employees have other responsibilities in pursuit of the organization's primary goals. For instance, a third-tier regional supervisor of a retail chain might be responsible for sales, marketing, hiring associates, and a number of other duties. Pressure to accomplish these duties often takes precedent. In addition, performing internal control audits and security checks can easily be ignored if there is a belief that lower tier employees are performing these functions.

**Circumventing Controls to "Get the Job Done":** Some employees purposely circumvent internal controls to "get the job done." These employees believe that some controls are a nuisance and hinder effective performance of their primary duty.

**Lack of Internal Control Audits**: Internal controls practices must be audited to ensure that procedures are being followed. For instance, say a policy exists where a procurement officer (buyer) is required to solicit four vendors for a particular material purchase. A supervisor should occasionally perform a second-tier review to ensure that the policy of soliciting four vendors is being followed. The review should be documented. Additionally, an internal auditor should regularly audit the supervisor's review and the buyer's soliciting practice. Failure to perform these functions will create an opportunity for the buyer to circumvent the policy causing a fraud hazard to exist.

**Contempt for Employer**: An employee's view of their employer is often attributed to their immediate supervisor. If the supervisor is dishonest or has a disregard for the organization, the employee could be negatively influenced. Additionally, if senior management is, or is perceived to be involved in unethical or questionable behavior, an employee might have contempt and is at a high risk of not following procedures.

**Apathy**: An employee who is apathetic might have no interest in performing up to standards. An employee's apathetic behavior can be caused by work-related disappointment, such as not receiving a promotion or a raise. It can also be caused by a boredom or work-related stress.

**Dishonesty**: A dishonest employee who has some level of internal control responsibility can purposely circumvent the controls to commit fraud. The fraud risk is greater if there is collusion with other employees or vendors.

An interviewer should be aware that an employee who does not follow internal controls could be less than truthful regarding the failure. In addition to obtaining the truth to resolve the matter under investigation, a goal should also include correcting the deficiencies that led to an asset loss.

## SUMMARY

The purpose of internal controls is to minimize an organization's risks; protect assets; ensure accuracy of records; promote operational efficiency; and encourage adherence to policies, rules, regulations, and laws. Internal controls begin with an organization's philosophy that should include a zero tolerance for fraud. Flowing from that, overarching polices are developed that fortify the philosophy. Flowing from the policies, internal control procedures are established that should be followed. The wild card is what the employees practice. It is beneficial for investigators to understand the reasons internal controls are not followed when conducting investigative interviews.

## EXERCISE 8.1. MULTIPLE CHOICE AND TRUE AND FALSE QUESTIONS

1. The purpose of internal controls is to:

_____ Minimize an organization's risks.
_____ Ensure accuracy of records.
_____ Promote operational efficiency.
_____ All of the above.

2. Fraud risk internal controls should be designed to deter and prevent fraud and losses.

   _____ True
   _____ False

3. In the four Ps of internal controls, an organization's philosophy should include a strong code of ethics that should eventually lead to effective internal controls procedures.

   _____ True
   _____ False

4. Policies are step-by-step measures that implement internal controls.

   _____ True
   _____ False

5. If practices do not conform to procedures, fraud hazard exists.

   _____ True
   _____ False

6. Familiarity is not a factor in not following internal control procedures.

   _____ True
   _____ False

7. When training an employee regarding an internal control procedure, an employer should stress its importance.

   _____ True
   _____ False

8. Some employees believe that "cutting corners to get the job done" is in the organization's best interest.

   _____ True
   _____ False

9. An employee who has a poor supervisory role model and contempt for their employer is not a high risk of not following internal controls.

   _____ True
   _____ False

10. If two or more persons collude to commit fraud, the fraud risk is greater.

    _____ True
    _____ False

## EXERCISE 8.2. ESSAY TOPICS

1. Discuss the importance of internal controls as it relates to the 10-10-80 rule.
2. Explain why it is important for an investigator to understand why internal controls are not followed.
3. Discuss the reasons employees might not follow internal controls.

## REFERENCE

Michigan Tech, Web, 11 November 2020, https://www.mtu.edu/internal-audit/control/what-is.

# 9

# Breaking Down Barriers and Gaining Trust

## LEARNING OBJECTIVES

- Discuss how to build rapport with an interviewee.
- Discuss the concept of proxemics in the interview room.
- List and discuss the six considerations when employing kinesics communication.
- Discuss the use of softer words instead of harsh or emotive words to break down barriers.
- Discuss how asking open questions assists in breaking down barriers.
- Describe how an interviewer can use paralinguistic communication to break down barriers.

## INTRODUCTION

Chapter 6 discussed understanding the attitudes of interviewees and what motivates an interviewee to be untruthful or truthful. Often an interviewee who is inclined to be untruthful will be honest if they trust the interviewer. An interviewer must earn that trust. The art of human interaction in union with employed skills will help the interviewer break down barriers and gain trust with a reluctant, uncooperative, or hostile interviewee. The objective is to receive complete, truthful information. This objective is difficult to achieve if there is a lack of trust. If an interviewee's attitude is less than cooperative, the interviewer should employ methods to break down barriers and gain trust. These methods include building rapport and utilizing nonverbal, verbal, and paralinguistic communication skills.

## BUILDING RAPPORT

Merriam Webster defines "Rapport" as "a relationship characterized by agreement, mutual understanding, or empathy that makes communication possible or easy." In building rapport with an interviewee, an applicable description could be, "the process of developing a connection with the interviewee by finding common ground and gaining trust." In the interview process, asking preliminary personal questions provides an excellent opportunity for building rapport.

Finding common ground must be a genuine attempt with an interviewee who is receptive. If the interviewee is not responsive to finding common ground, move on. If an interviewer can find common ground with a receptive interviewee, they should spend a few minutes relating the experiences. Following are some examples:

- The interviewee's neighborhood—Talk about a store, restaurant, or another landmark.
- Family—If the interviewee talks about their children, talk about children, nieces, nephews, grandchildren, or neighbors' children. If the interviewee is engaged or married, the interviewer might find common ground.
- School—Talk about school interests, such as sports teams or other school activities.
- Hobbies—For instance, if the interviewee mentions golf, the interviewer can discuss playing golf, or why they do not golf.
- Employment—Internal investigators for an organization can always find common ground.

## NONVERBAL COMMUNICATION

Various studies indicate that nonverbal behavior accounts for over 50% of communication. Nonverbal communication involves all nonspoken communication, including proxemics and kinesics. The following is a discussion on each topic.

## Proxemics

Proxemics is nonverbal communication that involves the nature, degree, and effect of the spatial separation people naturally maintain in social and interpersonal situations. For instance, intimate space is 0–2 feet, personal space is 2–4 feet, social space is 4–12 feet, and public space is 12 feet or more (Science Direct Proxemics). When conducting interviews, experience has shown that a distance of around 4–5 feet between the interviewer and the interviewee is optimal with no barriers. Having no table or desk situated between the interviewer and interviewee eliminates a physical barrier and assists in breaking down a psychological barrier. Having no physical barrier is conducive to a conversation, not a deposition or a "Question and Answer" session.

## Kinesics or Body Language

Kinesics is nonverbal communication relating to the interpretation of body movement, facial expressions, and gestures. When first engaging with the interviewee, an interviewer's body language should reflect a nonauthoritarian demeanor. The interviewer should appear relaxed, friendly, and professional. Kinesics includes posture, mirroring, hand gestures, facial expressions, and eye contact. An interviewer can use kinesics communication to break down barriers and gain trust. Following is a discussion on each topic:

**Posture**: The interviewer should sit upright, but not stiffly when first conversing with the interviewee. The interviewer should not cross their legs and keep their feet flat on the floor. Never slouch. A poor posture indicates an indifferent attitude and lack of energy. Also, sitting on the edge of the chair can convey nervousness and tenseness. During the interview, when listening to an interviewee's response to an open question, leaning slightly forward toward the interviewee shows interest in what the interviewee is saying. Nodding one's head shows agreement and understanding.

**Mirroring**: Mirroring is a behavior in which one person subconsciously imitates the gesture, speech pattern, or attitude of another. If an interviewee mirrors the interviewer, it is an indication that the interviewer has broken down some barriers and has gained some trust. On the other hand, an interviewer can consciously and artfully mirror an interviewee's gestures when appropriate. The interviewee will subconsciously relate with the interviewer, and a bond can form.

**Hand Gestures**: Hand gestures cause people to listen. Spencer Kelly, associate professor of psychology and codirector of the Center for Language and Brain at Colgate University, found that gestures make people pay attention to the acoustics of speech (Science of People Hand Gestures). Kelly said:

> Gestures are not merely add-ons to language – they may actually be a fundamental part of it.

When beginning the interview during the introductory statement and preliminary questions, it is customary to hold a pad and a pen, taking notes as needed. Later, when attempting to convey something important, it is natural to do so with open hands. Place the pad and pen on the table next to you. Hand movement should be genuine and contained within "the box." The "box" is the area from the top of the chest to the waist and just a few inches on either side of the body (Science of People Hand Gestures). If an interviewee becomes angry or upset, an interviewer can raise one hand in front, palm out, and elbow bent to instill calmness. The gestures must seem natural.

**Facial Expressions**: Facial expressions are a form of nonverbal communication A facial expression is one or more motions or positions of the muscles beneath the face's skin. According to one theory, these movements convey the emotional state of an individual to observers. There are seven universal microexpressions: disgust, anger, fear, sadness, happiness, surprise, and contempt. They often occur as fast as 1/15 to 1/25 of a second. The face is the best indicator of a person's emotions (Science of People Facial Expressions).

Facial expressions occur naturally in response to a particular emotional state. It is important not to show signs of anger, disgust, or contempt during the interview. A professional interviewer should control facial expressions and not reveal any actual negative emotion they are experiencing. An interviewer who is adept at the art of human interaction and confident in their ability will naturally present a facial expression that indicates they are cordial and empathetic.

Many people have a severe or stern disposition, which portrays an uninviting demeanor. Smiling when appropriate has a two-sided effect: (1) People look and feel pleasant and (2) smiling makes others more comfortable. During the interview, facial expressions can show other appropriate emotions, such as concern, urgency, and understanding. Facial expression must seem natural. If it is apparent that the interviewee is deceptive, do not display expressions of disbelief.

**Eye Contact**: Eye contact is a form of nonverbal communication and has a significant influence on social behavior. Eye contact is a meaningful sign of confidence, respect, and social interaction. Good eye contact in an interview means the interviewer is interested in what the interviewee has to say and appreciates their time. On the other hand, poor eye contact is considered disrespectful. The interviewee can perceive that the interviewer is not trustworthy.

When speaking to an interviewee, maintain eye contact for about 10 seconds, look away briefly, then reestablish eye contact. When listening to an interviewee, eye contact should be longer. It is important not to stare; that is unnerving and not natural. Staring can be intimidating and appear that the interviewer is challenging the interviewee.

## VERBAL COMMUNICATION

### Word Choices

Interviewers communicate verbally through word choices. The words used can help break down barriers, or they can have the opposite effect. As an example: When calling a potential interviewee to arrange an interview, instead of saying the word "interview," use the words "to discuss a matter." Many other softer or less emotive words can be substituted (Table 9.1). Below are some examples:

**Table 9.1** Emotive and Less Emotive Words

| Emotive Words | Less Emotive Words |
|---|---|
| Investigation | Inquiry, looking into a matter |
| Interview | Discussion, conversation |
| Evidence | Facts, details, information |
| Don't lie | Be straightforward, forthcoming |
| Guilt | Extent of involvement, responsibility |
| Excuse | Explanation, account |

**Table 9.2** Emotive and Less Emotive Words in Relation to Specific Crimes

| Emotive Words | Less Emotive Words |
|---|---|
| Embezzle | Take |
| Assault, battery | Touch |
| Kickback, bribe, illegal gratuity | Payment, inducement |
| Murder | Cause of death |

It also could be appropriate to use less emotive words when talking about a specific crime or crime element. For instance, instead of using the word "steal," use "take." Above are some other examples (Table 9.2).

The word choices will depend on the circumstances and the assessment of the interviewee's attitude.

## Ask Open Questions

Asking open questions has many benefits. Asking open questions allows the interviewee to answer with as much information as they want to offer. Open questions provide an opportunity for the interviewee to tell their story and fosters an environment where they have a voice. The interviewee believes the interviewer has not predetermined their involvement in the matter.

## Feel, Felt, and Found

Having empathy is a desired quality for an investigative interviewer. Three words, "Feel, Felt, and Found," is a powerful tool that shows empathy with a reluctant and uncooperative interviewee. For instance, an interviewee might say:

> I don't want to get anybody in trouble.

The interviewer can respond with:

> I understand how you feel. Many others have sat across from me and have felt the same way. However, what they have found is that I am fair, and the best course of action was for them to help resolve the issue and move forward.

## PARALINGUISTICS

Paralinguistics is spoken communication that does not involve words. Paralinguistics adds emphasis or shades of meaning to what people say by providing nuances to the words used and conveys emotion by using techniques such as:

- Pitch
- Volume
- Intonation
- Enunciation
- Verbal delivery speed

Interviewers can use paralinguistic communication in tandem with verbal communication and kinesics to break down barriers, gain trust, and convey various messages. These include empathy, compassion, fairness, urgency, seriousness, and confidence. For example, in conveying empathy, an interviewer might say, "I understand how you feel" in a soft, slow delivery. Another example is when an interviewer conveys seriousness, they can say, "Joe, listen, it's important that we get this issue resolved and we need your input," in a stronger voice and faster delivery.

## SUMMARY

The main objective of an interview is to obtain complete truthful information. This is difficult if the interviewee does not trust the interviewer. Interviewers can employ methods that assist in breaking down barriers and gaining trust with reluctant uncooperative and hostile interviewees. The methods include building rapport and using nonverbal, verbal, and paralinguistics communication. Building rapport is achieved by finding common ground with the interviewee. Nonverbal communication includes proxemics and kinesics. Verbal communication involves using less emotive words, and paralinguistics involve intonation, volume, deliver speed, enunciation, and pitch.

## EXERCISE 9.1. MULTIPLE CHOICE AND TRUE AND FALSE QUESTIONS

1. An interviewer can build, rapport by asking preliminary personal questions.

   _____ True
   _____ False

2. Building rapport involves exploring common ground with an interviewee.

   _____ True
   _____ False

3. Pick all that apply. Areas to find common ground include:

   _____ Family
   _____ Hobbies
   _____ Neighborhood
   _____ Employment

4. If an interviewee is not receptive to finding common ground, an interviewer should press the issue.

   _____ True
   _____ False

5. For the interviewer's safety, the interview room should be arranged so a table is placed between the interviewer and interviewee.

   _____ True
   _____ False

6. The interviewer and interviewee should sit around six feet apart.

   _____ True
   _____ False

7. Choose all that apply. Kinesics involves the following:

   _____ Body demeanor
   _____ Posture
   _____ Word choices
   _____ Facial expressions

8. It is recommended that an interviewer use less emotive words to break down barriers and gain trust.

   _____True
   _____ False

9. It is recommended that an interviewer not use hand gestures when talking. Hand gestures can be seen as threatening.

   _____ True
   _____ False

10. Paralinguistics is the aspect of language that involves word choices.

   _____ True
   _____ False

## EXERCISE 9.2. ESSAY TOPICS

1. Discuss what it means to build rapport.
2. Discuss how an interviewer can use kinesics to break down barriers and gain trust.
3. Discuss the use of word choices when arranging an interview.
4. Discuss how an interviewer can use paralinguistics to break down barriers and gain trust.

## REFERENCES

Merriam Webster, Web, 3 January 2021, https://www.merriam-webster.com/dictionary/rapport.

Science Direct, Web, 3 January 2021, https://www.sciencedirect.com/topics/medicine-and-dentistry/proxemics.

Science of People, Web, 3 January 2021, https://www.scienceofpeople.com/hand-gestures.

Science of People, Web, 3 January 2021, https://www.scienceofpeople.com/microexpressions.

# 10

# Evaluating Nonverbal Response Behavior

## LEARNING OBJECTIVES

- Discuss the basic concept of nonverbal communication.
- Identify the various body language anxiety indicators.
- Identify the various paralinguistic anxiety indicators.

## INTRODUCTION

As discussed in the previous chapter, interviewers can consciously employ word choices and nonverbal behavior to assist in breaking down barriers and gaining trust. With that said, in addition to interviewees responding to questions verbally, they unconsciously respond nonverbally. Studies have shown that nonverbal communication accounts for more than 50% of total communication.

As discussed in Chapter 12, during the introduction and preliminary questions, the interviewer should note an interviewee's verbal and nonverbal baseline behavior in response to preliminary nonsensitive questions. These questions should result in truthful answers with nonverbal communication supporting the response. An interviewer should compare these responses with the verbal and nonverbal response behavior to critical-sensitive questions.

When an interviewee answers a critical-sensitive question truthfully, their nonverbal behavior should support the response. However, when most interviewees answer a direct question with a lie, they will experience anxiety. This anxiety can manifest itself in telltale kinesics and paralinguistic changes immediately before, at the time of, or shortly after an interviewee responds deceptively to a direct question. On the other hand, interviewees who tell the truth, even if incriminating, will generally not experience the fight-or-flight stress and will not display kinesics or paralinguistic anxiety behavior. Keep in mind, some interviewees are skilled liars and seem not to display anxiety symptoms.

The author offers this instruction with an abundance of caution. Many people believe they can tell when someone is not being truthful by their nonverbal behavior. However, a little bit of knowledge can be dangerous when dealing with an interviewee who may be incorrectly judged due to a belief that their body language indicates deception. Indications of body language deception should not be considered evidence that leads to an accusation.

The author learned a valuable lesson many years ago when seeking a confession from an interviewee for theft from a petty cash box. The interviewee had the opportunity to take the money and she displayed indications of body language deception during the initial interview. During a second meeting, the author used a direct confrontational approach accusing her of the theft as follows:

> "—, our investigation shows without a doubt that you are the one who took the money from the petty cash box."
>
> She exclaimed
>
> "I did?"

This was not the expected response. The author retreated from the accusation and discussed the reason for the accusation. As it turned out, the interviewee did not take the money; however, she believed a colleague and close friend was responsible.

## KINESICS—BODY LANGUAGE ANXIETY INDICATORS

- Breathing gets heavier.
- Touching face.
- Face turns red/flushed.
- Covering mouth and eyes.
- Grooming gestures, including stroking mustache, removing nonexistent lint from clothes, smoothing hair.

- Changing posture.
- Fidgeting.
- Folding arms across the chest in a defensive posture.
- Shuffling feet.
- Sweating.
- Breaking eye contact with the interviewer (Figure 10.1).

**Figure 10.1** This interviewee is picking nonexistent lint off her clothes prior to responding to a direct question.

### Eye Direction When Answering Questions

Typically, when people look up and to the right, they are lying or tapping into their imagination. When they look up and to the left, they are remembering or recalling something, tapping into the memory part of the brain. However, it is important to assess an interviewee's natural baseline eye movements because this can be reversed for left-handed people (Science of the People. How to Read People's Eye Direction and Behavior).

## PARALINGUISTIC ANXIETY INDICATORS

- Change in pitch.
- Stuttering.
- Mumbling.
- Rambling.
- Delayed responses.
- Quick responses.
- Repeating the question. (Deceptive interviewees will often repeat the question or ask for clarification to alleviate anxiety and allow them time to determine their response.)
- Cancelling behavior. (Cancelling behavior includes coughing, clearing throat, laughing, or chuckling immediately after answering a critical question with a lie.)

When evaluating kinesics body language and paralinguistic anxiety indicators for deception, an interviewer must consider an interviewee's maturity and cultural differences. For instance, juveniles are known to fidget, shuffle feet, not make eye contact, and mumble. That does not necessarily mean their responses are deceptive or lies. Also, some cultures believe it is disrespectful to make eye contact. In addition, an interviewer must take into consideration if an interviewee is on medication, which could affect their behavior.

## SUMMARY

Studies reveal that more than 50% of communications is through nonverbal behavior. When an interviewee answers a question truthfully, their nonverbal behavior should support their verbal response. However, if an interviewee answers a question deceptively or with a lie, they might experience anxiety and their nonverbal behavior might betray their verbal response. The anxiety can trigger a fight-or-flight stress response.

Interviewers should be aware of kinesics and paralinguistic behavior that could be indicative of a deceptive verbal response. When evaluating nonverbal response behavior, the interviewer must consider an interviewee's maturity level and cultural differences.

## EXERCISE 10.1. MULTIPLE CHOICE AND TRUE AND FALSE QUESTIONS

1. Nonverbal communication accounts for less than 40% of communication.

   _____ True
   _____ False

2. When most interviewees answer a question with a lie, they will experience some level of anxiety.

   _____ True
   _____ False

3. Interviewees who tell the truth even if they incriminate themselves, generally do not experience anxiety.

   _____ True
   _____ False

4. An interviewer must evaluate nonverbal responses to preliminary nonsensitive questions and compare them to nonverbal responses to critical-sensitive questions.

   _____ True
   _____ False

5. Pick all that apply. Body language anxiety indicators include:

   _____ Beathing gets heavier.
   _____ Face turns red.
   _____ Change in intonation.
   _____ Grooming gestures.

6. If an interviewee's face turns red in when responding to a sensitive question, it could be an indication that the response is deceptive.

   _____ True
   _____ False

7. Pick all that apply. Grooming gestures include:

_____ Smoothing hair.
_____ Stroking mustache.
_____ Removing nonexistent lint from clothing.
_____ Polishing shoes.

8. If an interviewer breaks eye contact with an interviewer, the interviewer should conclude that the interviewee is being deceptive.

_____ True
_____ False

9. Choose all that apply. Paralinguistic anxiety indicators include:

_____ Change in pitch.
_____ Delayed responses.
_____ Cancelling behavior.
_____ Mumbling responses.

10. It is important that interviewers are aware of cultural differences when assessing an interviewee's body language and paralinguistic response behavior.

_____ True
_____ False

## EXERCISE 10.2. ESSAY TOPICS

1. Discuss the science of nonverbal response behavior.
2. Explain what an interviewer must do to effectively assess nonverbal response behavior for truth or deception.

## REFERENCE

Science of the People, Web, 3 January 2021, https://www.scienceofpeople.com/read-people-eyes.

# Part 3

# The Interview

Part 1 provided the legal foundation and forensic mindset a professional investigative interviewer should embrace. Importantly, it included instruction on confessions and false confession issues. Part 2 provided insight into the Human Factor, including an interviewer's desired qualities, understanding the interviewee and the offender, why employees do not follow internal controls, breaking down barriers and gaining trust, and understanding interviewees' nonverbal response behavior.

The teachings in Parts 1 and 2 are the basis to move forward in becoming a professional investigative interviewer. Investigative interviewing should be considered a craft, a critical component of an investigation. A craft, such as canoe building or piano tuning, employs best practice steps to achieve a desirable end result. Advances in technology or new tools could improve the process to achieve the best results. The same is true for investigative interviewing. The best practice steps might change due to interview circumstances, new rules, regulations, expectations, or laws.

Part 3 explores the interview process that begins when it is determined that information is needed from an individual. The process ends with writing a Report of Interview. The interview process is captured in the following chapters:

1. Preparing for and Arranging the Interview
2. Beginning the Interview
3. Evaluating Denials
4. Questions, Responses, and Follow-Up
5. Leading the Interviewee to the Truth
6. End, Evaluate, and Follow-up Interview
7. Writing a Report of Interview

# 11

# Preparing for and Arranging the Interview

## LEARNING OBJECTIVES

- To identify the importance of preparation basics.
- To explain the benefit of understanding the nature of the offense.
- To explain the benefit of evaluating available information prior to an interview.
- To discuss the importance of placing the interviewees in the appropriate category.
- To identify the various interviewee categories.
- To explain the concept of guilt in a legal and nonlegal context.
- To discuss the concepts in developing an interview strategy.
- To explain the benefit of performing interviewee background checks.
- To identify the four sections of a KTOT.
- To explain the various interview room arrangements.
- To discuss methods to arrange the interview.

## INTRODUCTION

The interview process begins once an interviewer determines that an individual needs to be interviewed pursuant to an investigation. The first step is to prepare for the interview. Preparation includes understanding the nature of the offense, evaluating available information, classifying the interviewees, developing an interview strategy, performing interviewee background, preparing a KTOT (Knowledge, Theory, Objective, and Topic List), and organizing the interview room. The next step is to arrange the interview. Many interview arrangements are made by phone depending on the nature of the investigation and the interviewee classification. This chapter discusses this first contact as an opportunity to break down barriers and gain trust using less emotive words. The interviewer must also overcome the individual's objections to participate in the interview.

## PREPARING FOR THE INTERVIEW

Preparation is the key to interview success. Most interviews that do not achieve interview objectives are due to the interviewer not being prepared. Basic preparation includes understanding the nature of the offense, evaluating available information, developing an interview strategy, and conducting an interviewee background check.

### Understand the Nature of the Offense

To investigate an allegation and conduct effective interviews, an investigator must understand how one commits the offense. For instance, if investigating a procurement fraud, the investigator should be a subject matter expert on the various procurement fraud schemes and how they are perpetrated. In this regard, it is also essential to understand the business procedures and policies that govern a particular entity's procurement of goods and services. Interviews of resource providers might assist. Understanding the nature of the offense and an entity's relevant policies and procedures allows the interviewer to prepare well-thought-out topics and questions.

### Evaluate Available Information

Investigations progress one step at a time. Prior to conducting any interview, it is prudent to gather and evaluate the information that is available at the time. Information can be provided by documents, forensic analysis of material and data, and people. As the case progresses, it is beneficial to evaluate as much information as possible prior to interviewing key witnesses, potential suspects, and suspects. The knowledge gained assists with well-thought-out topics and questions.

## Classify the Interviewees

Most teachings identify only three interviewee categories: victims, witnesses, and suspects. These three categories are typically those that involve a crime, such as murder, assault, theft, or robbery. These teachings place everybody who is not a victim or a suspect into the witness category. However, many investigations are complex and may include individuals that fall into different classifications. These include victims, accusers, whistleblowers, confidential sources, confidential informants, witnesses, possible witnesses, resource providers, persons of interest, subjects, potential suspects, suspects, co-conspirators, targets, and the individual responsible for or involved in the matter under investigation (the guilty individual). The classification of the various potential interviewees will assist in developing an interview strategy and preparing for the necessary interviews. In addition, the proper classification influences the interview objective and approach the interviewer takes with each.

Following is a brief discussion of each interviewee category:

- **Victim**: A victim of a crime could be an individual or an entity. If an entity is the victim, an entity representative would be interviewed.
- **Accuser**: An accuser is an individual who claims that someone committed a crime or infraction. An accuser could be a victim, a witness, or a whistleblower.
- **Whistleblower**: A whistleblower is usually an employee or a contractor who brings wrongdoing, such as fraud or safety issues, perpetrated by an employer or its employees to the attention of the government. Whistleblowers receive protection against retaliation for bringing the information forward. Not all whistleblowers are altruistic. Sometimes a whistleblower is involved in the fraud and, for one reason or another, reports it. In some circumstances, whistleblowers are entitled to a percentage of recovered monies by filing a *qui tam* lawsuit under the False Claims Act.
- **Confidential Source**: A confidential source is an individual that provides information to investigators and prefers to remain anonymous. They are not typically involved in the matter under investigation.
- **Confidential Informant**: According to the Attorney General of the United States Confidential Informant Guidelines, a confidential informant is "any individual who provides useful and

credible information to a Justice Law Enforcement Agency regarding felonious criminal activities and from whom law enforcement expects or intends to obtain additional useful and credible information regarding such activities in the future." Law enforcement agencies require the registering of Confidential Informants with the agency. However, law enforcement officers often utilize unregistered informants.

- **Witness**: A witness could be an actual witness to a crime or someone who has knowledge of the offense or infraction.
- **Possible Witness**: A possible witness is someone who might be an actual witness or might have knowledge of a crime or infraction.
- **Resource Provider**: Resource providers are individuals who are not involved in the investigation other than to educate the investigator on specific processes or functions that are unfamiliar. Also, a resource provider may provide documents or additional assistance in furtherance of an investigation.
- **Person of Interest**: A person of interest describes someone that law enforcement believes was somehow involved in a crime; however, they do not have enough evidence to charge them.
- **Subject**: Unlike a "person of interest," the term "subject of an investigation" has a particular meaning within the United States Department of Justice. According to the DOJ Handbook, a "subject" of an investigation is: "a person whose conduct is within the scope of a Grand Jury's investigation."
- **Potential Suspect**: A potential suspect is an individual who, based on information, could be the individual responsible for or involved in the matter under investigation. Also, a potential suspect could be an individual who had the opportunity, motive, as well as the ability to commit the offense. A potential suspect could also be an individual for which investigators have received uncorroborated information is responsible or involved. Based on information gleaned as an investigation progresses, potential suspects could be further classified as possible and probable suspects. However, investigators have not been able to determine with reasonable certainty based on clear and convincing evidence that the individual is a suspect.
- **Suspect**: A suspect is an individual that investigators determine with reasonable certainty based on clear and convincing evidence, is responsible for or involved in the matter under investigation.

- **Co-conspirator**: A co-conspirator is a suspect responsible for or involved with one or more other suspects in the matter under investigation.
- **Target**: A target is an individual that a government law enforcement agency or prosecutor has determined through credible information is involved in criminal activity.
- **Guilty Person**: In a legal context, a judge or jury determines guilt. However, in a nonlegal context, guilt can refer to an individual responsible for a criminal or administrative violation.

## Develop an Interview Strategy

Upon receipt of an allegation, a simple rule, albeit with some exceptions, is to first interview the person making the complaint. If on its face, the allegation is worthy of pursuing, the next step is to corroborate the complainant's assertion. If the complainant was anonymous, a determination must be made if the allegation meets an offense threshold or is at a minimum sufficient to begin a preliminary investigation.

Corroboration entails seeking information to support the allegation. More than likely additional interviews will need to be conducted to establish predication to open or continue an investigation. For instance, if a whistleblower alleges that a contractor is supplying inferior products that do not meet contract specifications (product substitution), the first step would be to establish the contract's existence and review the contract specifications. To do this, a resource provider might need to be interviewed.

Once predication is established to continue the investigation, subsequent interviews, and the order in which they are conducted will depend on the investigative case plan and the continual analysis of information received. As an investigation progresses, facts and evidence will be gathered. Cases are built one step at a time. Interviews assist in building a case and accumulating additional information. The analysis of the available facts will assist in preparing for subsequent interviews. A prudent interview strategy is to interview witnesses first to learn as much about the offense as possible. Often, a whistleblower or an accuser will be interviewed multiple times. In the product substitution example, an interview of the procurement official, the contract administrator, product experts, witnesses, and eventually individuals possibly or probably involved in the fraud will occur. For each interviewee, an interview objective, and an approach germane to that individual will be established.

With some exceptions, it is best to interview prime suspects last. Interviewing prime suspects last allows the investigator to acquire and analyze as much information as possible beforehand. Also, it is usually beneficial not to alert a prime suspect that an investigation is taking place, a goal which is often difficult to achieve.

The case plan, including the interview strategy, is a living document that could change as the case progresses. Some complex investigations require dozens, if not hundreds of interviews and the order of interviews will frequently change.

Legal issues, such as *Miranda, Garrity,* and *Kalkines* warnings, must be considered. If an interview involves a union employee, *Weingarten* might apply. Also, consideration should be made if the interview is to be audio or video recorded. These decisions will be based on interview room limitations, policies, laws, consultation with attorneys, and the availability of resources.

Additionally, if the organization's policy requires two investigators present during an interview, one should be designated the prime interviewer. The prime interviewer should conduct the interview. The second investigator can take notes. It is confusing and counterproductive to have two interviewers asking questions. It is also difficult to build rapport when two interviewers are interacting with the interviewee. At the interview's conclusion, the second interviewer can ask questions if needed.

## Interviewee Background

Once an individual is identified as a potential interviewee, it is beneficial to learn as much as possible and practical about the individual. The knowledge that is gleaned from performing the check can assist with an investigative theory. The knowledge along with the evaluation of gathered information, can lead to an interview objective, and well-thought-out topics and questions. The background can include the following:

- Criminal record
- Criminal associates
- Family
- Traffic record
- Civil record (lawsuits, bankruptcies, judgments)
- Real estate
- Autos
- Employment history

The extent of the background check is dependent on the matter being investigated and the interviewee category. A full background check, as detailed above, would not be necessary or appropriate for a resource provider.

## Preparing a KTOT

Preparing a KTOT is a recommended step in interview preparation for critical interviews. Armed with an understanding of the nature of the offense, knowledge of available case information, and as much background information about the interviewee as possible, prepare the KTOT.

A KTOT has the following sections:

- Knowledge
- Theory
- Objective
- Topics/Questions

Following is an explanation of each section:

**Knowledge**: The Knowledge section should include all the pertinent information learned about the interviewee. The Knowledge section should also include corroborated and uncorroborated information from other interviewees. If there is clear and convincing evidence that leads to an interviewee being classified as a suspect, it should be included here.

**Theory:** The Theory section flows from the Knowledge section. The theory is what is known or assumed about the interviewee's involvement or knowledge of the matter being investigated based on information and evidence. The theory could be that the interviewee has knowledge of, is a witness to, is possibly involved, or is involved in, or is responsible for the matter under investigation.

**Objective**: The Interview Objective flows from the Theory and should clearly state the objective(s) for interviewing the individual. For instance, if the theory is that the interviewee is involved in the matter under investigation, then the objective would be to have the interviewee acknowledge that fact if it is true. In this case the Interview Objective should include the words "if it is true," to maintain a forensic mindset. Also, the KTOT could be a discoverable document, so it is crucial to reveal objectivity.

**Topics**: The Key Topics flow from the Interview Objective and should be logically organized. The number of Key Topics depends on the complexity of the matter being investigated. For instance, the interview of an employee regarding misuse of a company computer, timecard fraud, and prohibited use of a company vehicle, should be covered in separate topics. The Topic section is a road map to achieve interview success. However, if the interviewee goes off-topic, be prepared to exercise mental agility.

## Benefits of Preparing a KTOT

The KTOT is an investigative tool that prepares the interviewer to achieve interview objectives. The KTOT is also a supervisory tool. The supervisor, who might not be immersed in the case, can review the Knowledge section to ensure that the interviewer's Theory, Interview Objective, and Topic list is appropriate. In many circumstances, the KTOT could be a mental exercise and a conversation with the supervisor or other investigators. With that said, it is recommended that the Topic section be prepared for most interviews.

### The Downside to the Topic Section

- If an interviewer reads from it, they do not appear knowledgeable about the subject matter.
- It is difficult to interact and build rapport when reading from a list.
- Verbal and nonverbal indicators of deception or truthfulness might be missed.
- An interviewer might not be able to exercise mental agility and transition to other topics and questions if they rely on the list.

It is best that the interviewer does not rely on the Topic List during the interview. The list should be memorized, understood, and absorbed. However, it is acceptable to refer to the List if needed. Near the end of the interview, it is common to review the list to ensure all topics were covered. The KTOT is beneficial for supervisors to review to ensure that the interviewer is on the correct path.

Review the KTOT Example in Appendix A.

## Organize the Interview Room

Interviews can take place in a variety of locations. Critical interviews of suspects, possible suspects, as well as reluctant, uncooperative, or hostile interviewees are ideally conducted in a dedicated interview room. The ideal interview room is described as follows:

- Size: 10′ by 10′ or thereabouts.
- No windows, phone, or other items that could distract the interviewee. The walls should be bare.
- The room should include two straight back chairs positioned facing each other around 4 or 5 feet apart. One chair is for the interviewer, and the other chair is for the interviewee. There should be room for two additional chairs.
- A small table should be placed against the wall next to the interviewer's chair. This table allows the interviewer to place files and a note pad on it.
- There should be no barriers, such as a table or desk between the interviewer and the interviewee.
- A dedicated interview room is ideally equipped with audio and video recording capability. The interview can be audio and video monitored from another location.

Depending on the circumstances, other interview room arrangements might be required. If an organization does not have a dedicated interview room or if interviews are conducted in the field, an interviewer must improvise. Conference rooms, offices, hotel rooms, or other appropriate spaces can be arranged. Remember that it is important to have no barriers between the interviewer and the interviewee, who should be seated around 4–5 feet apart. Also, keep in mind that interview privacy is the most important consideration when arranging an interview location. If conducting a noncustodial interview, the interviewee should be seated closest to the unlocked door. It is practical to interview resource providers at their location. The resource provider might easily retrieve needed documents from files located in their office.

The ideal interview situation is one interviewer and the interviewee. However, circumstances could dictate that additional individuals be included. If two interviewers are present, the secondary interviewer should be seated next to the prime interviewer, slightly angled facing the interviewee. If a union representative or attorney is participating, they should be seated next to the interviewee. Occasionally, an interviewer will request a non-involved interview observer to be present. The request might occur if the interviewer desires a witness to verify the interviewer's conduct and the validity of the interviewee's statement. This could occur if for some reason there is no audio or video equipment available. The non-involved observer should sit to the side and the rear of the interviewee. If an interpreter is required, they should sit next to the interviewer facing the interviewee at an angle.

If the interviewee is in custody, more than likely the interview is taking place in a law enforcement setting. The seating arrangements should be reversed from the noncustodial arrangements with the interviewer sitting closest to the door. In a custodial interview, it is best if only one law enforcement interviewer is present. Besides hindering the ability to build rapport, more than one interviewer can appear to create coercive environment. With that said, agency policy and case specifics could require two officers present. Other officers can observe the interview from a video monitor or an observation window. If the interview room does not have video monitoring capability or an observation window, then another officer can sit against the wall or at the table as an observer. Also, an attorney and interpreter, if needed, should be seated in the appropriate places relative to the interviewee.

## ARRANGING THE INTERVIEW

In some circumstances, it could be appropriate to arrive unannounced at an interviewee's location. This decision should be made during an interview strategy session. With that said, many interviews will be arranged. Most interviews are arranged by calling the individual.

Often, the individual is unaware of an investigation and is caught off-guard by the call. So, it is essential that the interviewer immediately set a positive tone. Breaking down barriers and gaining trust begins with the very first contact. When making the call, the interviewer should identify themself and their office. Be professional with a pleasant demeanor. Most people respond positively to someone who is cordial. During this call, the individual will assess the interviewer's attitude, while at the same time, the interviewer will evaluate the individual's attitude.

Do not use emotive words, such as "investigation." Use a softer word, such as "looking into a matter. Do not use the word "interview." Use "meet" or "discuss." Also, provide a general reason for the purpose of the meeting. For instance, if investigating a procurement fraud, do not use the word "fraud." Using the word "fraud" could cause concerns and resistance. It would be better to provide a broad reason, such as

> I am looking into the procedures for awarding contracts and I would like to meet with you to receive your input.

That is a broad, truthful reason for the interview. Review the "Word Choice" section in Chapter 9.

Occasionally, the individual will be aware that an investigation is taking place and is not surprised by the call. An individual involved in improper activity receiving a call to appear, will assume that their activity is the reason for the request. They are not 100% sure unless they are aware of an ongoing investigation. Many individuals will attempt to obtain as much information as possible. They will press for the reason why they need to appear. Just repeat the broad reason.

Many individuals will object to appearing or press for information and ask questions such as:

- "Am I in trouble?"
- "Do I need a lawyer?"
- "Do I need my union representative?"
- "Who else is being interviewed?"
- "Am I going to lose my job?"
- "Can't we just do this over the phone?"
- "What happens if I don't come in?"

An individual asking these questions provides insight into their attitude and their possible knowledge of or involvement in the matter. The interviewer should address these types of questions to overcome their objections. Following are some standard responses to the above questions:

- Q: "Am I in trouble?"
  - Response 1: "We are just beginning our inquiry. It is important that we receive your input. Okay?"
  - Response 2: "Is there a reason that you would be in trouble?" (Wait for response). "It is best that you come in and talk about it. Okay?"

- Q: "Do I need lawyer?"
  - Response: "I cannot advise you if you need to speak to a lawyer. That is your decision. Do you understand?"
- Q: "Do I need my union representative?"
  - Response: "I cannot advise you if you need your union representative. That is your choice. Do you understand?"

- Q: Who else is being interviewed?"
  - Response: "I am not going to discuss who else I talked to. Just like I would not tell anybody else that I talked to you. Okay?"
- Q: "Am I going to lose my job?"
  - Response 1: "I am in no position to tell you if you are going to lose your job. That is not my decision. We are just beginning our inquiry and would like your input. It is best if you come in and talk about it. Okay?"
  - Response 2: "I am in no position to tell you if you are going to lose your job. That is not my decision. Is there some reason you feel you might lose your job?"
- Q: "Can't we just do this over the phone?"
  - Response: "I understand you are busy; however, we are unable to do this over the phone. It is better that we meet to discuss this. Okay?" (Note: Many interviews can be conducted over the phone.)

Most entities have a policy that requires employees to appear for interviews and cooperate with management and entity investigators. It is advisable not to rely on it to gain compliance unless it is necessary. Citing the policy to seek agreement does not bode well for breaking down barriers. However, if needed, use it. With that said, the policy can be cited with an understanding response as follows:

- Q: "What happens if I don't come in?"
  - Response: "Well as you know, the policy requires that you appear to meet with us. If you choose not to, I merely report this to the appropriate individual. What happens is not up to me. It is best if you come in and talk with me. Okay?"

These are a few of the questions that might be asked. There are others. It is the interviewer's job to overcome the objections. It is advisable to end a response with the question, "Okay?" or "Do you understand?" Asking these questions causes the individual to reply with a "yes" or "no" answer. If they respond with "yes," the interviewer overcame the objection and gained compliance. A "no" answer provides additional insight into the individual's attitude. Ask why they do not understand or why it is not okay. If the interviewer receives further resistance from an employee governed by a cooperation policy, they will probably need to cite it. If the interviewer is dealing with a non-employee who refuses to appear, they might have to show up at the individual's location. Occasionally, an individual will object to the time and place of the interview. Listen to their reason and be flexible if warranted and possible.

Note: The author knows of one organization whose investigators send an email to the employee notifying them of the interview and instructing them what time to arrive for an interview. This policy is an option; however, it is not well suited for identifying the individual's attitude and gaining trust. With that said, the author's office was involved in two serious investigations that required over 100 expedited interviews for each case. Working with management and union officials, investigators formulated an interview schedule, and supervisors directed employees to appear. In both of these situations, the employees were aware of the investigation.

## SUMMARY

Once an interviewer determines that an individual needs to be interviewed pursuant to an investigation, the first step is to prepare for the interview. Preparation includes understanding the nature of the offense, evaluating available information, classifying the interviewees, developing an interview strategy, performing interviewee background, preparing a KTOT (Knowledge, Theory, Objective, and Topic List), and organizing the interview room. The next step is to arrange the interview. Many interview arrangements are made by phone depending on the nature of the investigation and the interviewee classification. This first contact is an opportunity to break down barriers and gain trust, using less emotive words. The interviewer must also overcome the individual's objections to participate in the interview.

## EXERCISE 11.1. MULTIPLE CHOICE AND TRUE AND FALSE QUESTIONS

1. Most interviews that fail to achieve objectives are due to a lack of preparation.

   _____ True
   _____ False

2. An investigator should be a subject matter expert of the offense for which they are conducting interviews.

   _____ True
   _____ False

3. Interview preparation can include evaluating available information from:

_____ Documents.
_____ Forensic analysis of material and data.
_____ Information from previous interviews.
_____ All of the above.

4. A suspect is an individual who the investigator has determined, with reasonable certainty based on clear and convincing evidence, is responsible or involved in the matter under investigation.

_____ True
_____ False

5. Upon receipt of an allegation, it is recommended to interview the suspect first to obtain their side of the story.

_____ True
_____ False

6. An interview strategy is separate from a case plan.

_____ True
_____ False

7. Upon receiving an allegation that meets a minimum threshold, the first step is to corroborate the allegation.

_____ True
_____ False

8. When preparing a KTOT, the Knowledge section flows from the Objective section.

_____ True
_____ False

9. In a noncustodial interview, the interviewer should be seated closest to the door.

_____ True
_____ False

10. When arranging an interview with an individual who is unaware of an investigation, the interviewer should provide the specific reason for the interview.

    _____ True
    _____ False

## EXERCISE 11.2. ESSAY TOPICS

1. Explain the importance of an investigator understanding the nature of the offense they are investigating.
2. Discuss the benefit of evaluating available information prior to an interview.
3. Discuss the importance of placing an interviewee in the appropriate category.
4. Discuss what developing an interview strategy entails.
5. Discuss the benefit of conducting a background check on interviewees prior to an interview.
6. Explain the KTOT section flow.
7. Describe the ideal noncustodial interview room arrangement.
8. Discuss the use of nonemotive words when arranging the interview.

# 12

# *Beginning the Interview*

## LEARNING OBJECTIVES

- Discuss the importance of the introduction.
- Explain what occurs during preliminary matters.
- Discuss the various Introductory Statements for different interviewee categories.
- Explain the three basic reasons to ask preliminary questions.
- Identify the importance of offering an appropriate Opening Statement.

## INTRODUCTION

An interview has a beginning and an end. How the interview begins will set the tone for the interview. The interviewer should strive to break down barriers and gain trust by being cordial and polite and not acting officious. Preliminary matters should be discussed at this time. The interview continues with an Introductory Statement that provides a broad reason for the interview. Following the Introductory Statement, preliminary questions are asked in an attempt to build rapport and note the interviewee's behavior response to nonsensitive questions. Following the preliminary questions, the critical Opening Statement addresses the specific reason for the interview and instructs the interviewee to be truthful and provide complete information.

## INTRODUCTIONS AND PRELIMINARY MATTERS

The introduction sets the tone of the interview. The mere fact that an interviewee has been asked to appear can cause them anxiety. It is the interviewer's job to break down barriers and gain trust. When the interviewee arrives, be professional, cordial, and polite. The interviewer's body language should reflect a nonofficious demeanor. Shake hands. Touch breaks down barriers. However, some interviewees do not want to shake hands. (**Note**: As this book is being written, the world is in the midst of a global pandemic. Shaking hands is not advised.)

The author recommends to not flaunt authority by using titles such as detective, investigator, or special agent. Use first names. Do not expose a badge or weapon. Do not display credentials unless asked to do so by the interviewee. (When conducting interviews in the field, it is appropriate to show credentials.) Ask the interviewee if they can be referred to by first name. If the say no, it provides a clue to their attitude. Introduce the second investigator if one is present. If the interviewee has a union representative or an attorney accompanying them, introductions should be made in the same fashion. Explain the interview parameters with the union representative or attorney. The interviewer should attempt to break down barriers and gain trust with these individuals.

Thank the individual for appearing, even if it was reluctant compliance. Have the participants sit in the designated seats as discussed in Chapter 11. If this is a noncustodial interview, show the interviewee that the door is unlocked. In most circumstances, refreshments or a chance to use the restroom should be offered. Keep in mind that an interviewee could use the drink to alleviate anxiety when responding to sensitive questions.

If the interview is going to be video or audio recorded, inform the interviewee and any other participant, and obtain their consent. Many states have two-party consent, wherein all parties must agree to the recording. Some states have one-party consent, wherein only one person needs to agree. That person would be the interviewer. However, it is still advisable to notify the interviewee and obtain agreement. When offering the Introductory Statement, again capture the interviewee and other participant's consent to having the interview recorded. The rules are different for custodial interviews by law enforcement and vary by state.

If an interviewee is an employee governed by a cooperation policy and does not agree to the recording, the interviewer should let them know it is policy to record the interview if that is the case. If they do not agree, the interviewer must decide if the interview takes place. If the interviewee is an employee governed by a cooperation policy, they should be informed that their noncompliance to policy will be reported to the appropriate individual.

## INTRODUCTORY STATEMENTS

Introductory Statements will vary depending on the interview category and interview objective. Many Introductory Statements can be rather informal. Even so, there should be a practiced structure. For instance, if an interviewer is interviewing a resource provider, after introductions the interviewer should thank them for their time and agreeing to meet. The interviewer can inform or remind the resource provider of the reason for the meeting. This is an excellent time to practice the art of human interaction and make small talk. The interview can begin with preliminary matters, such as the resource provider's current position and job responsibilities.

Introductory Statements for other interviewee categories are more structured. After the preliminary matters, ask the interviewee if they know the reason for the meeting. If a broad reason was given when arranging the interview, they will usually recite that reason. Often, an interviewee will know that an investigation is occurring and provide their understanding of the meeting purpose. If this is the case, agree with the interviewee and re-state the broad reason. If the interviewee claims not to know the reason, the interviewer should provide a broad reason.

If the interview is noncustodial, it is recommended the interviewer inform the interviewee that their participation is voluntary, and they are free to leave at any time. If *Garrity* or *Kalkines* warnings are required, this is the time to provide them. If the interview is custodial, recite the *Miranda* warnings. Next, the interviewer should ask the interviewee if they are aware of what their office or unit does. If they do, expound on their answer. If they do not, provide a brief explanation of the office's mission.

Next, seek the interviewee's agreement to answer preliminary questions. Very few interviewees will not agree. If they do not agree, it will provide further insight into their attitude. Some interviewees might not want to discuss personal matters that have nothing to do with the purpose of the interview. That is okay.

Following is an Introductory Statement for a noncustodial interview or of a witness or possible witness that is not video or audio recorded:

> Peter, thank you for agreeing to meet with us today. Do you know why we need to speak to you? **(Wait for a response).** As I mentioned on the phone, we are looking into a matter involving contract awards and would appreciate your input. Just to let you know, your participation is voluntary. You are free to leave at any time. Do you understand? **(Obtain an affirmation of understanding).** Are you aware of what our office does? **(Wait for a response).** We look into matters that affect the efficiency of the organization's operations, including waste, fraud, abuse, and mismanagement. Before I begin, I would like to obtain some preliminary information, okay?

Following is an Introductory Statement for an employee governed by an entity policy that requires employees to cooperate and participate in investigatory interviews. The interview is being audio recorded. The recorder is on.

> Today, is Monday, April 11, 2016, the time is 11:07 am. I am Jack Grant, Investigator with XYZ Corporation. Also present is Investigator Mary Duncan, and Fred Thompson, XYZ Procurement Officer. Fred, as I said earlier, you can call me Jack and you can call Ms. Duncan, Mary. Thank you for coming in and I appreciate your cooperation. As I mentioned, we are recording our discussion today. Do you agree with the recording? **(Fred agrees)** Great. I must tell you that notwithstanding XYZ's policy that employees must appear and cooperate with our office, your participation here today is voluntary. You are free to leave at any time. Do you understand? **(Fred states he understands).** Do you know why we need to speak to you today? **(Wait for a response).** As I mentioned on the phone, we will be discussing contracts between XYZ and a contractor and would love to have your input. Fred, are you aware of what our office does? **(Wait for a response).** We look into matters that affect the efficiency of XYZ's operations, including waste, fraud, abuse, and mismanagement. Before we get started, I would like to obtain some background information, okay?

Sometimes, the employee will say they do not understand that they are free to leave. It is the interviewer's job to obtain an affirmation of understanding from the interviewee. Repeat the statement and if necessary, add that the interviewee has a choice. Do not state that the employee will face discipline because that is not in the interviewer's control and is counter to breaking down barriers and gaining trust. Just say:

> Fred, if you choose not to participate and leave, I merely report your noncompliance to policy to the appropriate person here at XYZ. However, I hope that you will stay and provide your input. Do you understand?

If needed, recite the policy that refers to discipline for not complying. Having the interviewee acknowledge they understand breaks down barriers by causing the interviewee to participate in the conversation. Once the interviewee confirms their understanding, continue with the remainder of the Introductory Statement.

(**Note**: When the interviewer arranged the interview, a guilty interviewee often anticipates that they will be accused. Occasionally, an interviewee responsible for the matter under investigation will confess when asked if they know the purpose of the interview. If that is the case, move forward and have them relate the details.

Introductory Statements for a victim, whistleblower, or accuser are less rigid because they initiated the contact. Following are two examples:

Victim:

> "Today, is Tuesday. September 10, 2016, the time is 1:09 pm. I am Jack Grant, Investigator with XYZ Corporation. Also present is Emma Thornton. Thank you for coming in. Ms. Thornton has agreed to be referred to as Emma. Emma, we are looking into the sexual harassment complaint you made against your supervisor. I am going to ask you questions in this regard. As I mentioned, we will be recording this interview. Do you agree to the recording? **(Emma agrees).** Great. Before we get started, I would like to ask you some preliminary questions, okay?"

Whistleblower or Accuser:

> "Today, is Friday, January 6, 2016, the time is 10:25 am. I am Jack Grant, Investigator with XYZ Corporation. Also present is Robert Ramirez. Thank you for contacting us. Mr. Ramirez has agreed to be referred to as Bob. Bob, we will be examining the information you provided to us regarding a kickback scheme here at XYZ. As I mentioned, we are recording this meeting. Do you agree to the recording? **(Bob agrees).** Great. Before we get started, I would like to ask you some preliminary questions. Okay?"

The above Introductory Statements are offered as examples. An interviewer will develop statements that are appropriate with various interviewees.

## PRELIMINARY QUESTIONS

Asking preliminary questions will allow the interviewer to further assess the interviewee's overall attitude. If the interviewee displays an attitude that is less than cooperative, the interviewer should employ strategies to break down barriers and gain trust. Keep in mind that while an interviewer is assessing the interviewee's attitude, the interviewee is assessing the interviewer's attitude.

There are three basic reasons to ask preliminary questions:

- Obtain or verify necessary biographical information.
- Build rapport by finding common ground.
- Establish the interviewee's baseline response behavior.

### Biographical Information

One reason to ask preliminary questions is to obtain information that might be needed, such as full name, date of birth, address, and employment. Even though the interviewer might have this information, the questions should be asked for confirmation. With that said, asking these biographical questions should be done in a conversational tone and not sound like a deposition.

### Build Rapport

Asking preliminary questions also provides an opportunity to build rapport by finding common ground. Chapter 10 discussed Building Rapport. If common ground is found, spend a couple of minutes, not much longer on that topic. When asking the common ground questions, an interviewee might provide some insight into their motivation to be less than cooperative, as well as their possible involvement in the matter under investigation. For instance, if the investigation involves an internal theft, an employee might comment on personal or family financial troubles. Also, questions about employment can provide substantial insight into how employees might rationalize their behavior to fall on the wrong side of the fence. For example, the interviewee might comment that they were overlooked for a promotion that they thought they deserved. This insight may be beneficial later in the interview when seeking a truthful acknowledgment of responsibility.

### Establish Baseline Response Behavior

Asking preliminary questions allows the interviewer to establish the interviewee's response behavior to noncritical questions. Interviewees typically answer these questions truthfully and their nonverbal response behavior should coincide with truthful responses. The interviewer will compare these behavioral responses with behavioral responses to the key questions, evaluating for truth, deception, and lies.

After the preliminary questions, it is important to offer an appropriate Opening Statement.

## OPENING STATEMENTS

At this point in the interview process, the interviewer has hopefully identified the interviewee's attitude, broken down barriers, and gained trust. Now, the goal is to obtain as much truthful and accurate information as possible. The Opening Statement is a critical component of the interview. As discussed above, the Introductory Statement provided a broad reason for the interview. Now, the Opening Statement clarifies the specific purpose of the interview. Additionally, the Opening Statement encourages the interviewee to provide a full account even if they are not sure it is accurate and to let the interviewer know if that is the case. The interviewer should also instruct the interviewee not to fabricate any portion of the account. Opening Statements are beneficial for victims, witnesses, possible witnesses, accusers, whistle-blowers, potential suspects, and suspects. Following are examples:

Victim:

> "Okay Mary. As you know we are looking into the sexual harassment allegation you made against Joe Jones. It is important that you tell us everything you know. Do not leave anything out. Even something that might not seem important to you, could be. Also, if you are not sure about something, that is okay, just let us know that you are not sure. I am not saying that you would, but please do not fabricate any fact. Do you understand?"

Possible Witness:

> "Jerry, as I told you, we are looking into construction contract awards. Specifically, we are looking into information we developed that two contractors are paying certain employees a kickback to ensure that they receive the awards. It is imperative that we get to the bottom of this. We have reason to believe that you have

> information that could help resolve this matter. It is important that you tell us everything you know. Do not leave anything out, even something that might not seem important to you, could be. Also, if you are not sure about something, that is okay, just let us know that you are not sure. Jerry, I am not saying that you would, but please do not fabricate any information. Do you understand?"

Witness:

> "Fred, as you know, we are looking into construction contract awards. Specifically, we are looking into information that two contractors are paying certain employees a kickback to ensure that they receive the awards. It is imperative that we get to the bottom of this. It is important that you tell us everything you know. Do not leave anything out, even something that might not seem important to you, could be. Also, if you are not sure about something, that is okay, just let us know that you are not sure. Fred, I am not saying that you would, but please do not fabricate any information. Do you understand?"

Whistleblower or Accuser:

> "Bob, as you know, we will be looking into the complaint you filed regarding a procurement fraud here at XYZ. We appreciate you bringing this to our attention. It is important that you tell us everything you know. Do not leave any information out, even something that might not seem important to you, could be. Also, if you are not sure about something, that is okay, just let us know that you are not sure. Bob, I am not saying that you would, but please do not fabricate any information. Do you understand?"

Asking the above interviewees if they understand at the end of the Opening Statement causes the interviewee to acknowledge their understanding and become part of the conversation. The interviewer can further assess the interviewee's attitude depending on the answer.

## Potential Suspect

As previously discussed, a potential suspect is an individual for whom the interviewer has received uncorroborated information as being responsible for or involved in the matter under investigation. Also, a potential suspect is an individual who had the opportunity or possible motive to commit the offense. An Opening Statement for a possible suspect reveals the interviewer's objectivity. Additionally, the interviewer will ask the interviewee if they are responsible.

The Opening Statement for a possible suspect will differ depending on the incident being investigated. For instance, if the investigation involves a theft, assault, or another specific offense, the below Opening Statement could be offered:

> Peter, as I mentioned, we have been looking into the money missing from the safe. It is important that you are straightforward with us. Peter, if you did take the money, our investigation will conclude that you did. If you did not take the money, our investigation will conclude that you did not. Peter, if you took the money from the safe, it is best if you tell us now. Peter, did you take the money from the safe?

Peter will either deny taking the money or confess. If Peter states he did take the money from the safe, have him relate the details. If Peter denies taking the money, evaluate the strength of his denial, then proceed to the key questions. If the investigation involves a specific allegation without corroborating evidence, the following Opening Statement could be appropriate:

> Joe, as you know, we have been looking into the allegation that last Monday you came up behind Mary Reese in the hall outside of your office, put your arms around her, fondled her breast, and kissed her on the neck. Joe, is there any truth to this?

If Joe responds that there is truth or partial truth to the allegation, have him relate the details and fill in the blanks with follow-up questions. If Joe denies the allegation, evaluate the strength of his denial, then proceed to the key questions.

Below is an Opening Statement for a potential suspect who might be involved in fraud or other ongoing crime:

> Peter, we will be specifically discussing information that some employees are receiving kickbacks or payments to ensure certain firms receive contracts. Peter, we have been looking into this matter so, it is important that you are straightforward with us. If you are involved, our investigation will clearly show that you are. If you are not involved, our investigation will show that you are not. Peter, are you involved?

Peter will either admit or deny his involvement. If he denies involvement, evaluate the strength of his denial, then continue with the key questions.

### Suspect

An Opening Statement for a suspect could include an accusation. As previously discussed, a proper forensic mindset identifies a suspect as an individual for whom the interviewer has clear and convincing evidence is responsible for or involved in the matter under investigation. In a legal context, clear and convincing evidence is a standard to be considered by a trier of fact. It means that the evidence is substantially more probable to be true than not. In an interview context, clear and convincing evidence should be the minimum standard considered to accuse someone. Following is an Opening Statement with an accusation for a suspect involved in a procurement fraud:

> Fred, we have been looking into the circumstances surrounding John Simpson and Camden Contractors paying your daughter Anne's tuition at Granger University in return for you awarding a contract to Camden to build three stores. Our investigation shows that this in fact occurred. We would like you to explain the circumstances, okay?

Fred will either explain the circumstance or deny his involvement. Chapter 13 discusses evaluating and handling potential suspect and suspect denials.

## SUMMARY

Best practice interview steps begin with the Introduction and continues with an Introductory Statement. This is followed with preliminary questions and an attempt to build rapport by finding common ground. Depending on the interview objective and the interviewee classification, an appropriate Opening Statement should be offered.

## EXERCISE 12.1. MULTIPLE CHOICE AND TRUE AND FALSE QUESTIONS

1. If the interview is going to be video and audio recorded, it should be first addressed during the preliminary matters.

   _____ True
   _____ False

2. It is recommended that during the introduction, the interviewer exhibit their authority by volunteering credentials for the interviewee to review.

_____ True
_____ False

3. The same Introductory Statement should be used for all interviewee categories.

_____ True
_____ False

4. During the Introductory Statement, the interviewer should provide the specific reason for the interview.

_____ True
_____ False

5. It is advisable to inform noncustodial interviewees that they are free to leave at any time during the Introductory Statement.

_____ True
_____ False

6. It is advisable to show an interviewee who is not in custody that the door to the interview room is unlocked.

_____ True
_____ False

7. The basic reasons to ask preliminary questions are:

_____ Obtain or verify biographical information.
_____ Build rapport by finding common ground.
_____ Establish baseline response behavior.
_____ All of the above.

8. Suspect and possible suspect interviewees might provide insight as to their motive for committing an offense during preliminary questions.

_____ True
_____ False

9. An Opening Statement for a possible suspect reveals the interviewer's objectivity.

    _____ True
    _____ False

10. An Opening Statement for a suspect could include an accusation.

    _____ True
    _____ False

## EXERCISE 12.2. ESSAY TOPICS

1. Discuss how an interviewer should handle the introduction.
2. Explain the purpose of an Introductory Statement.
3. Discuss the purpose of asking preliminary questions.
4. Explain the importance of offering an Opening Statement.

# 13

# *Evaluating and Handling Denials*

## LEARNING OBJECTIVES

- To describe and discuss strong denials.
- To list the common weak denials.
- To explain the difference between a potential suspect denial and a suspect denial.
- To discuss follow-up responses to potential suspect weak denials.
- To discuss follow-up responses to suspect weak denials.
- To explain when, why, and how to retreat from an accusation.

## INTRODUCTION

As discussed in the previous chapter, a potential suspect when asked if they are involved or a suspect when accused of the offense will either confess or deny their involvement. Denials of responsibility are often the first reaction. Denials come in all shapes and sizes. A strong denial does not include modifiers or qualifiers. A strong denial is a simple, "no" or "I did not do it." As strong as those denials are, it does not necessarily mean they are true. Weak denials include evasive qualifiers, modifiers, and "word play" to convince the interviewer that the denial is sincere. A weak denial does not necessarily mean it is not factual; however, it should cause an interviewer to question its authenticity. Interviewers should be able to recognize weak denials and be prepared to follow up. It is also important to know when to retreat from an accusation.

## POTENTIAL SUSPECT DENIALS

If an interviewee is a potential suspect, the interview objective should be to determine the interviewee's knowledge of or involvement in the matter under investigation. At some point in the interview, often at the end of the Opening Statement, the interviewer will ask the interviewee if they did "it," if they are involved, or if there is any truth to the allegation. The interviewee will either deny involvement or confess. If the interviewee offers a denial, the interviewer must evaluate it for its strength.

Investigations may involve many elements of a larger issue. For instance, in a procurement fraud investigation involving kickbacks or bribes, a question at the end of the Opening Statement could be, "Are you involved?" If the potential suspect denies involvement, further questions could include, "Did you accept a free vacation?" *or* "Did you accept free sporting event tickets?" The interviewer must also evaluate any denials to those questions.

Keep in mind that even though the interviewee is classified as a potential suspect, they know if they are guilty. A guilty interviewee might be expecting an accusation and is prepared to offer a denial. The fact that the interviewer did not accuse them, did not alter their prepared denial when the interviewer merely asked if they did "it." An interviewee classified as a possible suspect who is not guilty, might also expect to be accused. They, too, could have prepared a denial. However, their denial is usually spontaneous and robust.

## SUSPECT DENIALS

If the interviewer has clear and convincing evidence that leads them to classify the interviewee as a suspect, the interview objective could be to obtain a truthful confession. If this is the case, the interviewer will accuse the interviewee of the offense, often at the end of the Opening Statement. Accusing a suspect is not the same as asking a potential suspect if they are responsible. Accusing an interviewee is *telling* them they are responsible. When accused, a suspect can provide the same common weak denials as a potential suspect.

As with a potential suspect, a suspect interviewee knows whether they are guilty.

## WEAK DENIALS

The author has identified the following types of weak denials:

- Simple evasive denial
- Present verb tense denial
- Future verb tense denial
- Reinforced denial
- Pre and Post-denial modifiers
- "Why would I" denial
- "I deny" denial
- "I resent the accusation" denial
- Technically correct denial

Other denial issues an interviewer must be aware of are:

- Re-defining words
- Interviewees possessing a different value system

If a potential suspect offers a weak denial, the interviewer has a choice to make. Do they immediately follow-up with a statement and questions that "catch" the interviewee in their weak denial? Or does the interviewer move on with questions that could move the interviewee from the potential suspect category to the suspect category? It depends. A weak, evasive denial begs for a follow-up with a response and a question or questions. It might be best to take note of other weak denials and move forward with questions. The interviewer will make the decision based on the interview circumstances.

If a suspect offers a weak denial, it is often best to make an appropriate comment and repeat the accusation. If the suspect again offers a denial, it could be appropriate to acknowledge the denial and reveal evidence that could convince the suspect to confess.

Following are examples of Opening Statement accusations along with weak denials and interviewer follow-up responses.

**Simple Evasive Denial**:

Implies the interviewee is telling the truth. Simple evasive denials are easy to detect.

**Potential Suspect**:

**Q**: "Pete, did you take the money from the safe?"
**Denial**: "I don't even have the combination to the safe."

**Note**: Besides this being a simple evasive response, it is also a present verb tense evasive response, as discussed next.

**Follow-Up Response**:

"Pete, I am glad to hear you do not have the combination to the safe. Have you ever had the combination to the safe?" *or* "Was the safe unlocked?" *or* "Was the safe on day lock?" *or* "Have you ever had access to the inside of the safe for any reason?"

Based on Pete's answers to these questions, the interviewer could ask him again if he took the money or move on.

**Suspect**:

**Accusation:** "Pete, our investigation shows that you took the money from the safe. Please tell me why you did this."

**Denial**: "I don't even have the combination to the safe."

**Follow-Up Response**:

"Pete, I am glad to hear you do not have the combination to the safe. That means that you did not plan this, it was a spur of the moment mistake. As I said, we know you did take the money from the safe. Was the safe unlocked, or was it on day lock?"

**Present Verb Tense Evasive Denial**:

An interviewee boldly offers this to suggest that the event never occurred, which prevents the interviewee who is guilty from either incriminating themself or lying.

**Potential Suspect**:

**Q:** "Joe, did you accept free sporting event tickets from a vendor?"

**Denial:** "I do not accept free sporting event tickets from vendors."

**Follow-Up Response**:

"Joe, I hear what you are saying; however, I need to know if you have ever accepted free sporting event tickets from a vendor. Have you ever?" *or* "When was the last time?"

**Suspect**:

**Accusation:** "Joe, our investigation shows that you did accept sporting event tickets from a vendor. Please explain the circumstances."

**Denial***:* "I do not accept free sporting event tickets from a vendor."

**Follow-Up Response**:

"Joe, I hear what you are saying; however, we know that you have. Please tell me about it."

**Future Verb Tense Evasive Denial:**

An interviewee offers this evasive response to suggest that it did not occur. However, the words "would never" means it will not happen in the future. It does not mean it did not occur in the past.

**Potential Suspect**:

**Q***:* "Joe, did you accept free sporting event tickets from a vendor?"

**Denial**: "I would never accept anything from a vendor."

**Follow-Up Response**:

"Joe, I'm glad to hear you would never accept free sporting event tickets from a vendor. I need to know if you have ever accepted free sporting event tickets from a vendor. Have you ever?" *or* "When was the last time?"

**Suspect**:

**Accusation***:* "Joe, our investigation shows that you did accept sporting event tickets from a vendor. Please explain the circumstances."

**Denial:** "I would never accept anything from a vendor."

**Follow-Up Response**:

"Joe, I hear what you are saying; however, we know that you have. Please tell me about it."

**Reinforced Denial**:

An attempt to convince the interviewer of the denial sincerity:

**Potential Suspect**:

**Q:** "Pete, did you accept a bribe from Zero Electronics?"
**A:** "I swear to God, I did not accept a bribe."
**Note**: I would take note of this response and move on with other questions.

**Follow-Up Response**:

"Okay Pete, let me ask you a few questions."

**Suspect**:

**Accusation:** "Pete, our investigation shows, without doubt, you did accept a bribe from Zero Electronics. Please tell me why you did this."
**Denial:** "I swear to God, I did not accept a bribe."

**Follow-Up Response**:

"Pete, like I said, we know that you did. I would like to understand why you did this."

**Pre-Denial and Post-Denial Modifiers:**

Sometimes, a denial will have a pre-denial or post-denial modifier that weakens the denial.

**Potential Suspect**:

**Pre-Denial Modifier**

**Q:** "Pete, is there any truth to the allegation that you accepted money from a contractor?"
**Denial:** "I can look you in the eye and swear I never accepted money from a contractor."
**Note**: Pete did not respond to the question with a simple yes or no answer. Pete's response does not mean that he did not accept money from a contractor. His modifier, "I can look you in the eye and swear," indicates just that. He could you in the eye and swear. It does not mean the second part of his response is true.

**Post-Denial Modifier**

**Q:** "Pete, is there any truth to the allegation that you accepted money from a contractor?"

**Denial:** "I did not accept money from a contractor. **That is my statement to you.**"

**Note**: Again, Pete did not respond to the question with a simple yes or no answer. Pete's response does not mean that he did not accept money from a contractor. His modifier of, "That is my statement to you," indicates just that. It is Pete's statement to you. It does not mean the first part of his response is true.

**Note**: I would move on to other questions.

**Follow-Up Response:**

"Okay Pete, let me ask you a few questions."

**Suspect**:

**Accusation:** "Pete, our investigation shows that you did accept money from a contractor. I would like you to explain the circumstances."

**Pre-Denial Modifier**

**Denial:** "I can look you in the eye and swear I never accepted money from a contractor."

**Post-Denial Modifier**

**Denial:** "I did not accept money from a contractor. That is my statement to you."

**Follow-Up Response**:

"Pete, as I said, our investigation shows that you did accept money from a contractor. We would like you to explain the circumstances."

**"Why Would I" Denial**:

An interviewee will deflect the question by asking, "why would I…," often with some qualified explanation.

**Potential Suspect**:

**Q**: "Pete, did you accept a bribe from Zero Electronics?"
**Denial**: "Why would I accept a bribe? I have a good paying job."

**Follow-Up Response**:

"Pete, I am not sure why; however, I am asking you if you did accept a bribe?"

**Suspect**:

**Accusation**: "Pete, our investigation shows that you did accept a bribe from Zero Electronics. We would like you to explain why."
**Denial**: "Why would I accept a bribe? I have a good paying job."

**Follow-Up Response**:

"Pete, that is what we want to understand, we know you did it, I just would like to understand why."

**"I Deny" Denial**:

An "I Deny" Denial is not the same as saying "no."

**Potential Suspect**:

**Q**: "Joe, did you accepted money from Camden Contractors in return for awarding them a contract?"
**Denial**: "I unequivocally deny receiving money from Camden Contractors."
**Note**: Joe did not say that he did not accept money from Camden Contractors. I would move on to other questions with a preamble.

**Follow-Up Response**:

"Okay Joe, let me ask you a few questions."

**Suspect**:

**Accusation**: "Joe, our investigation shows without doubt that you accepted money from Camden Contractors in return for awarding them a contract. I would like you to explain the circumstances."

**Denial**: "I unequivocally deny receiving money from Camden Contractors."

**Follow-Up Response**:

"Joe, like I said, we know that you did accept money from Camden Contractors for awarding them a contract. I would like to understand the circumstances."

**"I Resent the Accusation" Denial**:

This is a prepared deflection denial. It indicates that more than likely, the potential suspect was ready for an accusation. Often, the interviewee accompanies this weak denial with feigned anger.

**Potential Suspect**:

**Q**: "Joe, are you involved in the kickback scheme?"

**Denial**: "I resent the accusation."

**Note**: The interviewer did not accuse Joe. The interviewer asked Joe if he is involved.

**Follow-Up Response**:

"Joe, I did not accuse you, I just asked you. Are you involved?"

**Suspect**:

**Accusation**: "Joe, our investigation shows that you are involved in the kickback scheme. I would like to you to explain your involvement."

**Denial**: "I resent the accusation."

**Follow-Up Response**:

"Joe, like I said, we know that you are involved and would like to hear your explanation."

**Technically Correct Denial**:

In the United States Criminal Justice System, an accused individual is innocent until found guilty by a judge or a jury.

**Potential Suspect**:

**Q**: "Joe, did you take the money from the safe?"
**Denial**: "I am not guilty of taking the money from the safe."

**Follow Up Response**:

**Q**: "Joe, you certainly are presumed innocent until proven guilty in a court of law, which is not the same as being responsible. I asked if you took the money from the safe. Did you?"

**Note**: If the potential suspect again denies the allegation, the interviewer should acknowledge the denial and offer a statement such as:

"Okay. Let me ask you some questions so we can figure this out."

**Suspect**:

**Accusation**: "Joe, the results of our investigation show without doubt that you took money from the safe. We want to know why you did this."

**Denial**: "I am not guilty of taking the money from the safe."

**Follow-Up Response**:

"Joe, you are indeed presumed innocent until proven guilty in a court of law. However, as I said, our investigation shows that you did take the money from the safe. I want to understand why you did this."

**Redefining Words**:

Some interviewees will redefine words to assist in their seemingly strong denial.

**Potential Suspect**:

**Q**: "Bill, did you have sexual relations with the young girl?"
**Denial**: "I did not have sexual relations with that young girl."

**Note**: The interviewee has possibly defined what took place as not being sexual relations. In addition, the word "young" is subjective.

**Follow-Up Questions**:

**Q**: "What type of relations did you have with the girl?"
**Q**: "What is your definition of sexual relations?"

**Suspect**:

**Accusation**: "Bill, the results of our investigation show that you did have sexual relations with the young girl. I need you to explain how this happened."

**Denial**: "I did not have sexual relations with that young girl."

**Note**: The interviewee has possibly defined what took place as not being sexual relations. Also, Bill might have a different definition of "young."

**Follow-Up Questions**:

**Q**: "What type of relations did you have with the girl?"
**Q**: "What is your definition of sexual relations?"

After Bill answers these questions, you can again accuse Bill:

"Bill, like I said, our investigation shows that you did have relations with that girl. I would like you to explain the circumstances."

**Different Value System**:

Some interviewees have a different belief or value system and will not display nonverbal indications of deception or lies when asked a question. For instance, some cultures accept bribery, kickbacks, or payoffs as a usual way to conduct business without stigma.

**Q:** "Did you provide a kickback to Joe Green?"
**Denial:** "No"

**Note:** This is a strong denial due to the lack of stigma attached to the word kickback. Follow-up questions will have to be specific and not include "crime" words.

**Follow-up Question**:

"Did you give Joe Green money?"

**Suspect**:

**Accusation**: "The results of our investigation reveal you did provide a kickback to Joe Greene so he would award you the contract. Please tell me how this occurred."

**Denial**: "I did not pay a kickback to Joe Greene."

**Follow-Up Question**:

"Like I said we know you did give Joe Greene money for the contract. Please tell me how this occurred."

The following two denials are commonly offered only by suspects.

### "I Don't Know What You're Talking About."

**Suspect**:

**Accusation**: "Fred, we have been looking into the circumstances surrounding John Simpson and Camden Contractors paying your daughter Anne's tuition at Granger University in return for you awarding a contract to Camden to build three stores. Our investigation shows without a doubt that this occurred. I would like you to explain the circumstances. Okay?"

**Denial**: "I don't know what you are talking about."

**Follow-Up Response**:

"Fred, like I said, our investigation shows that John Simpson and Camden Contractors paid for your daughter Anne's tuition at Granger University in return for you awarding a contract to Camden to build three stores. You know that this is true, and we know this is true. I would like you to explain the circumstances."

### "What Proof Do You Have?"

**Accusation**: "Fred, our investigations show without a doubt that Camden Contractors paid your daughter's tuition at Granger

University in return for you awarding Camden three store contracts. I would like you to explain the circumstances."

**Denial**: "What proof do you have?"

**Follow-Up Response**:

"Fred, like I said, we know that this occurred You know this is true. I would like you to explain the circumstances without us having to show you our proof."

## EVALUATING NONVERBAL RESPONSE WITH VERBAL DENIAL

An interviewer should evaluate an interviewee's nonverbal and paralinguistic response behavior simultaneously with their denial. When a guilty interviewee is asked if they did "it," or accused, they will either confess or lie. The lie may cause anxiety. Often, a guilty interviewee who offers a weak denial will display some nonverbal behavior that does not match the verbal response:

- Breaking eye contact.
- Face turns red/flushed.
- Folding their arms.
- Shifting feet.
- Touching face.
- Feigning anger.
- Pitch changes.
- Rambling response.
- Mumbling.

An interviewee who is not guilty and offers a strong denial, should not experience anxiety. They usually do not display nonverbal behavior that is in contrast to their verbal denial. Be aware that not guilty individuals are concerned with being falsely accused, which could affect their behavior. However, if the interviewer broke down barriers and gained trust with the interviewee, their concern should be alleviated.

## RETREATING FROM THE ACCUSATION

The interviewer placed the interviewee in the suspect category based on clear and convincing evidence. "Clear and convincing" means the evidence is highly and substantially more likely to be true than not true. It is a high standard, and as discussed, it should be the minimum standard to classify a person as a suspect and accuse them. However, clear and convincing does not mean beyond all doubt. The interviewer could be wrong.

Chapter 4 discussed interviewer false confession risk factors. One being interviewer stubbornness. If the interviewee offers a more forceful denial, the interviewer could reveal some evidence and have the interviewee explain it. The interviewer could offer a statement, such as:

"Fred, I hear what you are saying. Let's examine the facts."

If Fred provides a satisfactory alternate explanation to the evidence, the interviewer should retreat from the accusation and move forward with key questions. Fred's responses to key questions could remove or keep him as a suspect. If the interviewer still determines that Fred is a suspect, the interviewer can make an accusation later in the interview. (Chapter 15 discusses making an accusation later in the interview.) Also, the interviewer might need to perform further investigation in an attempt to corroborate the information Fred provided. Keep in mind, not all suspects confess.

## SUMMARY

When a potential suspect is asked if they are involved in an offense or when a suspect is accused of an offense, they will either confess or deny their involvement. An interviewer should be able to recognize strong and weak denials and follow-up appropriately. If an interviewer accuses and interviewee, and the denial is strong, the interviewer must be prepared to retreat from the accusation.

## EXERCISE 13.1. MULTIPLE CHOICE AND TRUE AND FALSE QUESTIONS

1. If the interviewee is a potential suspect, the interview objective should be to determine the interviewee's knowledge of or involvement in the matter under investigation.

   _____True
   _____ False

2. It is appropriate to accuse a potential suspect of being responsible for the matter under investigation.

_____ True
_____ False

3. A strong denial is a simple, "no" or "I did not do it."

_____ True
_____ False

4. Weak denials contain modifiers and qualifiers.

_____ True
_____ False

5. A potential suspect or suspect who knows they are guilty might offer a prepared denial.

_____ True
_____ False

6. Pick all that apply. Nonverbal behavior that might accompany a weak denial includes:

_____ Breaking eye contact.
_____ Feigning anger.
_____ Sitting stoically.
_____ Face flushes.

7. Interviewees who are not guilty are concerned with being falsely confused.

_____ True
_____ False

8. An interviewee who is not guilty and offers a strong denial should experience anxiety and display nonverbal behavior that is indicative of deception.

_____ True
_____ False

9. If a suspect offers a denial, it is recommended to restate the accusation one time.

_____ True
_____ False

10. If a suspect offers a second denial, it could be appropriate to reveal evidence to convince the suspect to confess.

    _____ True
    _____ False

## EXERCISE 13.2. ESSAY TOPICS

1. Discuss various weak denials.
2. Discuss how an interviewer should handle a potential suspect's weak denial when asked if they are involved.
3. Discuss how an interviewer should handle a suspect's weak denial when they are accused.
4. Explain why and how to retreat from an accusation.

# 14

# Questions, Responses, and Follow-Up

## LEARNING OBJECTIVES

- To discuss the value of asking open questions.
- To discuss indicators of deception in a response to an open question.
- To explain the purpose of clarifying questions.
- To discuss the importance of asking properly phrased direct questions.
- To list the types of improperly phrased direct questions.
- To list the types of evasive responses.
- To discuss follow-up questions to evasive responses.
- To describe the various nonverbal responses indicating deception.
- To explain how to use a follow-up test question.
- To discuss the value of Attitude Assessment Questions.

## INTRODUCTION

If after the Opening Statement, a potential suspect did not confess, if a suspect offered an alterante explantion to revelaed evidence or if the interviewee is a victim, accuser, or witness, it is time to move forward with the key questions. The interviewer should ask properly phrased open and direct questions. The interviewer should listen for truth, deception, and lies. If the interviewer detects deception from an interviewee's response, then it could be appropriate to follow up with a direct question.

## OPEN QUESTIONS

In addition to providing an interviewee the opportunity to be heard, which breaks down barriers, asking open questions allows the interviewer to receive as much information as possible without having to ask specific direct questions. Also, asking open questions enables the interviewer to detect truth, deception, and fabrication more easily. Open questions are best when not phrased as a question. They are a request for information and can be offered as initial, clarifying, and follow-up questions. Open questions call for the interviewee to provide a narrative response instead of a specific response. The more open questions asked, the better. When asking an open question, it is valuable to use verbs such as:

- Explain
- Tell
- Describe

Following are some examples of open questions for various interviewee categories:

**Victim**

- "Please explain the circumstances that caused you to make the allegation."
- "Please tell me everything that happened last night."
- "Please describe everything that occurred."

**Witness or Possible Witness**

- "Please explain everything you know about the kickback scheme."
- "Please tell me what you observed."
- "Please describe what happened."

**Whistleblower or Accuser**

- "Please explain why you reached out to us."
- "Please tell me everything you know about the safety issue."
- "Please describe your role in the fraud."

**Resource Provider**

- "Please explain the accounts payable internal controls."
- "Please tell me how the company grants overtime."
- "Please describe the procurement process for construction contracts."

While listening to an interviewee's account in response to an open question, the interviewer should not take notes. The interviewer should just listen. It is distracting to the interviewee if the interviewer is writing on a notepad when they are telling their story. Also, verbal and nonverbal indicators of deception might be missed. It is best if the interview is audio recorded to alleviate this issue. The interviewer should pay attention to the interviewee and show signs of active listening, such as a head nod and leaning forward. If an interviewee provides an account that is not accurate, the interviewer should not interrupt. If an interviewee is deliberately falsifying information, again, do not interrupt. The interviewer must be aware not to allow his or her body language to reveal disbelief.

If an interviewee stops talking, the interviewer should wait a few seconds, and if the interviewee does not continue, the interviewer should ask them to continue. The interviewer should assume the interviewee has more to say. Telling an interviewee to continue, lets them know that the interviewer is expecting more information. An interviewee fabricating their story might falter at this point.

## EVALUATING RESPONSES TO OPEN QUESTIONS

Interviewees who are less than truthful in their response to an open question will omit important information and minimize their knowledge or involvement. Listen to the narrative. A deceptive response might sound rehearsed with a lack of emotion and contain contradictions and varying levels of detail. If an interviewee recounts an event for the first time, a complete honest recitation would most likely not be chronological as the interviewee recalls details. If the recounting of the event for the first time is in exact chronological order, the interviewer should suspect that the interviewee rehearsed the response. Furthermore, the recounting should comprise three parts: The pre-event, the event, and the post-event. The three sections should contain approximately the same level of detail. An indication of deception is an interviewee who provides little detail of the event. Also, when an interviewee is recounting an event, listen for deceptive phrases such as:

- "The next thing I remember…" (Unless the person blacked out)
- "I thought about…"
- "I was thinking about…"
- "I wanted to…"
- "I was going to…"

These phrases can be used by an untruthful interviewee to fill in gaps in a falsified account. If an interviewee is truthful in relating an event, they would not necessarily use phrases like these. Pay attention to the interviewee's eye contact when they are responding. Following is an open question and an interviewee's response regarding an alleged sexual assault.

**Q**: "Mary, please tell us everything that happened the day of the assault."

**Response**: "I was in my office working on a spreadsheet for the afternoon's budget meeting. I was getting hungry, so I decided to eat my lunch early. I had packed my lunch, which I usually do because the prices in the cafeteria are outrageous and the food is not that good. So, I ate my lunch at my desk as usual because I am so busy. When I finished, I went back to working on the spreadsheet. I was able to finish and make six copies around 10 minutes before the meeting, which was at 2 pm. I was in a hurry, so I gathered up my papers and my purse and left my office to go to the meeting. As I was walking down the hall Joe came up behind me and put his arms around me and fondled my breasts and kissed me on my neck. I thought about screaming for him to stop. The next thing I remember I was in the conference room handing out the spreadsheets to the other people there. I sat down to take notes. The meeting lasted for an hour. When it was finished, I went back to my office and thought about what happened. I continued to work as usual. I had transcribed the notes from the meeting, which took me over an hour. I finished work at 5 and locked up my office and walked to the parking lot, got in my car, and drove home. I fixed dinner for the kids. My husband was working late. I watched some television. My husband came home, and he had some dinner, then we went to bed. The next morning, my husband volunteered to get the kids off to school. I came to work and decided to report what Joe did."

The above account certainly should cause an interviewer to question its veracity. Mary provided minimal information about the event, compared to the pre-event and the post-event. Her statements "I thought about screaming for him to stop" and "the next thing I remember" are indications of deception. There is a plethora of follow-up topics that need to be explored. For instance:

- When did she realize it was Joe that came up behind her?
- How did she know it was Joe?
- How long did the incident last?
- What is her relationship with Joe?
- Did Joe say anything?
- Did she say anything to Joe?
- Has this happened before?
- Was she surprised this happened?
- What happened between the time she thought about screaming for Joe to stop and the next thing she remembered?
- Why didn't she scream for Joe to stop?
- How long does it take her to go from her office to the conference room?
- Did anybody witness the incident?
- Was there anybody else in the hallway?
- Did anyone in the conference room make a comment?
- Was Joe an attendee at the meeting?
- Did she tell her husband?
- Did she tell anybody else?
- Why did she decide to report this event?

Many more questions could be asked based on Mary's response to the above questions.

## FOLLOW-UP WITH CLARIFYING QUESTIONS

If the interviewee has completed their account, ask clarifying questions to elicit further information or explanation. These are especially helpful to confirm or break down an interviewee's alibi or to uncover a false report. Clarifying questions are best asked as open questions:

- "Please explain the reason you did not report this immediately."
- "Please describe how you felt about Joe doing this."
- "Please tell me why you think Joe did this."

An interviewee who fabricated their account might be caught off guard with these questions because they did not think about how they would feel or why Joe did this. An interviewee providing a truthful account will not have to think twice about their response to these types of questions because they experienced the incident.

As the interviewee is providing an account, listen for Freudian Slips. A Freudian Slip is an error in speech that is caused by the unconscious mind. In the following example, the interviewee is a potential suspect in his wife's disappearance.

**Q**: "Please tell me about you and your wife's relationship."
**A**: "Our relationship was wonderful...uh, is wonderful."

The interviewee's unconscious mind automatically placed the relationship in the past tense with "was." He corrected himself and put the relationship in the present with "is." It was too late.

Once the interviewee has completed their account, including answers to clarifying questions, the interviewer should determine what specific information the interviewee did not offer and ask direct questions to receive a specific response.

## DIRECT QUESTIONS

Direct questions are probing questions asked to elicit a specific response. The way a direct question is phrased will allow the interviewee to:

- Answer deceptively with a low chance of detection.
- Answer deceptively with a high chance of detection.
- Answer truthfully.

Following are examples of improperly phrased direct questions with an explanation, along with the proper phrasing.

**Do Not Ask Multifaceted Questions:**
**Improper**: "Did you see Bill or Joe last night?"

Asking the question like this can confuse the interviewee. It also allows the interviewee to easily be deceptive by answering truthfully to only one part of the question. The interviewee might have talked to Joe; however, he did not see him. The interviewee can boldly respond with a "No."

**Proper**: "Did you see Bill last night?" Wait for a response, then, "Did you see Joe last night?"

Asking the questions this way causes the interviewee to answer each question separately. A less than truthful answer can more easily be detected.

**Do Not Ask Negative Questions:**

**Improper**: "You don't know anything about the money missing from the safe, do you?"

Asking the question this way allows the interviewee to readily agree with your question: "That is correct, I do not know anything about the money missing from the safe."

**Proper**: "What do you know about the money missing from the safe?"

Asking the question this way will allow a less than truthful response to be more easily detected.

**Do Not Ask Memory Restricted Questions:**

**Improper**: "Do you recall where you were Friday night?"

Asking memory restricted questions allows a deceptive interviewee to easily claim they do not recall where they were Friday night.

**Proper**: "Where were you Friday night?"

Asking the question this way will allow the interviewer to assess the interviewee's answer with known information or to later determine whether or the response was truthful.

**Do Not Be Too Specific:**

**Improper**: "Did you take the $783.00 from the safe?"

Asking the question this way allows the potential suspect to boldly deny taking $783 if the amount is different or if the exact amount is unknown.

**Proper**: "Did you take the money from the safe?"

Asking the question this way eliminates the specificity, and a less than truthful response can more easily be detected.

## EVALUATING RESPONSES TO DIRECT QUESTIONS

Many deceptive interviewees will respond to direct questions with an evasive answer. When responding deceptively with an evasive answer, an interviewee might experience anxiety; however, the anxiety is not as high as when they tell a lie. When listening to the response, the interviewer should also look for nonverbal response behavior that indicate deception. Some interviewees attempt to manipulate the interview with misleading, vague, ambiguous, qualified, and incomplete responses. We are familiar with these types of replies in political debates and press conferences. A well-known political practice is to respond to the question they wanted asked, not the one that was asked. On the other hand, honest responses to direct questions are simple and unambiguous.

The following are types of evasive answers:

- Simple evasive response
- Incomplete evasive response
- Memory qualified evasive response
- Vague evasive response

If an evasive response is detected, offer a follow-up question to lead the interviewee to the truth. Ask either a direct question or an open question. The following are examples of evasive responses to direct questions along with follow-up question possibilities.

**Simple Evasive Response**: Implies the interviewee is telling the truth. Simple evasive responses are easy to detect.

**Q**: "How often do you conduct register audits?"

**Evasive Response**: "The policy is four audits per month for each cashier."

**Follow-Up**:

**Q**: "You are correct. But please tell me how often you conduct register audits."

**Incomplete Evasive Response**: Provides a truthful statement, but possibly not all of the truth:

**Q**: "How many times have you been treated to a golf outing by a vendor?"

**Evasive Response**: "A few times a couple of years ago."

**Follow-Up**:

**Q**: "Ok, let me ask you this. When was the last time a vendor treated you to a golf outing?"

Depending on the response, further questions can include:

**Q**: "Would the outings be noted on your personal calendar?"

**Q**: "What vendors treated you to a golf outing?"

**Q**: "What golf courses did the vendors take you to?"

**Q**: "Who else attended the golf outings?"

**Q**: "What will the vendors say?"

**Memory Qualified Evasive Response**: Provides the interviewee an "out" if there is information that contradicts their response:

**Q**: "Were you at the liquor store on Main Street last night?"

**Evasive Response**: "To the best of my knowledge, I was not in the vicinity of the liquor store last night." or "I don't recall."

Many follow-up questions can be asked to assist the interviewee with his or her memory:

**Follow-Up**:

**Q**: "If you were not at the liquor store last night, where were you?"

**Q**: "When was the last time you were in vicinity of the liquor store?"

**Q**: "How often do you go the liquor store?"

**Q**: "Will a review of the store video show you in the vicinity?"

**Q**: "Let us explore your activity yesterday. What time did you wake up?"

Continuing questions regarding activity for the day will continue to pin down the interviewee. If the interviewee continues to be evasive, ask the following question:

**Q**: "Is there anything that will assist you in refreshing your memory?"

If the interviewee responds with a "No," it is clear that the interviewee is uncooperative. The best course of action is to continue to ask direct questions to commit the interviewee to their statements.

**Vague Evasive Response:** Does not answer the question:

**Q**: "How often have you been treated to a sporting event by a vendor?"

**Evasive Response**: "Hardly ever," *or* "Rarely," *or* "Not often."

**Follow-Up Question**:

**Q**: "Ok, so hardly ever, So, please tell me how often a vendor treated you to a sporting event."

Other vague responses to the above question could be: "As a rule...,"

"Typically...," "Generally...," "As a matter of habit...,"

The interviewee's responses to the follow-up questions could cause the interviewer to ask further questions until the truth is obtained.

### Follow-Up to Deceptive Nonverbal Response Behavior

If the nonverbal response to a key question contradicts the verbal response, the interviewer can do one of the following:

- Immediately address the contradiction:

  Joe, you are saying that you haven't received any money from a contractor; however, it is obvious that you received something, correct? Please tell me what you received from a contractor.

- Address the contradiction later:

Take note of the contradiction and address it later in the interview or during another interview.

## FOLLOW-UP TEST QUESTIONS

Follow-up test questions can be used after a denial to see if the interviewee changes their response. These questions are asked as direct questions and are particularly useful if the interviewee's nonverbal communication indicates deception.

**Q**: "Ken, did you take the money from the safe?"
**A**: "No."
**Q**: "Have you ever been in the store safe?"
**A**: "No."
**Q**: "Have you ever had the combination to the safe?"
**A**: "No."

**Follow-Up Test Question**:

**Q**: "Ken, you know that it is common practice for us to install surveillance cameras in the ceiling above the office in case of a robbery or theft. Would there be any reason that our hidden surveillance camera in the ceiling would have recorded you entering the safe?"
**A**: "Well, maybe that one time the manager had me get some change."

The answer change could be an indication of guilt that should be explored. The interviewer is not telling Ken there is a recording of him entering the safe. The interviewer just asked a hypothetical question to see if Ken changes his answer.

## ATTITUDE ASSESSMENT QUESTIONS

Attitude Assessment Question responses provide insight into the interviewee's frame of mind concerning the matter being investigated. They are particularly valuable when interviewing reluctant witnesses and potential suspects. Attitude Assessment Questions can be asked throughout the interview when appropriate. Following are some questions with examples of responses that are indicative of a negative attitude toward the matter being investigated:

Why wouldn't you accept a kickback from a contractor?
"I would be afraid of getting caught."
Have you ever thought about accepting a kickback form a contractor?
Negative: "Yes, but I didn't go through with it."
How do you think this investigation is going to turn out concerning you?
"I don't know. I hope I am not being singled out."
What do you think should happen to a person who is involved in this activity?
"Maybe they should get a warning."
Do you believe this activity is going on here?
"No."
If you knew this activity was going on, would you report it?
"I don't know. I have to work here."
Would there be any reason someone would accuse you?
"Well possibly. Some people here do not like me."

Negative responses to Attitude Assessment Questions should not be considered clear and convincing evidence. Therefore, they should not be the basis for making an accusation.

Chapter 7 discussed the Fraud Triangle. The three sides are pressure, opportunity, and rationalization. An Attitude Assessment Question might provide insight into the three sides coming together that resulted in the offense. If later, the interviewee is classified as a suspect, their responses to Attitude Assessment Questions might be used to persuade the suspect to truthfully confess. Following is an example:

Why do you think an employee would be involved in taking bribes?

Pressure Responses:
Maybe they have personal financial problems.
Maybe they were threatened to do so.
Opportunity Responses:
Nobody here cares.
It's the way business is done.
Rationalization Responses:
It seems like everybody working here is dishonest.
This company doesn't pay that well.

If the interviewee has not been forthcoming in response to interviewer questions, Chapter 15 discusses strategies to lead the interviewee to the truth.

## SUMMARY

After the Opening Statement, the interview will progress to key questions. Interviewers should ask open questions, a request for information not phrased as questions. An interviewer can evaluate the response for indications of truth and deception. An interviewer can ask follow-up clarifying questions if necessary. Direct questions call for a specific response. The way a question is phrased can allow the interviewee to answer deceptively with a low chance of detection, answer deceptively with a high chance of detection, or answer truthfully. Interviewees who are intent on not being forthcoming may respond evasively. Interviewers should recognize the evasive response and ask follow-up questions. Follow-up test question can be asked to determine if an interviewee changes their answer to a direct question. Furthermore, this chapter discusses Attitude Assessment Questions that can provide insight into the interviewee's attitude toward the matter being investigated.

## EXERCISE 14.1. MULTIPLE CHOICE AND TRUE AND FALSE QUESTIONS

1. A properly phrased open question is designed to elicit a specific response.

   _____ True
   _____ False

2. A properly phrased open question implies that the interviewee has information to provide.

_____ True
_____ False

3. If an interviewee responds untruthfully in response to an open question, the interviewer should interrupt and ask for a truthful response.

_____ True
_____ False

4. If an interviewee stops talking in their response to an open question, the interviewer should do which of the following:

_____ Ask clarifying questions
_____ Ask direct questions
_____ Wait a few seconds then ask the interviewee to continue.
_____ Inform the interviewee that more information is expected.

5. Relating an event in perfect chronological order the first time it is provided, could be an indication the account has been rehearsed.

_____ True
_____ False

6. Clarifying questions can be beneficial to confirm or dispute an interviewee's alibi or to reveal a false report.

_____ True
_____ False

7. "Did you meet with Joe and Bill last night" is a properly phrased direct question.

_____ True
_____ False

8. The way a direct question is phrased will allow the interviewee to:

_____ Answer deceptively with a low chance of detection.
_____ Answer deceptively with a high chance of detection.
_____ Answer truthfully.
_____ All of the above.

9. A follow-up test question can be asked to see if an interviewee changes their answer to a previous direct question.

   _____ True
   _____ False

10. Negative responses to Attitude Assessment Questions can be an indication of guilt and used to make an accusation.

   _____ True
   _____ False

## EXERCISE 14.2. ESSAY TOPICS

1. Discuss the benefits of asking open questions.
2. Discuss what an interviewer should listen for when an interviewee is responding to an open question.
3. Discuss the purpose of asking clarifying questions.
4. Discuss the four types of evasive responses and how an interviewer should respond.
5. Explain when and how a test question can be used.
6. Explain how Attitude Assessment Questions can be used in conjunction with the Fraud Triangle.

# 15

# *Leading the Interviewee to the Truth*

## LEARNING OBJECTIVES

- To explain how to tell a witness they are not being truthful.
- To identify how to overcome an interviewee's objection to being truthful.
- To identify strategies to lead a suspect or potential suspect to the truth.
- To explain what interviewers should look for in a suspect's body language when persuading them to tell the truth.

## INTRODUCTION

The objective of the interview is to find the truth. As discussed in Chapter 6, interviewees have many reasons not to be forthcoming. The interviewer's job is to persuade the interviewee to provide complete, accurate, and truthful information. As the interview progresses, the interviewer should evaluate the interviewee's responses for truth and deception and ask appropriate follow-up questions. In addition, based on knowledge of the case, the interviewer should listen for discrepancies in the interviewee's account. If there are discrepancies or indications of untruthfulness, the interviewer should take steps to lead the interviewee to truth.

## NONCONFRONTATIONAL APPROACH

What happens if an interviewer determines an interviewee is not being truthful? At a strategic point, the interviewer should inform the interviewee of that fact. This can be accomplished in a nonconfrontational manner. The interviewer can make a statement such as:

- "Listen, I know you are not telling me the truth."
- "I know you are not being totally honest with me."
- "It is obvious you are not being straightforward with me."
- "I am trying to understand why you are not being truthful."
- "What you are saying does not make sense."
- "Based on the facts that we have, what you are telling me doesn't add up."

After offering one of these statements, the interviewer should follow-up with an open or a direct question such as:

- "Please tell me why you are holding back."
- "Is there a reason you are not being truthful with me?"
- "Why are you not being forthcoming?"

The statement followed by the question should cause a reaction and a response. If the interviewee still does not offer the complete truth, the interviewer might have to reveal knowledge or evidence that contradicts what the interviewee provided. However, the interviewer must be careful not to disclose information that would compromise the investigation or another individual. Based on understanding as to why interviewees might not be truthful as discussed in Chapter 6, the interviewer could offer possible reasons, such as:

- "Are you reluctant to get someone in trouble?"
- "Are you involved in the activity?"
- "Are you concerned with possibly having to testify?"
- "Are you involved in some other activity you are reluctant to talk about?"
- "Are you concerned you will be perceived as a snitch?"
- "Do you not want to provide information you are not 100% sure about?"

These are some of the questions an interviewer could ask a reluctant interviewee who is not being truthful or forthcoming. Based on the interviewee's responses, the interviewer might have to overcome objections. For instance, a common objection is:

"I'm reluctant to say anything that might get someone in trouble without proof."

The interviewer could offer a response using feel, felt, and found:

"I understand how you feel. Others sitting across from me have felt the same way. However, what they found is that the best course of action was to tell us what they knew so we can look into it and find the proof if it is there. That is what our office does. Do you understand?"

The interviewer should then ask the interviewee to tell the truth and ask the appropriate questions. Despite an interviewer's best efforts, some interviewee's will not be truthful.

## PERSUADING THE SUSPECT TO TELL THE TRUTH

If the interviewee is a suspect, the interviewer will accuse the interviewee at some point in the interview. The accusation usually takes place at the end of the Opening Statement. If the interviewee denies the accusation, the interviewer will evaluate the denial and repeat the accusation. If the suspect still denies the accusation, the interviewer can employee strategies to persuade him or her to confess. They are as follows:

- Reveal evidence.
- Appeal to common sense.
- Offer a reason for the offense.
- Relate similar behavior.

### Reveal Evidence

What evidence to reveal should be determined during an interview strategy session. The revealing of evidence can take place at the appropriate time during the interview. First, ask the suspect questions that will commit their responses for the record. For instance, if the offense being investigated is a residential burglary, then there might be fingerprint evidence at the point of entry or other areas throughout the house. Ask a direct question such as:

Have you ever been in the house?

If the suspect responds with a "yes" to any of the questions, have him explain the circumstances. If he responds with a "no," ask a question such as:

> How can you explain that your fingerprints were found throughout the house?

It is compelling to show the suspect the evidence. In this case, photos of the fingerprint lifts, a copy of his fingerprints, and the official crime lab analysis comparing the two. Continue with a statement such as:

> We know you broke into the house and you know you broke into the house, so there is no sense denying it. What we want to do here is figure out if you targeted this house or was it a random selection. Which was it?

Hardened or deviant offenders can easily deny their involvement unless they believe there is overwhelming evidence. They will often evaluate the evidence against them and determine the best course of action to minimize their consequences.

Sometimes, it is appropriate to immediately reveal evidence after the first denial, usually in response to the Opening Statement accusation. This will depend on the nature of the evidence and other corroboration. An Open Question can be an appropriate way to reveal knowledge. For instance, an investigation of a kickback scheme involving an employee receiving paid vacations by a contractor, the Opening Statement might be:

> Joe, we have been looking into a situation where you have been accused of receiving bribes and gratuities to ensure that a certain vendor receives favorable contracts. It is imperative that you are truthful with us today. Okay? Our inquiry shows that you have been receiving kickbacks and gratuities. Would you please explain how this began?

If Joe responds with:

> I don't know what you are talking about.

The interviewer can respond with:

> Joe, like I said we know that you have. So, it is imperative that you are truthful with us.

Joe responds with:

> I am being truthful.

The interviewer can respond with:

> Then please tell us about the paid vacation to Hawaii that Clifton Paper Goods provided.

At this point, Joe will either:

- Deny this occurred.
- Acknowledge that he took the trip, but claim it was not a gratuity or bribe.
- Acknowledge that the trip was a gratuity or bribe.

## Appeal to Common Sense

An appeal to common sense usually occurs near or at the end of an offender's interview who has not yet confessed. The interviewer can review the interviewee's responses to specific questions and expose inconsistencies with the evidence or other statements they made. The accusation can include an appeal to common sense, such as:

- Joe, what you're saying does not make sense. It is obvious that you are the one who took the money from the safe. Just tell me why you did this.
- Joe, based on what you told me and the facts that contradict what you are saying, it is clear that you are responsible for taking the money from the safe. Just tell me why you did this.

## Offer a Reason for the Offense

Based on knowledge of the interviewee, and the interviewee's responses to preliminary and attitude assessment questions, the interviewer can develop a reason for the offense that allows the offender to morally accept their action and more easily confess. For instance:

- Joe, I believe you took the money because you needed to buy food for your children and pay the rent. Isn't that right Joe?
- Joe, I understand that you did not receive the promotion you were expecting, so you only took the money because you felt you deserved it. Isn't that right Joe?
- Joe, I believe you are basically an honest guy. If it weren't for the negative example set by the bosses here, I am sure you would not have thought about doing this. Am I correct?
- Joe, I understand you were under extreme pressure to alleviate your financial difficulties. If it weren't for the company not following some simple control measures, I am sure you would have found another way, like finding a part-time job, right?

## Relate Similar Behavior

Another approach is to relate a personal situation or an incident of someone the interviewer knows about where they made a poor choice. An emotional offender might take comfort in knowing others have also made a mistake. For instance:

- Joe, you are not the only one who has made a mistake like this. You are only human. Us humans are not perfect. Let me tell you about a situation I was in, where I made a bad decision" (relate the incident). So, I moved forward. It will be best if you just let us know why this happened and move forward. Okay?
- Let me tell you about a good friend of mine who made a bad decision (relate the incident). It is not the end the world. We are still good friends. He found that the best course of action was to tell the truth and move on. So, Joe, it will be best if you just let me know why this happened. Okay?

An offender's body language will often provide a clue whether they are accepting the interviewer's persuasive strategies to truthfully confess. If they are not interested, they will often sit back with their arms folded and look at the interviewer with skepticism. The interviewer must decide if it is prudent to retreat from the accusation (Figure 15.1).

If the offender is accepting the interviewer's persuasive strategy, they will often begin nodding their head in agreement, slump forward, and look down (Figure 15.2). An interviewer should realize that this is the time to ask the interviewee to explain the circumstances or ask why the offense occurred. The interviewer should remain silent and wait for the interviewee to speak. If the interviewee again denies involvement, it is usually a weak last attempt. The interviewer can offer a reason for the offense and again ask the interviewee to explain their involvement or why the offense occurred.

Often, after sitting silent for a while, the interviewee might ask what is going to happen to them. This is an indication that the interviewee is ready to confess. An interviewer should respond with something like:

> Jill, I cannot answer that; however, it is important that you tell me why this happened. Then we can figure out what is going to happen to you. It is best if you tell us why this happened.

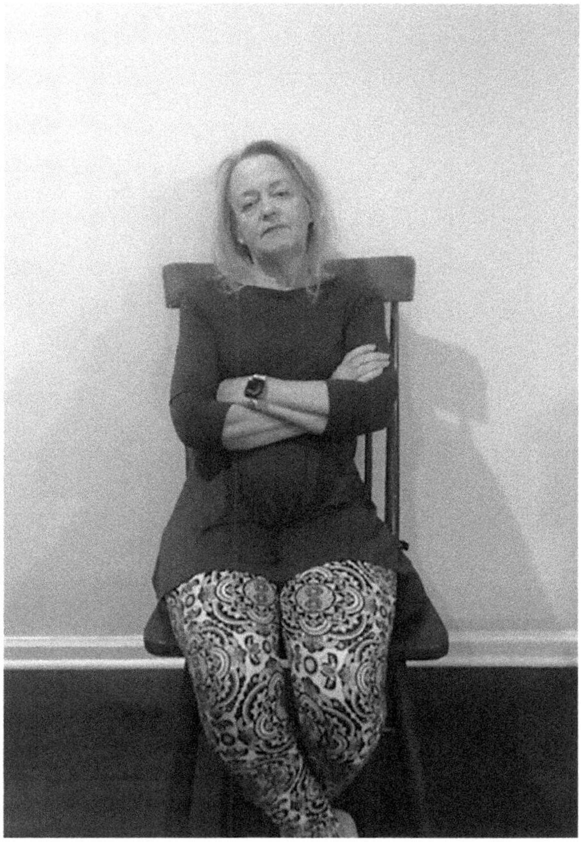

**Figure 15.1** The interviewee is not accepting the interviewer's persuasive strategy.

If the suspect interviewee continues to deny involvement, the interviewer must decide whether to continue with persuasive strategies or retreat from the accusation and conclude the interview. The decision should be based on the totality of circumstances including the length of the interview and the interviewee's demeanor. The interviewer must avoid using coercive tactics. Keep in mind, not all suspects confess.

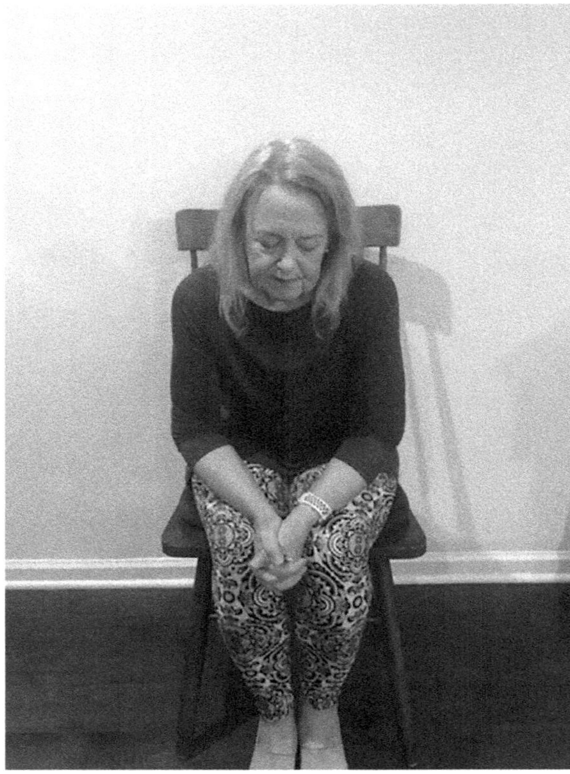

**Figure 15.2** The interviewee appears ready to make a truthful confession.

## SUMMARY

The objective of the interview is to find the truth. If the interviewee is not being truthful, the interviewer can let them know this with a nonconfrontational approach. The interviewer can overcome an interviewee's objections by asking the reason they are not telling the truth. The interviewer can use persuasive strategies to lead a suspect to a truthful confession. The strategies are revealing evidence, appealing to common sense, offering a reason for committing the offense, and relating another person's similar behavior. An interviewer should be aware of an interviewee's kinesics or body language behavior that could provide clues as to the acceptance or not of the persuasive strategy.

## EXERCISE 15.1. MULTIPLE CHOICE AND TRUE AND FALSE QUESTIONS

1. If an interviewer is aware that an interviewee has not been truthful, the interviewer should eventually inform them of that fact.

   _____ True
   _____ False

2. Informing the interviewee that they have not been truthful should be done in a stern manner to stress the importance of being truthful.

   _____ True
   _____ False

3. If a witness or possible witness has not been truthful, asking them why, is a recommended step.

   _____ True
   _____ False

4. Offering reluctant interviewees a possible reason they are not being truthful is not recommended.

   _____ True
   _____ False

5. If an interviewee offers an objection to providing information, an interviewee's job is to overcome the objection.

   _____ True
   _____ False

6. If a suspect denies an accusation, asking direct questions to commit their response for the record before revealing evidence could be appropriate.

   _____ True
   _____ False

7. Which of the following is not a strategy when persuading an interviewee to be truthful?

   _____ Appealing to common sense.
   _____ Offering an ultimatum.

_____ Offering a reason for the offense.
_____ Revealing related behavior.

8. Offering a reason for the offense can be based on the interviewer's knowledge of the interviewee and answers to Attitude Assessment Questions.

   _____ True
   _____ False

9. An appeal to commons sense, usually occurs at the beginning of the interview.

   _____ True
   _____ False

10. Related behavior can be offered to let the interviewee know they are not the only one who has made a mistake.

   _____ True
   _____ False

## EXERCISE 15.2. ESSAY TOPICS

1. Discuss strategies to persuade an interviewee to be truthful.
2. Discuss how an interviewer can reveal evidence to persuade a suspect to truthfully confess.
3. Discuss what interviewers should look for in interviewees' body language when persuading them to tell the truth.

# 16

# End, Evaluate, and Follow-Up

**LEARNING OBJECTIVES**

- To explain the importance of ending the interview on a positive note.
- To identify concluding questions to ask an interviewee.
- To discuss the importance of evaluating the interview results.
- To identify questions to ask when evaluating the interview.
- To identify Opening Statements in a follow-up interview.

## INTRODUCTION

All interviews come to an end. How an interview ends is as important as how it began. Upon completion, a professional interviewer should evaluate the conduct of the interview to determine what could have been done better. Often, a follow-up interview is required to verify or clarify information discussed in a previous interview or discuss new information that has come to light.

## END THE INTERVIEW

The interview should end on a positive note even if the interview objective was not achieved. When the interviewee appears to have no more to add, the interviewer should ask the secondary interviewer, if one is present, if they have any questions. The interviewer should review the Topic List to make sure they addressed all key issues.

After all issues have been discussed, the interviewer and interviewee should review and summarize the interview results. The interviewer can ask additional clarifying questions if needed and verify the answers the interviewee provided. Additionally, the following questions are valuable to ask the interviewee:

- "Did the interview go as you expected?"
- "Were there any questions I did not ask that you expected me to ask?"
- "How do you feel about the interview?"
- "Is there anything you would like to add that we did not discuss?"
- "If you were conducting this investigation, what would you do?" "Who would you talk to?"
- "How do you feel the investigation will turn out as it concerns you?"

The responses to these questions could begin a new series of questions. Be prepared to exercise mental agility.

Take the appropriate steps if a suspect provided a confession. For instance, if an employee confessed to an offense, notify the proper individual in the organization. They would decide the employee status, such as suspension pending further investigation, or removing a union employee from service pending a company hearing. If the interview was not recorded, it is recommended that an interviewee write a statement if they confessed. However, having an interviewee write out a confession is awkward and sometimes controversial. Defense attorneys could challenge the statement as being coerced and dictated by the interviewer. Recording the interview alleviates this issue.

At the interview conclusion, the interviewer should thank the interviewee for appearing and inform them that there might be a need for further discussion. Obtain agreement for future contact. The interviewer should provide a business card and advise the interviewee to call if they can think of anything else.

## EVALUATE THE INTERVIEW

Interviewers should always evaluate the conduct of the interview. Self-evaluation is a hallmark of a professional. The interviewer should take this step even if they achieved the interview objective. The interviewer should ask what they could have done better. Did the interviewer:

- Effectively arrange the interview?
- Offer an effective introductory statement?
- Break down barriers, gain trust, and build rapport?
- Find common ground during the preliminary questions?
- Offer an appropriate and effective opening statement?
- Ask properly phrased questions?
- Miss indications of deception?
- Remain even-tempered?
- Miss asking appropriate follow-up questions?
- Effectively handle denials?
- End the interview on a positive note?

If a secondary interviewer was present, the interviewer should discuss the interview with them. There is always room for improvement!

## FOLLOW-UP INTERVIEW

As a case progresses and more information is obtained, an interviewer might need to re-interview someone. A follow-up interview might be needed of resource providers, accusers, whistleblowers, victims, witnesses, potential suspects, or suspects. If the interviewer broke down barriers and gained trust with the interviewee during the original interview, and ended it on a positive note, a follow-up interview is usually more easily arranged.

Follow-up interviews with a whistleblower are less formal, almost casual. The whistleblower feels they are part of the investigative team. It is normal to interview whistleblowers many times during the course of an investigation. Accusers, victims, and witnesses also can be interviewed more than once. After preliminary matters, a simple Opening Statement could be:

> Mary, thanks for meeting with me again. I need to go over a few things that have come up since we last met. First, let me ask you this. Has there been any new developments that you know about?

The interviewer can again stress the importance of providing total accurate information. Also, the interviewer can ask the interviewee if they want to add anything they forgot to include during the initial interview.

After an initial interview of a potential suspect who denied involvement, further investigation could uncover clear and convincing evidence that would place the individual in the suspect category. A follow-up interview could include an Opening Statement with an accusation, such as:

> Pete, since we met last time, we continued our investigation into the kick-back scheme. We have uncovered evidence that shows without a doubt that you are involved. I would like you to explain your involvement.

Pete will either confess or deny his involvement. If Pete confesses, the interviewer should have him relate the details by asking open and direct questions. If Pete denies his involvement, the interviewer will gauge the strength of denial and follow the steps previously discussed.

## SUMMARY

All interviews come to an end. It is important to end them on a positive note. The interview results should be reviewed with the interviewee and any clarifying and follow-up questions should be asked. The secondary interviewer, if one participated, should ask questions at the end if needed. The Topic List should be reviewed to ensure all topics were covered. Once the interview has ended, an interviewer should evaluate the conduct of the interview, even if interview objectives were achieved. Self-evaluation is the hallmark of a professional. Occasionally, a follow-up interview will be necessary to clarify information from the initial interview or to go over new information that has come to light. If the interviewer succeeded in breaking down barriers and gaining trust during the initial interview and if it ended on a positive note, a follow-up interview should be easily arranged.

## EXERCISE 16.1. MULTIPLE CHOICE AND TRUE AND FALSE QUESTIONS

1. How an interview ends is as important as how the interview began.

   _____ True
   _____ False

2. At the conclusion of the interview, it is appropriate to ask the secondary interviewer, if one is present, if they have any questions of the interviewee.

_____ True
_____ False

3. After the interview has concluded, the interviewer should review the Topic List to ensure all appropriate issues have been discussed.

_____ True
_____ False

4. Pick all that apply. At the conclusion of the interview, it is recommended the interviewer ask the following questions.

_____ How do you believe the interview went?
_____ Are there any questions I did not ask that you were expecting?
_____ How do you think the investigation will turn out as it concerns you?
_____ Is there a reason you were not truthful with me today?

5. If an interviewee confesses to an offense, the best practice is to have them write a statement.

_____ True
_____ False

6. The hallmark of a professional is self-evaluation.

_____ True
_____ False

7. If the interview objective was achieved, it is not necessary to evaluate the interview.

_____ True
_____ False

8. If an initial interview ended on a positive note, it is often easier to arrange a follow-up interview.

_____ True
_____ False

9. A follow-up interview should include the same preliminary questions that were asked in the initial interview.

_____ True
_____ False

10. A good follow-up interview question would be "Is there anything new since we last met?"

_____ True
_____ False

## EXERCISE 16.2. ESSAY TOPICS

1. Discuss the importance of ending an interview on a positive note.
2. Discuss the questions an interviewer should ask when evaluating the interview.
3. Describe the difference in a follow-up interview's Opening Statement with an initial interview's Opening Statement.

# 17

# Writing a Report of Interview

## LEARNING OBJECTIVES

- To explain the reasons to write an ROI.
- To discuss the basic rules when writing an ROI.
- To discuss the proper use of verbs.
- To discuss the proper use of pronouns.
- To explain what it means to write an ROI in logical order.
- To describe peripheral information that should be captured in an ROI.

## INTRODUCTION

The last step in conducting an investigative interview is to prepare a Report of Interview (ROI). Organizations have different names for an ROI, such as Memorandum of Oral Interview, Interview Report, or a Form number, such as the FBI's 302. For purposes of this instruction, we will use the term "ROI." An ROI should be prepared even if the interview was audio-recorded. ROIs should not be a list of questions asked and the interviewee's word for word response. It is burdensome to read a report structured that way. It would read like a deposition. It would be tiresome, tedious, and often confusing to read, and it is not necessary to capture the interview facts. Always consider the reader.

Armed with interview notes, recording, transcript if available, and memory, a clear, thorough, accurate, concise, and logical narrative of the interview should be placed on paper. It is best if the ROI is completed immediately following the interview. However, most agencies have a 3-day rule. If an interviewer conducts multiple interviews in one day, it would be challenging to write all the reports immediately following each interview. So, time must be taken within 3 days to prepare the ROI, at least the best draft that is ready for supervisor review.

ROIs provide a record for the case file and give the reader a clear understanding of what transpired. The reader could be another investigator, a supervisor, an attorney for the prosecution, an attorney for the defense, a trier of fact, and any other individual who needs to know. An investigator should keep in mind that ROIs will be held in perpetuity and possibly reviewed years after the interview. The author has written and reviewed thousands of ROIs throughout his career. Following are some basic rules the author has followed when writing an ROI.

## ROI RULES

### Short Paragraphs

A good rule to follow with ROIs, as with most writings, is to write short paragraphs, which make the paper much easier to read. The chapters in this book offer easy-to-read paragraphs.

### Proper Grammar, Punctuation, and Syntax

Many interviewees do not speak in complete sentences, do not use proper grammar, and often use colloquialisms or slang. That does not mean the ROI should be written that way. With a narrative form of writing, ROIs should use proper grammar, punctuation, and syntax. Colloquialisms should not be used in the ROI. For instance, if an interviewee uses the word "Feds" in an interview, referring to a Federal Government authority, the ROI reflects what the colloquialism meant. That could be the United States Attorney's Office, the FBI, the IRS, etc.

### Use Active Voice

Active voice is easier to read. For instance, write:

> I interviewed John Smith…

Do not write:

> John Smith was interviewed by me…

## Minimal Use of Quotes

When writing an ROI, the use of quotes should be minimal and only used when the writer believes it is crucial to capture a critical response by the interviewee. For example, if a suspect confesses or makes an admission of culpability, then quote the exact words used. Another instance where quotes would be encouraged is if the interviewee states something profound or significant that would help other readers know what was said. Additionally, if a crime victim or witness reports the exact words used by a suspect, then that phrase should be placed in quotes.

## Proper Tense

The interview took place in the past, so ROIs should be written in the past tense. For instance, write:

> Harris *stated* he is the owner of ABC Retail Company.
> Do not write in the present tense:
> Harris states he is the owner of ABC Retail Company.

## Appropriate Verbs

An ROI should not be considered creative writing. With that said, it could be appropriate to use verbs that more adequately capture the essence of an interviewee's response. Following is a list of verbs and their usage.

**Stated**: When reporting information provided by an interviewee, that is not controversial. For example, "Smith stated that he has lived at 1234 Main St. for ten years."
**Claimed**: When reporting information that needs to be corroborated. For example, "Smith claimed Jones gave him three checks."
**Acknowledged**: When reporting information provided by an interviewee that is known. For example, "Smith acknowledged that he and Jones are cousins."
**Asserted**: When reporting a forceful statement by an interviewee. For example, "Smith asserted that he did not believe that his actions violated company policy."
**Provided**: The interviewee provided information in response to a question. For example, "Smith provided the following information regarding his employment."
**Offered**: Same as Provided.

**Opined**: When reporting an opinion. For example, "Smith opined that Gannon needed the money to support a drug habit."

**Admitted**: When reporting the interviewee's reluctant acknowledgment of a fact that is true. For example: "Smith admitted that his actions were probably a violation of company policy."

**Confessed**: When reporting the interviewee's acknowledgement of their responsibility for the matter under investigation. For example, "Smith confessed that he accepted money from Jones to ensure that Jones received the contract."

Other past tense verbs to use when appropriate are shown in Table 17.1.

Do not overuse verbs when describing an interviewee's responses. It can be very tedious and burdensome to read. As an example, read the following paragraph:

> Smith stated that he and Jones are first cousins. Smith also stated that he and Jones are like brothers. Smith stated that Jones spent a lot of time at the Smith house when both of them were growing up. Smith stated that his and Jones mother are sisters and have a close relationship.

The above example was one paragraph. Imagine reading an entire ROI written that way. Compare the above paragraph with the one below:

> Smith provided that he and Jones are first cousins and are like brothers. His mother and Jones's mother have a close relationship. Jones spent a lot of time at the Smith house when they were growing up.

It is a good practice to use a minimum number of interview action verbs when relating an interviewee's narrative response to an open question. The following example captures a response to an open question regarding employment history:

> Smith provided the following information regarding his employment history. He has worked at ABC for thirteen years and is currently a procurement officer reporting to the AVP of Finance. (And so on)

**Table 17.1** Past Tense Verbs Appropriate for Report Writing

| | | |
|---|---|---|
| Responded | Professed | Denied |
| Added | Argued | Refused |
| Declared | Alleged | Explained |
| Maintained | Contended | Related |
| Verified | Affirmed | Proffered |

## Proper Pronouns

Do not confuse the reader with overuse of pronouns. Read the following paragraph:

> Smith stated that he and Jones were first cousins. He also said that they are like brothers. He always spent time at his house when they were growing up.

In the above paragraph, the writer knows who spent time at who's house; however, the reader would have to guess.

Do not start a paragraph with a pronoun:

"He (Incorrect)/ Smith (Correct)" claimed that Jones is not aware of the investigation.

## Identifying Individuals and Entities

Fully identify an individual or entity the first time they are mentioned, followed in parentheses by the name referred to throughout the report. For example:

> On March 18, 2014, I interviewed Frederick Webster (Webster), the owner of XYZ Clothing Outlet (XYZ). Webster stated he has owned XYZ for approximately ten years.

An investigation might involve many interviews with the same individuals and entities referred to in each ROI or activity report. Each report stands on its own and should follow the identification rule.

## ROI Organization

A prepared topic list acts as a "roadmap" for the interview. However, the conversation often deviates from the charted course. The interviewee might respond off-topic. Additionally, an interviewee might add information that refers to an earlier part of the interview. For instance, an interviewee might state something early in the interview, then correct themselves later or near the end of the interview. This can happen when an interviewer seeks clarification, or if the interviewee spontaneously interjects. Take a look at the following example:

**Interviewer**: "Jeff, what is the name of the person you met with the other night?"
**Jeff**: "Bob."

Then, later in the interview Jeff interjects:

> **Jeff**: "I'm sorry, the name of the person I met with was Bill, not Bob."

If the interviewer feels that the discrepancy was an honest mistake, write the ROI like this:

> Jeff identified the individual he met with the other night as Bill.

If the interviewer feels that the discrepancy is significant to capture for the record and the reader, then write the ROI like this:

> Jeff initially identified the individual he met with the other night as Bob; however, later in the interview, he claimed he was mistaken and identified the individual as Bill.

It would be confusing to the reader if in one section of the ROI, it read:

> Jeff identified the individual he was with the other night as Bob.

Then near the end of the ROI, it read:

> As I concluded the interview, Jeff interjected and stated he was mistaken about the name of the individual he met with the other night. Jeff stated the individual's name was Bill, not Bob.

Writing the ROI in this manner would be disrupting to the reader. While reading the report, the reader believes the individual was Bob. Then near the end of the ROI, the reader learns the individual was Bill. Just because the interviewer experienced this disruption does not mean the reader should experience it. ROIs are not necessarily written in the chronological order of the interview. Doing so can be confusing to the reader. It is best to write the ROI in a logical order.

In another example, interviewees will often downplay their involvement in a matter under investigation. Some interviewees are psychologically unable to leap from denying involvement to making a complete, truthful statement of their responsibility. It is an interviewer's job to assist the process.

For instance, an interviewee might first deny not ringing up sales and pocketing cash. As a result of further questioning, the interviewee might admit to doing so, minimizing the amount taken, say $100. With further interview questioning, the interviewee might increase the amount taken to $300. With further questioning, the interviewee might reveal the actual amount to be $1,000. It would be burdensome and confusing to the reader if the ROI were written with all the detail it took for the interviewee to admit to taking $1,000 over a 2-month period. This section could be written as follows:

> Harris first denied not ringing up sales and pocketing the cash. However, in response to further questioning, Harris confessed to doing so, taking $1,000 over a two-month period.

## Preliminary and Peripheral Information

Many organizations have "fill-in-the-blank" forms that assist with preliminary and peripheral information such as date, time, and location of the interview. However, it is beneficial to also include this information in the body of the report. It does happen that a form that is stored on a computer will have the preliminary information from a previous ROI captured. Occasionally, the interviewer writing the report will neglect to overtype that information with the new information. That can be a problem if the information is not captured in the body of the report.

ROIs should also include necessary preliminary information to "set the stage" for the reader. For example, if an interviewee had been interviewed previously, it would be beneficial to let the reader know this either in a footnote or parenthetically as follows:

> On Tuesday, May 2, 2013, I interviewed Fred Smith (Smith), owner of Smith Industrial Supplies (SIS). The interview took place at Smith's office, located at 1232 Foster Blvd, Baltimore, MD, 21230. (I previously interviewed Smith on Sunday, April 30, 2013. See ROI dated May 1, 2013.)

Another example would include related activity that took place before the commencing of the interview as follows:

> On Tuesday, May 2, 2013, I interviewed Fred Smith (Smith), owner of Smith Industrial Supplies (SIS). The interview took place at Smith's office, located at 1232 Foster Blvd, Baltimore, MD, 21230. As requested, Smith provided four file boxes relating to the SIS contract with ABC Retail Company (ABC). I reviewed the files prior to the interview.

**Note**: The results of the file review would not be captured in the ROI. The results would be captured in a separate investigative activity report.

ROIs should also include any peripheral activity, such as a restroom or refreshment break. You should capture the time the breaks were offered and when they occurred in a footnote. Since ROIs are not necessarily written in the chronological order of the interview, this footnote can be captured at the beginning or end of the ROI. Documenting this activity could be important, especially if the interviewee makes a complaint about the interview conduct. In this regard, the use of footnotes in an ROI should be minimal. It is distracting for a reader to move from the body of the report to the bottom of the page. If the information can be easily be included in the body of the report, do so.

See the Interview and ROI example in Appendix B.

## SUMMARY

A Report of Interview (ROI) must be prepared even if the interview was recorded. The ROI will become a part of the case file for others to read, including supervisors, attorneys, other investigators, and anyone else who has a need to know the interview results. ROIs should be prepared in a narrative style versus a "Question and Answer" session. In this regard, it is important to follow certain rules when preparing the ROI. The rules include writing short paragraphs, using proper grammar and syntax, writing in the active voice, and using a minimal number of quotes. In addition, the proper verbs and pronouns should be used. Furthermore, the ROI should be written in a logical order and include necessary peripheral information.

## EXERCISE 17.1. MULTIPLE CHOICE AND TRUE AND FALSE QUESTIONS

1. If an interview is recorded, there is no need to prepare an ROI.

   _____ True
   _____ False

2. An ROI should be written in a "Question and Answer" format.

   _____ True
   _____ False

3. A basic ROI rule is to write short paragraphs.

   _____ True
   _____ False

4. If an interviewee speaks using improper grammar, the ROI should be written in the same manner to capture its accuracy.

_____ True
_____ False

5. When writing an ROI, using active voice is preferred.

_____ True
_____ False

6. When writing an ROI, the use of quotes should be minimal. From the following, choose what should Not be placed in quotes.

_____ A witness or victim relating the exact words of a suspect in the commission of a crime.
_____ A suspect's admission or confession.
_____ An interviewee exclaims something profound that a reader would want to know.
_____ An interviewee asks for a restroom break.

7. Once an individual is fully identified in and ROI using the parenthetical rule, subsequent ROIs only need to utilize the shortened identification.

_____ True
_____ False

8. The interview took place in the past, so the interviewee's responses should be written in the past tense.

_____ True
_____ False

9. Using the appropriate verbs captures the essence of the interviewee's responses.

_____ True
_____ False

10. An ROI should be written in the exact chronological order of the interview.

_____ True
_____ False

## EXERCISE 17.2. ESSAY TOPICS

1. Discuss the basic rules of preparing an ROI.
2. Discuss why it is important to capture peripheral information in the ROI body.
3. Discuss what should be captured in quotes.
4. Discuss why an ROI should be written in a logical order instead of a chronological order.

# Part 4

# Case Study

The Case Study is a microexamination of an investigation that somewhat parallels an actual case. The Case Study involves procurement fraud schemes against Nationwide Retail Company, a Fortune 100 entity with stores throughout the United States. Nationwide Retail Company as well as the names of involved individuals are fictitious. Any resemblance to the names of actual individuals is merely a coincidence.

The Case Study involves a whistleblower, two prime contractors, and four involved employees. The Case Study consists of six parts with six interviews that are captured in interview notes or transcripts. These interviews are presented as learning tools. In addition to the interviews, the Case Study includes other investigative activity that is presented to provide context to the case.

The first section provides a basic overview of procurement fraud, which is necessary to appreciate the Case Study. Procurement fraud prevention methods are not offered in this instruction.

# A Basic Overview of Procurement Fraud

## GLOSSARY

- **Change Order:** Change orders are addendums to the contract. Often a change order is requested by the vendor to change the price of a product due to changes in the market.
- **Contract Administrator:** The Contract Administrator ensures that the selected vendor abides by the term of the contract. The Contract Administrator facilitates addendum to the contract, including change orders.
- **Cost Plus Contract:** A contract that is based on what it cost the vendor to fulfill the contract plus a fixed percentage for profit.
- **Fixed Price Contract:** A contract that is based on a price that has been determined by the vendor's bid amount.
- **Prime Contractor:** A prime contractor receives the contract award for a large project.
- **Procurement Officer:** A Procurement Officer, or a buyer, is the employee of an organization who solicits potential vendors for a purchase of goods or services, reviews the bids, and awards the contract.
- **Project Manager:** The Project Manager (PM) manages the project, ensuring the materials meet contract specifications. The PM also facilitates vendor change order requests. The PM is usually an employee; however, they can also be a contractor hired specifically to oversee a project.
- **Sole Source Contract:** An end user of the goods or services suggests that the contract be awarded to a specific firm or individual with no competing bids based on the firm or individual's unique ability to fulfill the contract.
- **Subcontractor:** The Prime Contractor will hire subcontractors to assist with the fulfillment of the contract.

## PROCUREMENT PROCESS

Many organizations utilize similar procurement processes. Below is a simplified version. There are many variables depending on the organization and the value or complexity of the project:

1. A department (end user) requires goods or services.
2. The end user receives approval for the purchase. The approval level depends on the level of the requester and the budgeted dollar amount.
3. The approved request is sent to the appropriate Procurement Officer (PO) in the Purchasing Department. (In a large organization a PO can specialize in specific goods or services.)
4. The PO evaluates the request and sends out a Request for Proposal (RFP) to a known list of vendors who are capable of fulling the contact. The PO might seek new vendors who might be interested and send an RFP to them.
5. Interested vendors will submit a bid based on the specifications listed in the RFP.
6. The PO or a committee will review the bids, select a vendor, and issue a contract.
7. Once the contract is awarded a Contract Administrator (CA) will oversee the contract progress.
8. The CA is responsible for approving payments and facilitating change orders.

## COMMON FRAUD HAZARDS

- **Bid Manipulation:** Competing vendors can manipulate the awarding of contracts through:
  - Bid rotation (Firms take turns bidding high or low).
  - Complimentary high bid by a vendor who has no intention of winning.
  - A competing vendor bids high then is hired by the prime contractor as a subcontractor.

- **Change Order Fraud:** Change orders requesting an increase in payment for goods or services can be easily falsified and approved. The vendor, the PM, and the CA can be in collusion. Often a vendor will recoup a low-bid monetary loss this way.

- **Conflict of Interest:** An employee has an undisclosed interest with a potential vendor.
- **Product Substitution:** A vendor will surreptitiously substitute inferior, less expensive products than the ones specified in the contract, causing the vendor's profit to increase. This fraud can be in collusion with the PM.
- **Phantom Employees and Equipment:** In a cost plus contract, the vendor factors in the cost of a certain number of employees and equipment to submit the bid. The vendor can employ a lesser number of employees and the profit will increase. Falsified payroll documents can be prepared for the PM and any auditor to review. Equipment usage can be falsified. One scheme involves having an inoperable piece of equipment on site costing the end user X number of dollars per hour, however, it is never used.
- **Vendor Collusion with Influential Employees:** Vendors collude with influential employees to commit the above mention fraud schemes. The influential employee can include the end user, the project approver, the PO, the PM, and the CA. The employee can overlook the irregularities or actively participate in the fraud. Vendors provide employees:
  - Bribes
  - Kickbacks
  - Gratuities

Bribes, kickbacks, and gratuities can take the form of cash, trips, merchandise, college tuition, company stocks, family member employment (actual or only on the books), and any number of other methods.

# Case Study—Part I

Jack Grant (Grant) is a new investigator with the Office of Investigation (OI) for Nationwide Retail Company (Nationwide), a fortune 100 company with headquarters in Baltimore, Maryland. Grant recently retired from the United States government with 30 years as a special agent with several Cabinet level Office of Inspectors General. He is a Certified Fraud Examiner (CFE) and a Certified Forensic Interviewer (CFI). Grant is attached to the Headquarters Investigative Unit along with four other investigators. He reports to Chief Investigator Herman Williams (Williams).

On the morning of Monday, April 21, Grant arrived at the office and listened to Hotline voicemails. One call was registered on Sunday, April 20 at 8:04 pm. The caller was a male. The transcription of the voicemail is as follows:

> I'm calling to report that one of your Project Managers has been taking kickbacks from two construction firms for over ten years. One million dollars at least. Call me tomorrow between four and five o'clock at this number. 302-555-1242.

Grant reported the call to Williams who instructed Grant to look into it.

## INVESTIGATIVE ACTIVITY

Grant reviewed various internet sites and public and propriety data bases and discovered the following:

- A reverse check on the phone number provided revealed that it is listed to a Robert Lanier (Lanier), 9373 N. Hyde St., Chicago, Illinois 60917.
- Nationwide Retail Company personnel records revealed no employee with the last name of Lanier.

- Robert Lanier is the owner of Lanier Electrical Supply (LES), located in Chicago.
- Lanier and LES is being sued by three electrical supply manufacturers for nonpayment.
- Cook County, Illinois, property records reveals that Lanier's home is valued at $450,000 and is co-owned by Dorothy Lanier. Lanier and his wife Dorothy have lived there for 25 years.
- A public record criminal and traffic violation check for Illinois reveals that Lanier has no published criminal record. He has had several speeding tickets in the past year. Records did not reveal criminal or traffic violations for Dorothy.
- The Nationwide Retail Company Procurement Database (NPD) was reviewed. The NPD has been in existence for 2 years. NPD can be searched for Projects, Contracts, Contract Types, Completed Projects, Project Costs, Project Managers, Contractors, and Subcontractors. (At the inception of the NPD, contractors submitting a bid must include the identity of subcontractors they intend to use on a contract.) The NPD data population is handled by the Procurement Office. Data input began 2 years previous. Contracts and Projects prior to NPD's launch have not and will not be entered. The following information was discovered:
    - LES was listed once as a subcontractor for Premier Construction Company (Premier).
    - Premier is identified as the Prime Contractor for Nationwide's Mid-West Distribution Center in Octavia, Illinois. The construction began 2 years ago, corresponding with the creation of the NPD.
    - NPD listed 11 other subcontractors that Premier is using for the Midwest Distribution Center, including a HVAC company, two plumbing companies, and other various firms. One subcontractor was ABC General Construction (ABC).
    - The Nationwide Project Manager (PM) for the project is identified as Raymond Burke (Burke) of the Central Division.
- Nationwide personnel records reveal Burke, a nonunion employee, has been employed with Nationwide for 23 years. He has been a PM for 13 years. Burke's current annual salary with Nationwide is $80,000.
- A public records check revealed that Burke owns a home in Lyle, Illinois. Laura Burke is listed as a co-owner. The home is valued at

$1.2 million. Burke and his wife, Laura have lived there for 3 years. The Burkes sold their previous home located in Chicago's north side 3 years ago for $370,000. The Burkes lived there for 18 years.

- Public records reveal no criminal, traffic, or civil, records on the Burkes.
- Burke is listed with the Illinois Secretary of State as the President of Northside Chicago Electric, Inc. (NCE). Laura Burke is listed as Secretary of NCE. NCE organizational documents list its purpose as providing residential and commercial electrical services. The address was listed as the Burke home in Lyle.
- An internet and phone search for NCE revealed no phone listed or web references.
- A check on Premier revealed it to be a large Construction firm based in Chicago, Illinois, and has been operating for 26 years. A Dun & Bradstreet (D&B) check indicates that Premier has annual revenue of around 100 million dollars. Premier's list of clients includes large retailers, manufacturers, sports arenas, colleges, as well as local, state, and federal government contracts. The President and CEO of Premier is identified as John Novak.
- A public record background on Novak revealed that he is 59 years old. He has a criminal record including old charges of assault, weapons violations, theft, and racketeering. The most recent charge was the federal racketeering charge 14 years previous. Dispositions for those cases could not be found.
- An online search of Chicago area newspaper archives revealed stories that claim and hint that Novak is a Chicago area Organized Crime member. One story revealed that Novak was found not guilty of the racketeering charge.
- A check on ABC found that it is a Chicago area construction company. D&B reports annual revenue of around 20 million dollars. ABC lists clients as commercial and government. ABC has been operating for 13 years.
- Illinois Secretary of State records reveal that the president of ABC is Roger Billings. (Billings) Billings is 45 years old.
- A public record search reveals Billings has been arrested several times 18–27 years ago for auto-theft and receiving stolen goods. Dispositions on those charges were not discovered.
- A search of Chicago area online newspaper archives revealed no stories concerning Billings or ABC.

Grant reported the findings to Williams. Williams instructed Grant to make the call as instructed. He also suggested that Grant become familiar with Nationwide's procurement policies, specifically as they pertain to construction projects. A review of the Nationwide Organizational Chart determined that it would be beneficial to interview Assistant Vice President (AVP) of Procurement John Nelson. Grant contacted Nelson's office and a meeting was scheduled for 3:00 PM.

## AVP JOHN NELSON INTERVIEW

On Tuesday, April 22, at approximately 3:00 PM, Grant interviewed Nationwide's AVP for Procurement John Nelson (Nelson) to learn about procurement policies and procedures, specifically as it relates to construction contracts. The interview took place in Nelson's office on the fifth floor of Nationwide Headquarters. Grant thanked Nelson for taking the time to meet.

During the preliminary conversation, Grant learned that Nelson has been employed with Nationwide for 37 years. He began his career as a clerk in his senior year of high school at the Philadelphia Distribution Center. Nationwide chose him to participate in the management trainee program and paid for his college. Nelson worked his way up the corporate ladder and has been the AVP of Procurement for 7 years. Grant learned that Nelson's younger brother is a special agent with the FBI. Grant did not inform Nelson of the allegation made by the hotline caller. Nelson provided answers to questions, which were captured in the following notes:

- Nelson supervises Nationwide's Procurement Officers (PO).
- Construction contracts are handled differently than other procurements made by a Nationwide.
- Construction contracts are "cost plus" contracts. That means that the Prime Contractor will bid what it will cost to do the job and add 15% for profit.
- Nelson estimated that Nationwide uses approximately 35 Prime Contractor construction firms throughout the country on a consistent basis.
- Once a construction firm is used as a Prime Contractor, it is beneficial to continually use them due to their knowledge of store construction requirements. The learning curve is eliminated with a seasoned Prime Contractor.

- It is beneficial for Nationwide's area Project Managers (PM) to have a good working relationship with the Prime Contractors. It makes things work smoothly.
- The PMs report to the AVP Store Operations, Wilbur Gunn.
- The Prime Contractor hires the subcontractors for the project.
- Beginning with the existence of the Nationwide Procurement Database (NPD) 2 years previous the subcontractors are identified. Prior to the NPD, Nationwide did not keep track of the subcontractors hired by the Prime Contractor.
- Nationwide's area POs are the individuals who make the decision to award a contract based on the Prime Contractor's bid and ability to deliver on the contract.
- Nationwide does not "sole source" construction contacts.
- Nelson believes that it is possible that only two construction firms would bid for a job; however, the policy calls for the PO to solicit bids from at least four Prime Contractors for each project.
- The PO is the first line of defense in preventing and detecting bidding irregularities.
- Once the contract has been awarded, The PO's duties are finished for that contract.
- Nationwide's area Contract Administrator (CA) takes over to ensure that the Prime Contractor is meeting the terms of the contract.
- The CA for each area report directly to the AVP Contract Administration, Henry Ernst.
- The area PMs supervise project construction.

  (**Note:** Even though Nelson and the Procurement Officers he supervises are not responsible for change orders, he explained the change order process.)
- If a "change order" to the contract is required, the CA will amend the contract. For example, if the price of a specified piece of equipment has increased since the time of the contract award, the Prime Contractor will ask for a change order so they can be paid appropriately for the equipment.
- The PM will facilitate the change order request with the CA. Nationwide does not want the Prime contractor to lose money because of something out of their control.

**The interview concluded at 4:00 PM.**

---

## CASE STUDY—PART 1 EXERCISE

- Prepare an ROI of the John Nelson Interview.
- Based on Grant's investigative activity, discuss what assumptions he should have to either prove or disprove.
- Discuss Grant's next investigative step. Who should he interview next?

# Case Study—Part 2

On Tuesday, April 22 at 4:10 pm, Grant called the phone number left by the caller. A male answered and when asked, he acknowledged he was Robert Lanier. Grant identified himself. Lanier acknowledged that he called the Nationwide hotline number and left the message. Grant questioned Lanier about the message. Lanier stated that before he provides information, he wants assurances that Nationwide would assist him with an IRS issue. Grant informed Lanier that it would be best to meet in person. Lanier agreed to meet the next day. Lanier did not want to meet at his home, his business, or at Nationwide's office due to fear of being observed. Lanier suggested to meet him at the Holiday Inn on 3rd street in Withers, Illinois.

Grant booked a flight to Chicago and a room at the Holiday Inn in Withers for two nights. Grant contacted the Office of Investigation's Central Office and arranged to have Investigator Mary Duncan (Duncan) meet him at the airport and accompany him to the Holiday Inn to interview Lanier. Grant arrived at Midway Airport on April 22 at 11:40 am and was picked up by Duncan. Grant and Duncan arrived at the Holiday Inn and secured a small conference room for the interview. Duncan agreed that Grant would be the primary Interviewer and she would be the second and take notes.

## PRELIMINARY MATTERS—ROBERT LANIER INTERVIEW

Lanier arrived at the Holiday Inn at 2 pm. Introductions were made. Grant informed Lanier he could call him Jack and investigator Duncan, Mary. Lanier asked to be called Bob. Grant thanked Lanier for meeting and asked him if he wanted something to drink or use the restroom. Lanier declined. Grant informed Lanier that the meeting would be recorded, and he agreed. (The transcript speakers are noted as Jack Grant (JG), Mary Duncan (MD), and Robert Lanier (RL).

## ROBERT LANIER INTERVIEW TRANSCRIPT

**JG**: "The date is April 22, the time is 2:22 pm Central Time. I am Jack Grant of the Nationwide Retail Company Office of Investigation. Also present is Mary Duncan, Nationwide's Office of Investigation, and Robert Lanier, owner of Lanier Electrical Supply. We are in a first-floor conference room at the Holiday Inn in Withers, Illinois. We have agreed to refer to each other by first names. Bob, thank you for contacting us and agreeing to meet. As I mentioned earlier, we are recording this meeting. Do you agree to the recording?"

**RL**: "Yes."

**JG**: "Great. Bob, before we get to the reason you reached out to us, I would like to obtain some preliminary information. Okay?"

**RL**: "That's fine."

**JG**: "Great. Please tell me a little bit about yourself, your age, family."

**RL**: "Okay, well I'm 53, born on September 13, 1961. I'm married for thirty years to Dorothy. I have two grown children, a boy and a girl."

**JG**: "I have two grown children. Girls. No matter how old they are I still worry about them."

**RL**: "Yeah."

**JG**: "Where do you live?"

**RL**: "I live Chicago. I grew up in Chicago. I was a Chicago cop for 10 years. My boy is a Chicago cop. You talk about worry."

**JG**: "Oh yeah, I was on the job in Baltimore for eight years, then worked for the Federal Government at a few agencies as a special agent for thirty years. I retired from the government last year. However, you can see I'm still working. So, tell us about Lanier Electrical Supply."

**RL**: "Okay. As a teenager I started doing electrical work for a company. I joined the PD when I was 21 and continued to do electrical work on the side. Everybody had side jobs to make ends meet."

**JG**: "Yeah. When I was on the PD, I use to do roofing with a guy I worked with. My wife and I were young when we had our children. She stayed home when they were little. You have to do what you have to do to supplement a cop's pay. So, when did you start your business?"

**RL**: "I left the PD in 1992. I had an opportunity to buy an electrical supply outfit in Chicago. Apex Electrical Supply. The owner was getting old and had no family to keep it going. He made me a sweet offer, so I bought it. I changed the name."

**JG**: "Bob as I told you, we are interested in listening to you about the kickbacks you mentioned on the phone. We appreciate you bringing this to our attention. It is important that you tell us everything you know. Please do not leave anything out, even if it something you do not think is important. It could be. Also, if you are unsure of something, that is okay. Just let us know that you are not sure. And, I am not saying that you would, but please do not fabricate any information. Okay?

**RL**: "Yeah, but before I go into all of this, I want to see how you could help me with my problem I mentioned on the phone."

**JG**: "The IRS problem. Tell me about it."

**RL**: "Well, I got behind in paying my business taxes, and my personal taxes. I haven't filed for three years and haven't paid taxes for the last six or seven years. Things are going to hell."

**JG**: "Okay, how much do you owe?"

**RL**: "I owe over $100,000, and it is growing everyday with penalties and interest. I haven't paid my wholesale suppliers. They are getting ready to sue me."

**JG**: "Okay. Tell me what you are expecting us to do?"

**RL**: "I would like, in return for the information I provide, for Nationwide to use its influence to have the IRS grant me amnesty. Or for Nationwide to pay my back taxes."

**JG**: "Bob, first, I am not sure if Nationwide would have any influence with the IRS. I am also not sure about Nationwide paying your taxes. Right now, it is premature to discuss any type of arrangement. Your best course of action is to provide the information and we will see how it pans out. If the information you provide is true and significant, and you cooperate throughout the length of any investigation, we would inform whoever was handling the IRS issue that you came forward, cooperated, and were truthful throughout the investigation. If the information is significant and you cooperate, I will talk to my supervisors regarding your request for financial help. That is all I can promise you at this point. Do you understand?"

**RL**: "Oh, what I have to tell you is significant."

**JG**: "Okay. Why don't you tell us what you have?"

**RL**: "I also want to remain confidential."

**JG**: "Bob, I understand. At this time, your identity will be kept confidential by our office. However, depending on what you tell us, there could come a time when keeping you confidential is out of our control. Again, it is premature to talk about this until we hear what you have to say."

**RL**: "One more thing. I want immunity from prosecution."

**JG**: "Bob, I cannot offer you immunity. Only a prosecutor can offer you immunity. If what you tell us is serious enough to refer to a prosecutor, I would inform the prosecutor of your total, truthful, and significant cooperation, as long as it is total, truthful, and significant. Do you understand?"

**RL**: "I guess. What I have to tell you is significant. I'm taking a big risk here."

**JG**: "Bob, I understand. Why don't you tell us?"

**RL**: "Okay, one of your project managers has been taking kickbacks from two construction contractors for twelve years or so. Over a million dollars."

**JG**: "Okay. Go on"

**RL**: "Well his name is Ray Burke. The two contractors are Premier and ABC."

**JG**: "Okay. Bob, please tell us everything you know about Ray Burke receiving kickbacks from Premier and ABC."

**RL**: "All right. I met Ray 12 or 13 years ago the first time I was a subcontractor for Premier on a Nationwide job. I came to know Ray pretty well and we started hanging out together. I was hired by Premier as a sub to provide electrical supplies for a store construction. The owner, John Novak instructed me to add 30% of my actual costs to my proposal to Premier. He told me all of the other sub-contractors did the same. Novak used the padded proposals for his bid on the job. Novak kicked backed 25% from my padded proposal. Novak took 50% and Burke gets 25%. Novak told me that Burke ensures that Premier wins the bid. With the other subcontractors being involved in the same scheme, Burke and Novak are making a killing.

**JG**: "Go on"

**RL**: "What do you want to know?"

**JG**: "You mentioned ABC as the other contractor."

**RL**: "Yeah, Novak referred me to Roger Billings, the owner of ABC. They also do construction projects for you. Billings has the same scam going with the subs and Burke."

**JG**: "Okay, tell me what you supply as a sub for Premier and ABC."

**RL**: "Wire, switches, breakers, boxes, and any other electrical supply they need. I have subbed on all of Premier and ABC jobs with Nationwide for the past 12 or 13 years."

**JG**: "Who are the other subcontractors?"

**RL**: "You name it, it is usually the same ones. HVAC, painters, roofers, a few other ones.

**JG**: "Okay. Tell us how the kickbacks are paid."

**RL**: "Novak and Billings pay my actual invoice. Then they pay me my extra by check."

**JG**: "Do they make the check out to you or your business?

**RL**: "To Lanier Electrical Supply."

**JG**: "Okay. Go on."

**RL**: "What do you want to know?"

**JG**: "How is Burke paid?"

**RL**: "Well, Burke has a company, Northside Chicago Electrical. Burke's money was paid to the company. Burke told me they paid him as a consultant. Around nine years ago or so, Burke asked if some of the money could be paid to my company. Premier and ABC would write a check to my company. I would write a check to Burke's business minus 30% that I would keep. I did this for around two years. I became wary of this situation. Too much money coming through my account. My wife has access to the books, and she is unaware of all this. She and my children would be devastated if they found out."

**JG**: "So, what happened then?"

**RL**: "Burke instructed me to form a company with one of his foremen. He became aware of the kickbacks and Burke wanted to keep him quiet by giving him a percentage. So, we formed a company, FBN Enterprises. Now Premier and ABC pay Burke's share to FBN, and I distribute the payments to Burke. I handle the banking."

**JG**: "Who is the foreman?"

**RL**: "Peter Taylor."

**JG**: "Okay. What do you, and what does Taylor receive in this arrangement?"

**RL**: "I receive 15% of Burke's money and Taylor receives 15% of Burke's money."

**JG**: "Okay How long have the kickbacks been paid to FBN?"

**RL**: "Around seven years."

**JG**: "How much money are we talking about going through FBN?"

**RL**: "A lot, maybe 2 million."

**JG**: "Okay. So, based on what you are saying, you and Taylor have each received $300,000 and Burke received $1.4 million in the past seven years from FBN."

**RL**: "Maybe not that much, but close. I have the records. The biggest chunk of money has been in the past couple of years with the Distribution Center construction. Can I use the restroom? "

**JG**: "Sure. Let's take a break. It is now 3:10 PM and the recorder is being turned off."

**JG**: "Okay, we are back. The time is 3:32 and the recorder is back on. We were talking about the Distribution Center. Tell us about that."

**RL**: "Well, as you know the construction began about two years ago. Premier was able to get the contract as the Prime. Novak hired ABC as a sub because the project is so big. I was a sub at first, but I had to be replaced because my wholesalers won't supply me since I haven't paid them."

**JG**: "Okay. Bob, you mentioned that Novak told you that Burke ensures that Premier wins the bid. Please tell us how this occurs."

**RL**: "Burke controls the operation through intimidation. The procurement guy awards the contracts. But Burke tells him what to do."

**JG**: "Who is the procurement guy?"

**RL**: "Gary Shelton."

**JG**: "Tell us about Gary Shelton."

**RL**: "I only know what Burke tells me. I don't have to deal with him. Burke called Shelton a wimp. Burke gives him a little bit of money to go along with all of this. He is afraid of Burke. I know that Premier and ABC have an arrangement where Premier will bid high and ABC low on some jobs and vice versa. But Ray makes all that happen."

**JG**: "Okay. How much money has Burke given Shelton?"

**RL**: "Based on what Burke told me, I'm guesstimating around $50,000 over the years. He also treats Shelton to meals all of the time."

**JG**: "How does Burke pay Shelton?"

**RL**: "Cash. A little bit here, a little bit there."

**JG**: "What else?"

**RL**: "I don't know."

**JG**: "Besides the subs padding the proposals, what else is happening?"

**RL**: "What do you mean?"

**JG**: "What about change orders?"

**RL**: "Oh yeah. Most jobs require change orders. Burke told me that many of the change orders Premier and ABC submit are padded or false. I don't get involved with them. Burke and the Contract Administrator handle those. Around four years ago when Nationwide announced they would be building the Distribution Center, Burke realized that there would be a few million dollars that they would be able to take with the padded subcontractor scam and with fabricated and padded change orders. Novak was able to arrange with Burke to get a pal of his hired as the Contract Administrator, Jeffry Freeman. The other Contract Administrator quit because he didn't want to go along with it. All change orders are approved by Freeman. Burke told me he gets a percentage of the pad. Prime and ABC generates the change orders and Burke signs off on them and Freeman approves them. Nobody is checking."

**JG**: "Tell me about the previous Contract Administrator."

**RL**: "Burke told me he didn't want to play ball. He quit after the Distribution Center plan was announced. I don't know where he went."

**JG**: "What is his name?

**RL**: "I don't remember. I didn't have any dealings with him."

**JG**: "Okay. To be clear. With regard to the change orders, Burke receives a percentage of the padded amount. Correct?"

**RL**: "Yes."

**JG**: "And that amount is paid to FBN, is that correct?"

**RL**: "Yes."

**JG**: "And you and Taylor each receive 15% of the money paid to FBN?"

**RL**: "Yes."

**JG**: "Does FBN provide actual service?"

**RL**: "No. It's a company on paper only."

**JG**: "Okay. Let's go over a few things. When Burke's kickbacks were being paid to your company for those two years, how much are we talking about?"

**RL**: "I'm not sure, probably around 200 to 300 thousand dollars."

**JG**: "And you received 30%, correct?"

**RL**: "Yes."

**JG**: "So then you would have received between 60 and 90 thousand, and Burke would have received between 140 and 210 thousand, correct?"

**RL**: "I guess."

**JG**: "How do you give Burke his money?"

**RL**: "I write him checks to his company, Northside Chicago Electric."

**JG**: "Okay. So, in addition to the percentage of Burke's kickbacks you receive, how much have you received from the padded proposal kickbacks paid to your company?"

**RL**: "Geez, I don't know offhand. It could be a couple hundred thousand over the years."

**JG**: "Okay. Is there anything else?

**RL**: "Well, no."

**JG**: "Bob, it seems like you are hesitating. Remember what I said, don't leave anything out. You have gone this far, so it makes sense to tell us everything okay?"

**RL**: "Okay. This is really where I could use help. Novak is being investigated by the FBI and the United States Attorney's Office for paying kickbacks to a government contracting officer to receive federal construction projects. I'm afraid my name will be brought up. I was a sub for Premier. I padded my proposals by 30% and received 25 percent of the pad. I assume the kickback scheme is the same as the one with you. Novak told me to play dumb if the FBI interviews me or if I am called to a Grand Jury. I cannot stand the pressure of the IRS, the kickbacks, the lawsuits and now the federal investigation. I want this all to end. I have heart problems. I do not want to go to jail."

**JG**: "I understand. Bob the best thing you can do is to continue to cooperate with us. Let's go over a few things. Interrupt me if I am incorrect. Okay? You met Burke around 12 years ago when you first subbed on a job for Premier at Nationwide. On that job, Novak instructed you to pad your proposal by 30%. You received a kickback of 25%, Burke received 25%, and Novak received 50% of the pad. Correct?

**RL:** "Yes"

**JG**: "All of the other subcontractors were involved. You also subbed for ABC who had the same padding proposal and kickback scheme in place."

**RL**: "Yes."

**JG**: "How many construction jobs in the past 12 or 13 years are we talking about?"

**RL**: "Man, a lot. At least fifty across the Midwest. Premier is huge, so is ABC, but not as big as Premier. Premier has offices throughout the Midwest. You guys have been expanding so fast, building new stores, and remodeling the old ones and the stores you bought from Q Mart when they went bust."

**JG**: "Okay. So, let me go over this. Your proposals to Premier and ABC were padded 30% above your actual cost that you billed them. Right?"

**RL**: "Yes."

**JG**: "Can you please explain how this works. Can you give an example?"

**RL**: "Sure. I buy the supplies from the manufacturers and wholesalers at wholesale prices. I sell the material to whoever needs it at retail cost, double the wholesale price. This is normal. On the large construction jobs, I offer a ten percent discount. If I need to supply material that cost me at wholesale, say $50,000, I will normally sell the material for $100,000. For the construction jobs, to Premier and ABC, I would discount it at 10% and sell it for $90,000. I would pad my proposal to Premier and ABC by 30%. That would be, hold on, let me see, $27,000. So Premier and ABC will use a figure of $117,000 included in their bid to Nationwide. I would invoice Premier and ABC my actual charge of $90,000. You guys would pay Premier and ABC. They would pay me a kickback of 25%, or in this case $6,750. Burke would receive $6,750 and the rest is extra for Premier and ABC. And like I said, all the subs do the same. So, if there are ten subs on a job and they all are involved, Burke is making a killing. So is Novak and Billings. "

**JG**: "Okay. Let's go over this. When you first met Burke, his kickbacks were being paid to his company, Northside Chicago Electric. Right?"

**RL**: "Yes."

**JG**: "Does Northside perform any service?"

**RL**: "Burke told me he used to do side jobs. He hasn't done anything since I've known him."

**JG**: "Then Burke's kickbacks were being paid to your business for about two years and you would write a check to his company."

**RL**: "Right."

**JG**: "Okay. So, when Burke's kickbacks were being paid to your company, did you receive a separate payment for your padded proposal kickback."

**RL**: "Yes."

**JG**: "Okay. After you stopped receiving Burke's payments to your business, you formed FBN with Taylor. You estimate that Premier and ABC have paid FBN around two million dollars and you and Taylor each receive fifteen percent of that total. Let me ask you this. Why did Burke ask you to have the payments go through your business? Why didn't he just continue to have Premier and ABC pay his business. It would have saved him thirty percent?"

**RL**: "Well, I've been thinking about that. At first, I thought it was because he was making so much money and him and I became good friends and he wanted me to share. But I also think it was to entrench me in the scam to keep from ever, well do what I'm doing, blowing it wide open. I was in deep. The same thing he is doing with Taylor. Burke told me Taylor shook him down."

**JG**: "Okay Bob. This is a lot to take in. What documents can you provide us?"

**RL**: "I have seven years of the FBN bank statements and cancelled checks and payment to my business. I have shredded a lot of the checks and invoices that are past seven years."

**JG**: What will the FBN bank documents show?"

**RL**: "It will show payments from Premier and ABC that I deposited, and checks issued to Burke and Taylor?"

**JG**: "What about payments to you?"

**RL**: "Yes, checks I wrote to my business."

**JG**: "Okay. When can you provide the documents?"

**RL**: "Is next week okay?"

**JG**: "Yes, let's meet next Tuesday, here. I will call you to confirm a time. I have to go home and pack some bags and head back."

**RL**: "That works."

**JG**: "Mary, do you have any questions for Bob?"

**MD**: "Yes. What are the full names of Premier and ABC?"

**RL**: "Premier Construction Company. ABC General Construction."

**MD**: "Thank you. Is there anybody else involved?"

**RL**: "Not that I know of."

**MD**: "Okay. Thanks."

**JG**: "Bob, can we please verify your home address."

**RL**: "9373 N. Hyde St. Chicago, 60917.
**JG**: "And you phone number?"
**RL**: "Your have it. My cell is: 302-555-9876
**JG**: "Okay. Bob, thank you for bringing this to our attention. We take this very seriously. I will provide my boss an update and tell him what we discussed. Here is my card. If you can think of anything else that we need to know before Tuesday, give me a call. I advise you to not talk to anybody else about this. Oh. Bob. I need to ask you. Have you reported this to any other agency?"
**RL**: "No."
**JG**: "Does anybody know that you are reporting this?"
**RL**: "No."
**JG**: "Does anybody know that you were meeting with us today?"
**RL**: "No"
**JG**: "Okay. Let's end here. The time is 4:33 pm. I am turning the recorder off."

---

The next day Grant contacted Chief Investigator Williams and provided a briefing of Lanier's interview. Williams agreed that there is predication to move forward with opening a case. Williams agreed to assign Duncan to assist in the investigation. He told Grant to come home, spend time with his family because he will probably be staying in Chicago for a while.

Grant asked Duncan to perform background investigations on Taylor, Shelton, Freeman, and FBN. Grant also asked Duncan to identify the previous Contract Administrator and determine his whereabouts. Grant checked out of the hotel a day early and flew back home.

## CASE STUDY—PART 2 EXERCISE

- Prepare a ROI of the Robert Lanier interview.
- Identify the Introduction, Preliminary Matters, the Introductory Statement, the Preliminary Questions, and the Opening Statement.
- What next step(s) should Grant take and why?
- Of the names Lanier provided, develop a preliminary interview order. Who should Grant interview next and why?

# Case Study—Part 3

## INVESTIGATIVE ACTIVITY

Duncan checked Nationwide's employment records and other public records for Peter Taylor, Gary Shelton, and Jeffrey Freeman. Duncan identified the previous Contract Administrator as Sean Flannigan. She found the following information:

### Taylor

- Taylor has worked for Nationwide for 15 years as a carpenter, then as a foreman. He is a union employee represented by the International Association of Retail Construction Workers (IARCW).
- As a union employee, Taylor earns $22.55 per hour. He has been subject to a reduction in force (RIF) three times during his tenure with Nationwide. The first time was 8 years ago for 4 months, the second time was 5 years ago for 3 weeks, and the third time was 3 years ago for 2 months. As a union employee, Taylor received union benefits and state unemployment totaling $225.00 per week when he was furloughed.
- Taylor is married and has three daughters, ages 7, 10, and 11. They reside in a home he and his wife Lisa purchasd 4 years ago in Chicago.
- There are two civil judgments against Taylor for nonpayment of hospital bills in in the past 4 years.
- No criminal record could be found.

### Shelton

- Shelton is Nationwide's Procurement Officer for the Central Division, a nonunion position. He has been employed with Nationwide for 25 years. He has worked in the Finance Department

in various positions his entire career. He has been the Procurement Officer for the Central Division for 13 years.
- Shelton is married with two children, a boy and a girl, ages 20 and 21.
- Shelton and his wife, Nancy, own a home in a suburb north of Chicago for 25 years.
- No record of civil judgements or criminal record for Gary or Nancy Shelton.

### Freeman

- Freeman was hired 3 years ago to his current position as Contract Administrator, a nonunion position. He is single. Freeman listed his previous employer as Premier Construction Company where he worked for 10 years in the position of Business Manager. The reason noted for leaving Premier was "to seek other employment."
- The address listed in Freeman's personnel record is a high-rise apartment complex on Lake Michigan in Chicago.
- There is no record of property ownership.
- No criminal or civil record could be found.

### Flannigan

- Flannigan was employed at Nationwide for 8 years, leaving 3 years previous. He currently resides in Boise, Idaho.

### FBN

- FBN is a registered corporation in the state of Illinois, chartered 7 years ago. The President is listed as Robert Lanier. The Secretary and Treasurer is listed as Peter Taylor. The Registered Agent is Jerome Hartnett. The business purpose is listed as Consulting Services.

## RELEVANT NATIONWIDE POLICIES

Grant checked Nationwide's policies regarding employee honesty and found "Conflict of Interest and Integrity," policy, # 09-12, that reads as follows:

> All employees must act with the highest integrity and honesty and provide loyal and faithful service to Nationwide Retail Company in the course of their duties, Including not accepting

> anything of value from a vendor that could or could appear to influence business decision made on behalf of Nationwide. In addition, employees conducting Nationwide business should refrain from illegal, immoral, or unethical conduct.

Additionally, Grant found the policy that refers to employee cooperation with matters being investigated by the Office of Investigations: "Employee Responsibilities and Duties," policy # 99-55, that reads as follows:

> All employees have an obligation to cooperate with any matter being investigated by any member of senior management, Loss Prevention, Security, Office of Investigations, and Office of Internal Audit. This includes making oneself available for interviews and answering questions honestly, thoroughly, and candidly. Lack of compliance in this regard can lead to discipline, including termination.

On Tuesday, April 29, Grant kissed his spouse and dog goodbye and flew to Chicago. Duncan picked Grant up and drove to the Withers Holiday Inn.

## ROBERT LANIER SECOND INTERVIEW

Duncan secured the same small conference room at the Withers, Illinois Holiday Inn. Lanier arrived at approximately 4:00 pm with two boxes of FBN bank statements and cancelled checks.

> (Note. Once a relationship has been established with a whistleblower like Lanier, meetings and interviews are more casual in nature. Trust has been gained and the whistleblower often has a sense of being part of the team. In the actual case, investigators met with the Lanier character dozens of times over the three-year investigation. Even with this "casual" relationship, the whistleblower still has to be prompted for information. Also, information provided still has to be corroborated.)

While Lanier sat in the room, Grant and Duncan performed a quick review of the records. The bank statements revealed deposit entries from Premier and ABC in varying amounts ranging from $15,235 to $62,410. Cancelled checks were made payable to NCE, LES, and Taylor. In addition, some cancelled checks were made payable to a Lucy Bennett in the amount of $5,000 and were dated on or near the first day of each month. All the cancelled checks were issued by Lanier.

After the quick review of the records, Grant asked Lanier if there was anything new since they last talked. He said that Burke is worried about federal investigation of Novak and Premier. Burke is aware that Lanier is involved in the federal kickback scheme. Burke is concerned that the investigation could broaden with his name being implicated due to his illegal activity at Nationwide.

**In response to questions, Lanier provided the following information captured by Duncan taking notes. The interview was not recorded.**

- Since last Tuesday, Lanier has not reached out to any other entity or agency regarding the kickback schemes, nor has he discussed his coming forward to report the kickback scheme with anybody.
- Lucy Bennett is a woman he has been seeing for a couple of years.
- His wife Dorothy is not aware of Bennett.
- He pays Bennett using FBN checks to help her with her apartment rent and expenses in Chicago. He does not believe Bennett is aware of Lanier's illegal activities.
- He and Bennett have socialized with Burke and a woman Burke is seeing, Brenda Jansen.
- Jansen is Novak's niece.
- Lanier does not believe that Burke and Taylor know he is paying Bennett using FBN checks.

**Lanier provided the following information in response to direct questions:**

- Lanier believes Novak and Billings hand deliver Premier and ABC kickback checks to Burke. Burke hand delivers them to Lanier. Lanier personally deposits the checks at the bank.
- Lanier hand delivers FBN checks to Burke, Taylor, and Bennett.
- The FBN checks to Burke are made out to NCE.
- Burke deposits his checks in his NCE bank account.
- Taylor deposits his check in his personal bank account.
- Bennet deposits her checks in her personal bank account.
- FBN Bank statements and cancelled checks are delivered by US Mail to a Post Office Box Lanier rents in FBN's name.

> (Note: The above questions concerning the method checks are delivered are routine questions to determine if the federal Mail Fraud Statute, 18 U.S.C. Section 1341 could be applied. In this case, the hand delivery of the checks was a concerted attempt

to avoid that charge. However, the statements and cancelled checks mailed from the bank to the FBN PO Box would be sufficient to charge many counts of Mail Fraud.)

**Grant asked questions about Taylor, Shelton, and Freeman. Lanier responded as follows:**

- Burke said that Taylor is anxious and is worried about the federal investigation, even though he is not involved in the federal kickback scheme.
- Taylor will probably crack under pressure and divulge the Nationwide kickback scheme.
- Gary Shelton is a weak individual and will probably "sing like a bird" if confronted.
- Freeman will not cooperate. He is loyal to Novak.

**Duncan asked the identity of the other subcontractors involved. Lanier provided the following information:**

- There have been many over the years. Some have been consistent subcontractors since he began. The consistent subcontractors who are currently involved in the Distribution Center are:
    - Jenkins Plumbing and Heating (Owner: Greg Jenkins)
    - Syzmanski Contractors (Owner: Richard Syzmanski)
    - Thorpe Concrete (Owner: Theodore Thorpe)
    - Walburn Electric (Owner: Ryan Walburn)
    - Cook County Lighting (Owner: Elizabeth Peterson)
    - Precision Grinding (Owner: Jorge Rodriguez)

Grant told Lanier that he will call him on Friday to clarify any of the information learned from the FBN Bank records review and to find out if anything else is happening. Grant instructed Lanier to call his cell phone if he thought of anything else.

## The interview concluded at 5:20 pm

- On Wednesday, April 30 Grant contacted Williams and briefed him on the Lanier interview. Williams agreed the next task was to perform a forensic examination and analyses of the FBN bank records provided by Lanier. Duncan was assigned that task. After the FBN bank record examination is complete, it was decided that the next interviews should be, Shelton, Taylor, and Freeman.

Ideally, the interviews should be conducted on the same day, one right after another.

- Williams instructed Grant to hold off contacting the United States Attorney's Office until there is substantive information to provide.

## REVIEW OF FBN BANK DOCUMENTS

- On Friday May 2, Duncan reported that she completed her examination of the FBN bank records. The records covered the past 7 years. In brief, her findings were as follows:

**Table Case 3.1** FBN Bank Records

| | | | |
|---|---|---|---|
| Checks from Premier and ABC | $1,874,645 | | |
| Breakdown: | | Premier 22 deposits | $1,125,487 |
| | | ABC 14 deposits | $749,158 |
| 36 checks to NCE | $1,225,105 | | |
| 36 checks to Taylor | $260,500 | | |
| 16 checks to LES | $160,000 | | |
| 21 checks to Bennett | $105,000 | | |
| **Account balance** | **$124,040** | | |

## CONTACT WITH SHELTON, TAYLOR, AND FREEMAN

### Shelton

On May 5, Grant contacted Gary Shelton and asked him to appear at the OI office the next day at 9:00 am. Shelton asked why Grant needed to talk to him. He asked if he could just talk to on the phone. After Grant's responses, Shelton reluctantly agreed to come appear.

### Taylor

It is OI policy to notify a union employee's supervisor to arrange an interview of the union employee. There are exceptions. Due to Burke being Taylor's supervisor, Grant contacted Taylor directly by phone at his home on Monday, May 5, at 7:00 pm. Grant identified himself and asked Taylor to appear at the OI office the next day at noon.

Grant detected that Taylor became immediately nervous. He wanted to know what it was all about. He asked if he needed an attorney. He asked if his coworkers would know that he is there. He also asked who else is being asked to appear. He asked what is going to happen to him. He also asked what would happen to him if he refused to come in. He stated that if he left to go to the offices at noon, others will know. He also asked if he would need a union representative. Grant responded appropriately to each of Taylor's concerns.

### Freeman

Grant contacted Freeman at his home and asked him to appear at the OI office at 4:00 pm the next day. Freeman asked, "What's this all about?" After Grant's response, Freeman asked "What if I refuse to come in?" Grant responded. Freeman was non-committal regarding his intention to appear.

---

## CASE STUDY—PART 3 EXERCISE

- Prepare a ROI of the Lanier second interview.
- Prepare KTOTs for Shelton, Taylor, and Freeman. (What interviewee category would you place each.)
- Prepare and Introductory Statement and Opening Statement for Shelton, Taylor, and Freeman.
- How would you respond to Shelton's questions?
- How would you respond to Taylor's questions and concerns?
- How would you respond to Freeman's questions?

# Case Study—Part 4

## PRELIMINARY MATTERS—GARY SHELTON INTERVIEW

On May 6, at 9:10 am, Shelton arrived at the OI office. Grant met Shelton in the lobby, introduced himself and led Shelton to an interview room. The interview room is equipped with audio and video recording equipment.

The following conversation took place prior to the interview commencing and was not recorded.

**JG**: "Thank you for coming in. You can call me Jack, and this is Mary Duncan, you can call her Mary. May I call you Gary?"

**GS**: "That's fine."

**JG**: "Great. Gary, we are going to video and audio record this meeting to make sure that everything that is said is captured accurately. Are you okay with that?"

**GS**: "I guess so. Will I be able to obtain a copy of the recording?"

**JG**: "There may come a time that you will be able to receive a copy; however, right now we would be unable to provide one to you. We will be preparing a report of our conversation today and if you feel the need, we can allow you to see the report after it is completed."

**GS**: "Okay."

**JG**: "Would you like something to drink or use the restroom before we get started?"

**GS**: "No."

## GARY SHELTON INTERVIEW TRANSCRIPT

**JG**: "Okay, it is Tuesday, May 6, the time is 9:37 am. I am Investigator Jack Grant from Nationwide Office of Investigations. Also present is Investigator Mary Duncan from Nationwide Office of Investigations and Nationwide Procurement Officer Gary Shelton. We have agreed to use first names. We are in interview room #

2 at the Nationwide Office of Investigations Chicago office. Mr. Shelton has agreed to allow the interview to be video and audio recorded. Is that correct Gary?"

**GS**: "Yes"

**JG**: "Gary, thank you for agreeing to meet with us today. Do you know why we need to speak with you?"

**GS**: "I have no idea."

**JG**: "As I mentioned on the phone, we are looking into procedures involving awarding construction contracts and would like your input."

**GS**: "Okay."

**JG**: "Gary, I need to tell you that notwithstanding Nationwide's policy that employees must cooperate with inquiries by our office, your presence here today is voluntary. You are free to leave at any time. If you do leave, I merely report that fact to the appropriate management official. Do you understand?"

**GS**: "Yeah."

**JG**: "Gary, are you aware of what our office does?"

**GS**: "Not really."

**JG**: "We look into internal matters that affect the efficiency of Nationwide's business operations. This includes waste of resources, mismanagement, and fraudulent activity, including theft and embezzlement and misappropriation of assets. Before we get started, I would like to ask you a few questions. Okay"

**GS**: "Okay."

**JG**: "Please tell me about your employment here at Nationwide."

**GS**: "Okay. I have worked here for about 25 years."

**JG**: "I'm relatively new here. It seems that everybody I talk to at Nationwide has twenty plus years on the job."

**GS**: "Yeah."

**JG**: "How long have you been the Procurement Officer?"

**GS**: "About thirteen years."

**JG**: "Who do you report to?"

**GS**: "John Nelson."

**JG**: "He's the AVP for Procurement, correct?"

**GS**: "Yes."

**JG**: "How do you like it here at Nationwide?"

**GS**: "It's okay, it puts food on my table."

**JG**: "Please tell me a little bit about your family?"

**GS**: "Am I here to talk about my family?"

**JG**: "No, I just like to know a little about the employees. You are not required to talk about your family."

**GS**: "Okay. I just want to know what this all about."

**JG**: "I will tell you. Gary, we will be discussing information we received that a couple of construction contractors are paying kickbacks to employees in return for receiving contracts. We will be discussing your role in this situation. We have been looking into this, so it is imperative that you are truthful with us today. If you are involved in this matter, our investigation will clearly indicate that you are. If you are not involved, our investigation will clearly indicate that you are not. So, Gary, if you are involved, it would be in your best interest to let us know now. Gary, are you involved?"

**GS**: "I resent this accusation."

**JG**: "Gary, I am not accusing you, I am merely asking you. Are you involved?"

**GS**: "I don't know anything about any kickbacks."

**JG**: "Okay, so let me ask you some questions. Let's start by telling me your duties as the Procurement Officer."

**GS**: "Okay. I receive Statements of Work from Operations or requests for supplies and materials. I then solicit bids from qualified vendors or contractors. I review the bids and determine who can best deliver on the request and award a contract."

**JG**: "Please tell us how you go about awarding prime contracts to construction firms."

**GS**: "Operations sends a Statement of Work for a proposed construction project. I send out a Request for Proposal to qualified contractors seeking bids for the job…."

**JG**: "Go on."

**GS**: "I pick the best bid and award the contract. What's this all about?"

**JG**: "Gary, as I said, we received information that some construction firms are paying kickbacks to employees in return for receiving contracts. And we need to ask you some questions concerning this. Do you understand?"

**GS**: "I feel like I am being singled out."

**JG**: "Gary, we are not singling you out. We have been conducting the inquiry and it is a normal step to talk with the Procurement Officer. You can understand that, right?"

**GS**: "I guess."
**JG**: "How do you deliver the Request for Proposals?"
**GS**: "I send them out by FedEx."
**JG**: "How are the bids returned to you?"
**GS**: "They are usually returned by FedEx."
**JG**: "Usually?"
**GS**: "Sometimes by mail."
**JG**: "Okay, Gary, let me ask you this. How many contractors do you solicit for a typical construction project?"
**GS**: "The policy is four."
**JG**: "So, you always solicit four?"
**GS**: "Well, most of the time"
**JG**: "Why not all of the time?"
**GS**: "Sometimes contractors have made it known that they are not interested in a project, so I might only solicit two or three in the geographic area."
**JG**: "How many times does that occur?"
**GS**: "I don't know, maybe 50% of the time."
**JG**: "How do you reconcile that with the policy of soliciting four contractors?"
**GS**: "What do you mean?"
**JG**: "What I mean is, is there some process or approval needed from your boss, Mr. Nelson, or somebody else before you solicit less than four contractors for a project?"
**GS**: "No."
**JG**: "So, you are able to decide if less than four contractors will be solicited?"
**GS**: "It is just the way it is done."
**JG**: "Gary, when we review the procurement files, are we going to see a notation or justification statement as to why less than four contractors were solicited?"
**GS**: "Uh No."
**JG**: "What will we find?" …… "Gary, what will we find?"
**GS**: "They will show that I solicited four contractors."
**JG**: "Even though you did not?"
**GS**: "Yes, it's the way it's done, to get the job done. Even if I do solicit four, some do not bid."
**JG**: "Do you solicit contractors that you know will not bid?"
**GS**: "Yeah, sometimes."

**JG**: "Okay. Just to be clear, sometimes you solicit contractors that you know will not bid, correct?

**GS**: "Yeah."

**JG**: "And sometimes you add the names of contractors to the file that you did not solicit. Is that correct?"

**GS**: "Yes, but I know they wouldn't submit a bid anyway."

**JG**: "So, do you do this so the procurement file will appear to meet policy if reviewed?"

**GS**: "Well, I guess, but it's the way it's done, to make sure the project is contracted to meet the demands of the Operations Department."

**JG**: "Has anyone, like Mr. Nelson, questioned you about this practice?"

**GS**: "No, he's just happy that things run smooth out here."

**JG**: "Does Mr. Nelson know that you don't solicit four contractors?"

**GS**: "Uh, not specifically, he probably realizes it. I am sure the other Procurement people do…to get the job done and have things run smoothly."

**JG**: "Are you sure, or are you just assuming?"

**GS**: "Assuming."

**JG**: "Has anybody ever reviewed your files?"

**GS**: "Some auditor came out once, a few years ago."

**JG**: "What did the auditor find?"

**GS**: "Nothing, he didn't say anything."

**JG**: "Do you know the name of the auditor?"

**GS**: "Andre…something."

**JG**: "Okay. Let me ask you this. What contractors do you always solicit?"

**GS**: "Uh, I guess Premier Construction and ABC Construction."

**JG**: "Do they always submit a bid?"

**GS**: "Yes, pretty much."

**JG**: "Pretty much?

**GS**: "Okay, always"

**JG**: "Is either Premier or ABC always awarded the contract that they bid?"

**GS**: "Well, yes. One of them wins but it's not fifty-fifty. Premier wins more than ABC. They are the best for the job and know how to work on Nationwide projects. They work well with the Project Manager. That's important."

**JG**: "Who is the Project Manager?"

**GS**: "Ray Burke."

**JG**: "You say that it is not fifty-fifty between Premier and ABC. What is the breakdown?"

**GS**: "I am not sure, but Premier does more work. Maybe sixty-forty."

**JG**: "Gary, I need to ask you this. Have you ever received anything from a contractor?"

**GS**: "No."

**JG**: "Have you ever been treated to a meal by a contractor?"

**GS**: "No."

**JG**: "Have you ever accepted money from a contractor?"

**GS**: "No Way!"

**JG**: "Have you ever borrowed any money from a contractor?"

**GS**: "No."

**JG**: "Have you ever received anything from another employee?"

**GS**: "Uh, like what?"

**JG**: "Money?"

**GS**: "Uh, No."

**JG**: "Gary, I see you hesitated before answering, are you sure?"

**GS**: "Well, I have borrowed money from time to time."

**JG**: "Okay, who from?"

**GS**: "Well, my assistant, Maria, just when I'm short for lunch. I pay her back on payday."

**JG**: "Who else?"

**GS**: "That's it."

**JG**: "Gary, I need you to think about this. Remember I said that we have been looking into this for a while. We know the answers to some of the questions we are asking, so it is imperative that you are truthful with us today."

**GS**: "Oh, let me think."

**JG**: "Gary, you certainly should be able to remember what other employees you have received money from."

**GS**: "Oh Yeah, I have borrowed money from Ray Burke."

**JG**: "Borrowed?"

**GS**: "Yeah"

**JG**: "Okay, how many times have you borrowed money from Mr. Burke?"

**GS**: "I don't know. A few times."

**JG**: "Gary, can you be more specific?"

**GS**: "I don't know, maybe 10 or 15 times."

**JG**: "Okay, when was the last time you borrowed money from Mr. Burke?"
**GS**: "I think last week. Why, what does this have to do with anything? Is it a crime to borrow money from an employee?"
**JG**: "Gary, we are just trying to understand what is happening here so we can look into the information we received. We want to make sure that any type of money being transferred from one employee to another or from a contractor to an employee can be explained. Do you understand?"
**GS**: "I guess."
**JG**: "Okay Gary, let's continue. How long have you been borrowing money from Mr. Burke?"
**GS**: "I don't know, maybe a few years."
**JG**: "Can you be more specific?"
**GS**: "Geez, I don't know, four or five years. So what?"
**JG**: "When was the last time you borrowed money from him?"
**GS**: "Maybe last week."
**JG**: "How much did you borrow last week?"
**GS**: "I think it was a hundred dollars."
**JG**: "Did you pay it back?"
**GS**: "No."
**JG**: "When will you pay it back?"
**GS**: "Well, the thing is, Ray never asks to be paid back, I offered, but he says not to worry about it."
**JG**: "Let me ask you this. How much money have you borrowed from Ray over the past few years?"
**GS**: "I don't know, it could be a few hundred dollars or so."
**JG**: "Gary, you said you borrowed a hundred dollars from Burke last week. So, since you have been borrowing money from him for the past few years, I have to believe it has been more than a few hundred dollars. So, how much could it be?"
**GS**: "It has to be a few thousand dollars or so."
**JG**: "A few thousand dollars. Could it be as much as $20,000?"
**GS**: "No way, not that much."
**JG**: "Could it be as much as $15,000?"
**GS**: "I don't think it has been that much. I haven't really thought about it."
**JG**: "If we ask Mr. Burke, how much money will he say he has given you over the years?"

**GS**: "I don't know what he will say."
**JG**: "Will he say he has given you over $20,000?"
**GS**: "I don't know. Maybe."
**JG**: "How much over $20,000 will he say?"
**GS**: "I don't know, I don't know."
**JG**: "Have you ever paid him back?"
**GS**: "I offered, but he said not to worry about it."
**JG**: "Do you offer every time?"
**GS**: "No, it is understood that he doesn't want to be paid back."
**JG**: "Why does he not want to be paid back?"
**GS**: "I don't know, he is a nice guy I guess, and he knows I struggle with two kids in college."
**JG**: "Do you do anything for him because of this?"
**GS**: "Nothing, what could I do?"
**JG**: "How does this happen? Do you call Ray and say, 'can I borrow a hundred dollars?'"
**GS**: "No, I have never asked him. He just drops by my office and says, 'Can you use some cash?' I say sure and he hands me some money."
**JG**: "Has he asked you to do anything for him?"
**GS**: "No, nothing."
**JG**: "Gary, do you find it strange that he has given you thousands of dollars over the past few years and wants nothing in return?"
**GS**: "No. He is just a nice guy and he likes me and knows it is hard with two kids in college."
**JG**: "Do you socialize with Burke?"
**GS**: "Not really."
**JG**: "Not Really? Tell me about meals he has treated you to."
**GS**: "Okay, he has taken me to lunch on a few occasions. So what?"
**JG**: "Where does he take you to lunch?"
**GS**: "Sam's Deli, uh, The Corner Bistro, and once in a while at Ruth Chris' Steakhouse. Actually, he took me to dinner at Ruth's Chris Steakhouse a couple of times."
**JG**: "Does anybody else go with you?"
**GS**: "Well a couple of times Jeff went with us, along with the owner of Premier."
**JG**: "Jeff?"
**GS**: "Jeffrey, Jeffrey Freeman. The Contract Administrator."
**JG**: "Who is the owner of Premier?"

**GS**: "John Novak, but Ray pays, so it wasn't like I was receiving anything from a contractor."
**JG**: "What do you talk about?"
**GS**: "We talk about the Cubs and the Bulls."
**JG**: "Did you discuss any Nationwide construction projects?"
**GS**: "Well, yeah, we did talk about the Distribution Center. Is that a problem?"
**JG**: "What about the Distribution Center?"
**GS**: "Well it would be natural to talk about it. Just that it is going well and that some change orders have to be issued due to lack of availability of some electrical supplies and the new supplier's costs are a little higher. That's all. Jeff handles that."
**JG**: "Who is the prime contractor for the Distribution Center?"
**GS**: "Premier."
**JG**: "Have you ever socialized with Novak without Ray being present?"
**GS**: "No."
**JG**: "Have you ever socialized with Jeff?"
**GS**: "He has taken me to lunch a few times."
**JG**: "Where has he taken you?"
**GS**: "He likes Luigi's."
You: "So, is that where he takes you?"
**GS**: "Yes"
**You**: "How many times?"
**GS**: "I don't know, a dozen?"
**JG**: "Does he always pay?"
**GS**: "Yeah."
**JG**: "What do you talk about with Jeff?"
**GS**: "Just work issues, Nationwide, stuff like that."
**JG**: "Who is the owner of ABC Construction?"
**GS**: "That would be Roger Billings."
**JG**: "Have you ever socialized with Billings?"
**GS**: "Never."
**JG**: "Okay, Gary, you mentioned that when you have a meal with Novak and Ray, you discuss the Distribution Center. Please explain how the solicitation and award for the Distribution Center occurred."
**GS**: "Well, we placed national advertisements in the papers and trade magazines around four years ago asking firms to send a

letter of interest with a resume and evidence that they have the ability to handle the project. I had lots of interest because the job is huge. I picked four companies to solicit, which I did around three years ago."

**JG**: "What firms did you solicit."

**GS**: "Tri-State from Iowa, an uh, uh a firm from Milwaukee. Uh, I can't think of their name."

**JG**: "That makes three with Premier."

**GS**: "Oh yeah, ABC."

**JG**: "Yes, you said you always solicit Premier and ABC."

**GS**: "Yes. Premier hired ABC as a sub since the job is so big."

**JG**: "Gary, let me ask you this. Are you aware of any employee receiving anything from a contractor?"

**GS**: "No."

**JG**: "Gary, I need to ask you this. Is Ray receiving money from Novak-Premier?"

**GS**: "If he is, I wouldn't know about it."

**JG**: "Do you believe Ray is receiving money from Premier?"

**GS**: "I wouldn't know."

**JG**: "Is Ray receiving money from Billings-ABC?"

**GS**: "If he is, I wouldn't know about it."

**JG**: "Okay Gary, please tell me about the trips Novak has provided."

(Note: Grant had no information that Novak or anybody has provided a trip; however, due to the methods employed by contractors to gain favor with influential employees, trips are a usual unallowed gratuity or bribe. Grant was "fishing" with this Open Question.)

**GS**: "Trips?"

**JG**: "Yes, trips."

**GS**: "Do you mean the golf retreat?"

**JG**: "Tell me about the golf retreat."

**GS**: "Well, Novak flew us to Las Vegas for a golf retreat."

**JG**: "Us?"

**GS**: "Us, me, Ray, Jeff, and a few others. It was all on the up and up."

**JG**: "Who are the few others?"

**GS**: "Roger, and some guys that work at Premier."

**JG**: "Roger?"

**GS**: "Roger Billings.

**JG**: "You said you never socialized with Billings."

**GS**: "I forgot. Plus, I thought you meant if Roger paid."

**JG**: "Who are the guys that work at Premier who went to Las Vegas?
**GS**: "It was two guys I never met them before. I can't remember their names. Mike and uh, Louis, I think."
**JG**: "Did your wife go?"
**GS**: "No. Nobody's wives went"
**JG**: "Okay, nobody's wives went. Did you take somebody else?"
**GS**: "Uh, No. Novak had some women there. I didn't do anything though."
**JG**: "You didn't do anything with the women? Is that what you are saying?"
**GS**: "Yes, Ray and the others did though?"
**JG**: "But not you."
**GS**: "No."
**JG**: "Where did you stay?"
**GS**: "The MGM Grand."
**JG**: "How long were you there?"
**GS**: "Four or five days. We mostly played golf."
**JG**: "When was this?"
**GS**: "Three years ago."
**JG**: "Did Novak pay for the entire trip?"
**GS**: "Yeah, but it was all on the up and up. It had nothing to do with Nationwide. I didn't do anything for it. Its just that Burke asked me if I wanted to go along. I've never been to Vegas."
**JG**: "What other trips?
**GS**: "Huh? No, that's it."
**JG**: "What about Roger? Did he provide you with any trips?
**GS**: "Never."
**JG**: "Okay, Gary, let's move on. "Do you have any dealings with the sub-contractors for the projects?"
**GS**: "No, I just contract with the prime contractors. They employ the subs. Ray and Jeff would deal with the subs."
**JG**: "Gary, do you have any other source of income other than Nationwide?"
**GS**: "No."
**JG**: "Does your wife work?"
**GS**: "Yeah, she is a part time librarian."
**JG**: "Does she have any other source of income?"
**JG**: "No"
**JG**: "Gary, how many bank accounts do you have?"

**GS**: "Just one checking and one savings both with my wife. Why do you want to know that?"

**JG**: "I'm just asking. "You have two children in college, is that correct?"

**GS**: "Yes."

**JG**: "Do either of your children work?"

**GS**: "They both work part time sometimes."

**JG**: "Where do they work?"

**GS**: "My son works at Pizza Supreme."

**JG**: "What about your daughter."

**GS**: "She sometimes works at the Campus Coffee Corner."

**JG**: "Do they have separate bank accounts?"

**GS**: "Yes, why?"

**JG**: "Would there be any reason if we examined all of the Shelton's bank accounts, that we would find any deposits from sources other than from known employers?"

**GS**: "No."

**JG**: "Gary, would there be any reason that during the course of our investigation someone would tell us that you have taken money to award a contract to a particular contractor?"

**GS**: "No, …not unless someone would think that the money that Burke lent me was to award a contract. Did someone say that I have?"

**JG**: "Gary, just like we are not going to tell anybody what you have told us here today, we are not going to tell you what anybody else has said. Who would think that the money you have taken from Burke is to award particular contracts?

**GS**: "I don't know. Nobody."

**JG**: "Let me ask you this, and I want you to think carefully about your answer. "Is the money you received from Burke to ensure that either Premier or ABC are awarded contracts?"

**GS**: "I just send out the RFPs and they just submit the bid, whoever is lowest wins."

**JG**: "And you said that Premier and ABC always win, correct?"

**GS**: "Yes, that's the way it works out."

**JG**: "Okay, let's go over a few things that you told us that I want to be clear about. You said that you send RFPs to contractors that you know will not bid, correct?"

**GS**: "Yeah"

**JG**: "And sometimes you include names of contractors in your file that you do not solicit for a bid, correct?"

**GS**: "Yeah, but like I said, I know they wouldn't bid anyway, and it is to make things run smoothly out here."

**JG**: "And, you stated that Ray has given you money over a few years that might be over $20,000 and you have not paid him back, is that correct?

**GS**: "Yeah."

**JG**: "Okay. Gary, do you suspect that ABC and Premier are involved in bidding irregularities?"

**GS**: "Um, listen, I don't know what they do amongst themselves. How would I know what they do?"

**JG**: "Gary, you seem like a reasonable and an intelligent person. I find it hard to believe that you do not know what is going on. What do you think a judge would believe when they hear that you have been receiving money from Ray, falsifying the procurement files, have taken a trip to Vegas with Novak and Billings, paid for by Novak at the time you solicited bids for the Distribution Center? Plus, Novak and Billings win all of the bids?"

(Note: It is difficult to detect Shelton's attitude, as well as experience his non-verbal and paralinguistic communication during the interview without listening to the audio and viewing the video. Initially, Shelton's attitude was combative, but nervous. He did not want to talk about his family. He wanted to get to the point of the interview. At the end of the Opening Statement when Grant asked him if he was involved, he replied that he resented the accusation. This is a defensive exclamation. He really did not resent the accusation. As the interview progressed, Shelton's answers were incriminating; however, he tried to mitigate his involvement by claiming "It's the way things are done to run smoothly," and "Is it a crime to borrow money from an employee?" When asked what a judge would think and his responses reviewed, Shelton's resistance almost ended. He physically withdrew in his chair and kept his head down.)

**GS**: "Judge?"

**JG**: "Yes, a Judge. This is serious business. Let me tell you what I think. I think that you are deeply involved in this and know exactly what is going on."

**GS**: "All I know is that Ray gives me money, which is not a crime, and I do what is necessary to make things run smoothly out here. This is the way it works."

**JG**: "Okay Gary. I want to clarify some things that we talked about. I need to ask you this and I want you think before answering. Have you received money from a contractor?"

**GS**: "Never."

(Note: This was a strong denial. He was eager to say he never took money from a contractor. So, more than likely he has not, at least directly.)

**JG**: "Let me ask you this. Have you ever been offered money from a contractor?"

**GS**: "No."

**JG**: "Have you ever thought about taking money from a contractor?"

**GS**: "Well, it crosses my mind, because I know how much money they make. But I never would."

**JG**: "Why wouldn't you take money from a contractor?"

**GS**: "I would be too afraid of getting caught."

(Note: At the beginning of the interview there was not clear and convincing evidence to accuse Shelton. There certainly is now. This is the time to make the accusation. Shelton's resistance has ended. He is waiting to tell the truth.)

**JG**: "Okay Gary, like I told you before, we have been conducting this investigation for a while and know what is going on. We wanted to talk to you today to give you an opportunity to be honest with us. Let me say this, you have not been totally honest with us. Our investigation shows without a doubt that Novak and Billings are paying Burke to ensure that they receive all the store construction contracts in the region, and to ensure Premier was awarded the contract for the Distribution Center. And Ray is giving you money to ensure you award Premier or ABC the contracts and not to ask questions. Gary, we know that you are not the main person involved here. You have been a dedicated employee for many years and a good family man. It was just easier, and safer for you to go along and not ask questions. It's not like Burke gave you millions of dollars, he just gave you a small amount over the years compared to others. You know the money Burke gives you is not a loan. You are awarding the contracts to Premier and ABC and not questioning their bidding practices because it is easier to go along. Isn't that correct?

(Note: This is a soft accusation. Grant told Shelton that he knows that he is not the main perpetrator in this scheme and that he is only receiving a small amount of money compared to others. Shelton is able to psychologically minimize his participation in the scheme and more readily confess at this time.)

**GS**: "Things just run smoothly out here."

(Note: One last effort to mitigate his culpability.)

**JG**: "Gary, you know what I'm saying is true, right?"

**GS**: "Yes."

(Note: Shelton just confessed!)

**JG**: "Okay Gary. I appreciate your honesty. Gary, tell me how it started."

**GS**: "I don't know, some years ago, when I first was promoted to Procurement Officer, Burke came to my office and introduced himself. He was the new Project Manager. He took me to lunch. He said that he and I would be working together, and it was my and his job to make things run smoothly. He is an intimidating person. He said that he knows the best construction firms to handle all the construction requirements in the area. He said he thinks it would be best for us if they received the contracts. He identified one of the firms at that time as Premier Construction. He told me that the owner was involved in some organized crime, but not to worry because they do a good job. He said the owner would really appreciate the consideration.

**JG**: "Go on."

**GS**: "Later, when the first store remodeling job was proposed, Burke took me to lunch and told me to remember the conversation we had. He said Premier wants the job. He said another firm, ABC should be solicited. He told me I should choose the lowest bidder of the two. I asked him what if another firm bids lower. He looked at me and told me to make sure that doesn't happen. He said, 'Remember who we are dealing with'."

**JG**: "Okay, then what?"

**GS**: "That's it."

**JG**: "What about ABC?"

**GS**: "One day when another small construction job was proposed for an outdoor pavilion at one of the larger stores, Burke came to my office and said the job should go to ABC. Premier and ABC both submitted bids. I did not solicit any other firm but added two names to the file. ABC bid low and was awarded the contract.

After that, Burke came in and asked if I could use a couple hundred dollars. I said, 'sure'." Then it just continued."

(Note: The interview continued with more details about different construction contracts, falsified files, lunches, money received, conversations with Burke, etc. This additional information was eliminated from this instruction. The important lesson here is how the interview was structured, developing incriminating information, leading Shelton to the truth, and obtaining a truthful, legal, and ethical confession.)

**GS**: "What's going to happen to me?"

**JG**: "As this investigation continues, you are going to have some choices to make. You will have to think about what is best for you and your family."

**GS**: "Am I going to lose my job?"

**JG**: "Gary, when we finish our investigation, we will report our findings to the bosses. They will make any decision concerning your job. We are going to continue the investigation and see where it takes us. Let me ask you this. Who else is involved?"

**GS**: "Nobody that I know of. I don't like one of Burke's foremen, Peter Taylor, but I don't know if he knows anything."

**JG**: "Okay Gary, before we end this interview, do you have anything you want to add?"

**GS**: "No. I just don't want to lose my job"

**JG**: "I understand. Do you have any questions for us?"

**GS**: "No."

**JG**: "Are there any questions that I didn't ask you that you thought I was going to ask you?"

**GS**: "I didn't' know what to expect."

**JG**: "Mary, do you have any questions?"

**MD**: "Not at this time."

**JG**: "Gary thank you for coming in today. If you think of anything you want to tell us, please give me a call. I advise you not to discuss this interview with anyone else, other than an attorney if you choose to consult with one.

**GS**: "Do you think I need an attorney?"

**JG**: "Gary, I am unable to advise you whether or not you need an attorney. That is your choice. If you do retain an attorney have them call me. Here is my card. We will probably need to talk to you again soon. We will let you know. Thanks. Okay the time is 11:34 am."

**End of Interview Transcript**

After the interview ended and the recorder was turned off, Grant asked Shelton if he would wait in Duncan's office for a few minutes. Grant called Williams and gave him a summary of Shelton's interview. Williams told Grant to stand by. Ten minutes later Williams called Grant and told him Shelton will be suspended and not allowed to return to his office pending the outcome of the investigation. Williams instructed Grant to have Shelton call AVP Nelson. Grant went down the hall to Duncan's office Shelton called Nelson. After the phone call, Shelton told you he has been suspended and was ordered to go home and not to return to his office and to not speak to anybody about this investigation. Shelton, visibly upset, asked Grant what he should tell his wife. Grant responded that it was up to him. Shelton left.

## CASE STUDY—PART 4 EXERCISE

- Identify Shelton's evasive responses.
- Evaluate the interview.
- Prepare an ROI of the Shelton interview.

# Case Study—Part 5

On Tuesday, May 6 at 12:10 pm Peter Taylor called the OI Office. He informed Duncan that he wanted his union representative present; however, the representative was in St. Louis and will not be available until Thursday. Duncan told Taylor to arrive with his union representative on Thursday, May 8, at noon.

Duncan obtained the former Contractor Adminstrator Sean. Flannigan's home address and phone number in Boise, Idaho. Duncan called him at his home. After introductions and stating the purpose of the call, Flannigan told Duncan that he did not want to talk and asked her not to call back.

After lunch at Luigi's, Grant and Duncan went to Shelton's office with a cart and boxes, packed the pertinent procurement files, and took them to Duncan's office.

Freeman, who was non-committal with Grant's request to appear at 4:00 pm, had not arrived by 4:30 pm. Grant called Freeman's office and left a voicemail. Grant called Freeman's home number. Freeman answered and advised that he did not report to work today because he was sick. He stated he will probably be available by Friday. Tentative arrangements were made for Freeman to appear on Friday, May 9 at 9:00 am.

Between the afternoon of May 6 and the morning of May 8 Grant and Duncan reviewed the procurement files removed from Shelton's office. There were many indications of falsified files. Premier and ABC had in fact been awarded all the contracts in the geographic area. The files consistently listed that four firms were solicited, two of those always being Premier and ABC. Some files revealed that only Premier and ABC submitted bids of the four firms listed as being solicited. Other files revealed that two firms other than Premier and ABC who submitted bids, submitted high bids which caused them to lose the award.

## PRELIMINARY MATTERS—PETER TAYLOR INTERVIEW

On Thursday, May 8, at 12:15 pm Taylor arrived at the Office of Investigations offices with his union representative, William Menendez. Grant led Taylor and Menendez to the interview room. Grant introduced Duncan. Grant informed Menendez that he was allowed to counsel Taylor during the interview; however, unnecessary interruptions would end the interview. Grant also informed Taylor and Menendez that the interview would be recorded, and they agreed. Duncan offered Taylor and Menendez refreshments and a chance to use the restroom. They declined.

### Peter Taylor Interview Transcript

**JG**: "Today is Thursday, May 8. The time is 12:36 pm. I am Investigator Jack Grant from Nationwide Office of Investigations. Also present is Investigator Mary Duncan from Nationwide Office of Investigations, Peter Taylor, Nationwide Foreman, and Mr. William Menendez, union representative from the International Association of Retail Construction Workers. We are in interview room # 2 at the Nationwide Office of Investigations Chicago office. Mr. Menendez is here at Mr. Taylor's request. Mr. Taylor and Mr. Menendez have agreed to allow the interview to be recorded. Is that correct Mr. Taylor?

**PT**: "Yes."

**JG**: "Mr. Menendez?"

**WM**: "Yes."

**JG**: "OK, Mr. Taylor, may I call you Peter?"

**PT**: "Yes."

**JG**: "Mr. Menendez, how should I refer to you?"

**WM**: "You can call me Bill."

**JG**: "Great, Thank you. As I mentioned earlier you can call me Jack, and this is Mary. First, I must tell you that I appreciate you appearing here today."

**PT**: "Did I have a choice?"

**JG**: "Peter, yes. We cannot force you to be here and participate. Even though it is Nationwide's policy that employees cooperate with inquiries by our office, including appearing for interviews and answering questions honestly, you have a choice. You are free to leave at any time. You are here voluntarily. If you decide not to participate and leave, I merely report this to management and if they decide to take disciplinary action because you did not follow company policy, that would be their choice. However, I would hope you will stay and listen to what I have to say and answer some questions. Do you understand?"

**PT**: "Some choice."

**JG**: "Peter, do you understand that you have a choice. You are here voluntarily. You can leave at any time. Do you understand that?"

**WM**: "May I interject?

**JG**: "Please do."

**WM**: "Peter, you can leave if you want, but you will face company consequences if you do. I advise you to listen to what they have to say."

**PT**: "OK."

**JG**: "So Peter, do you understand what I told you, that you are here voluntarily and can leave at any time?"

**PT**: "Yes"

**JG**: "Great. Peter, do you know why we need to meet with you today?"

**PT**: "Just what you told me on the phone."

**JG**: Yes, we are looking into the awarding of construction contracts and would like your input."

**PT**: "I don't know how I can help you."

**JG**: "Okay. Peter, are you aware of what our office does?"

**PT**: "Not Really."

**JG**: "We look into internal matters that that affect the efficiency of Nationwide's business, such as waste of resources, mismanagement, and fraudulent activity. Before we get started, I would like to ask you some preliminary questions. Okay?"

**PT**: "Go ahead."

**JG**: "Peter, does anybody other than Bill know that you are meeting with us today?"

**PT**: "I didn't tell anybody."

**JG**: "Okay, but does anybody know you are here?"

**PT**: "I don't think so."

**JG**: "Okay, Thanks., Please tell me about your employment here at Nationwide."

**PT**: "What do you want to know?"

**JG**: "How long have you been employed with Nationwide?"

**PT**: "About fifteen years."

**JG**: "Okay. What positions have you held?"

**PT**: "I was hired as a carpenter. I have been a foreman for seven or eight years."

**JG**: "What do you do as the foreman?"

**PT**: "I supervise carpenters and electricians and make sure the contractors are on the job and doing their job."

**JG**: "Who do you report to?"

**PT**: "The Project Manager, Ray Burke."

**JG**: "How do you like working here?"

**PT**: "You know, I have been laid off 3 times. That has not been easy for me. Trying to raise a family and everything."

**JG**: "I understand. Tell me about your family."

**PT**: "I have a wife and three young girls."

**JG**: "How old are your girls?

**PT**: "The oldest is eleven, Leslie is 10, and Julie, the youngest is seven."

**JG**: "Girls can be a handful."

**PT**: "Yeah."

**JG**: "Does your wife work?"

**PT**: "Yeah, at Lumber Depot. I worked there before I worked here."

**You**: "Is that where you met your wife?"

**PT**: "No, she started working there a couple of years ago."

**JG**: "Okay. Peter, how far did you go in school?"

**PT**: "I finished High School then went to trade school to be a carpenter."

**JG**: "Okay Peter, thank you.

**PT**: "Can you tell me why I am here?"

**JG**: "Yes. Peter we are looking into information we received that some construction contractors are paying kickbacks to some Nationwide employees for the purpose of being awarded contracts and overlooking bidding and contracting irregularities. We need to ask you some questions regarding this information. You should understand that we have been looking into this for a while, so it is imperative that you are straightforward with us today. Peter, our investigation shows that you are involved. Could you please tell us about your involvement?"

(Note: Peter should be classified as a suspect. Information from Lanier revealed that Taylor is involved. Lanier stated that Taylor found out about the relationship between Burke and

Premier and ABC. Burke is paying him to remain silent. Lanier and Taylor formed FBN to facilitate the payments. The Illinois Secretary of State's records corroborates that Taylor is a principal of FBN. In addition, Lanier provided bank documents that show Taylor received payments from FBN that originated with Premier and ABC. So, with this clear and convincing evidence, accusing Taylor, and asking him to explain his involvement is appropriate.)

**PT**: "What?"

**JG**: "Please tell us about your involvement"

**PT**: "How could I be involved in anything like that? I mean, I am just a foreman. What would I know about that?"

**JG**: "Peter, I want you to think about this. Like I said, we have been looking into this for a while and know a lot. It is imperative that you are truthful with us today."

**PT**: "I am being truthful."

**JG**: "Peter are you saying that you are not involved?"

**PT**: "I am just a foreman. How could I receive kickbacks?"

**JG**: "Peter, we know you are involved. If you are not receiving kickbacks, tells us what your involvement entails."

**PT**: "I don't know what you are talking about."

**JG**: "Okay Peter. Let me go over a few things with you. Please explain your involvement with an entity known as FBN Enterprises.........................Peter, can you please tell me your involvement with FBN Enterprises?"

**PT**: "Uh, I need to speak to Bill. In private."

(Note: FBN was certainly a Topic to ask Taylor about. Since Taylor did not readily confess to his involvement with the fraud, it was best to reveal knowledge of FBN. If the FBN payments to Taylor were legitimate or not connected to a fraud scheme, then Taylor's response would be different. He could explain the legitimate or alternate purpose of the payments. He did not.)

**JG**: "Okay. Peter, we will give you a few minutes. It is now 12:59 pm. Mary Duncan and I will leave the room to provide privacy for Peter Taylor and William Menendez. The recorder is now being turned off."

**JG**: "OK, it is now 1:07 pm. Mary Duncan and I are back in the interview room and the recorder has been turned back on. Approximatively one minute ago, Mr. Menendez exited the interview room to retrieve Mary Duncan and me. Are we ready to continue?"

**WM**: "Yes."

**JG**: "Peter?"

**PT**: "Yeah, I guess."

**WM**: "I talked to Peter. He is willing to talk about FBN Enterprises. However, he wants assurances, that he will not lose his job."

**JG**: "Bill, Peter. I can offer no assurances. Peter has choices to make. He can participate in the interview and answer questions truthfully, he can answer untruthfully, or he can leave. We will continue with our investigation and report the findings to senior management. If Peter is untruthful or decides to leave, we will report that to senior management. They will make any decision regarding job status. If Peter is truthful with us today and continues to be truthful and cooperates with us now and in the future, the only thing that I will assure both of you is that I will let whoever needs to know, that Peter was in fact totally truthful and cooperated and continued to cooperate with us during our investigation. Do you understand?"

**WM**: "OK. Peter?"

**PT**: "I don't want to lose my job."

**JG**: "Peter, I understand how you feel. I have had many people like you in similar situations sitting across from me who felt the same way. What they found is that the best course of action to take was to be truthful and cooperate. You know that this is the right way to go, don't you?"

**PT**: "Do I need an attorney?"

**JG**: "Peter, I cannot advise you whether or not you need an attorney. That is your choice. Can we continue?"

**PT**: "Go ahead."

**JG**: "OK. Peter, tell me about FBN Enterprises."

**PT**: "Alright. A few years ago, Ray told me to form this company with Bob Lanier. I didn't know what it was about. I assumed he had some business deal going where he didn't want his name on it. He said I would be paid a little bit of money for my trouble. So, I met with this guy Jerry, a friend of Ray's and he filled out some paperwork and I signed it."

(Note: The above statement is Taylor's posturing, trying to explain his involvement. His statement is in contradiction to what Lanier told Grant and Duncan, that Taylor found out about

Burke, Premier, and ABC, and Burke is keeping Taylor silent by paying him. So, Burke had Lanier and Taylor form FBN to funnel the kickbacks. According to the review of FBN Bank documents, Taylor received 36 checks totaling $260,500. That is not a little bit of money. What Taylor told you is a good start; however, it is your job to lead Taylor to a total truthful statement.)

**JG**: OK, go on.

**PT**: "That's it"

**JG**: "OK. Tellme about Bob Lanier?"

**PT**: "He is a friend of Ray's. He is a sub-contractor and provides electrical supplies to the job."

**JG**: "OK. Go on."

**PT**: "What else do you want to know?"

**JG**: "I would like you tell me your total involvement with FBN."

**PT**: "That's all I know."

**JG**: "OK, let me ask you this. Does FBN provide any service?"

**PT**: "No, Bob and I just went to see Jerry and sign papers. I don't do anything."

**JG**: "Tell me about Jerry?"

**PT**: "He is some lawyer friend of Ray's."

**JG**: "OK. When did you and Bob sign the FBN papers with Jerry?"

**PT**: "I don't know, a few years ago. Six, maybe seven years ago. Shortly after I became foreman."

**JG**: "OK. You said that Burke would pay you a little bit of money for your trouble. How much did he pay you?"

**PT**: "Uh, I don't know, a few hundred dollars, maybe."

**JG**: "A few hundred dollars? Peter, you know that you received more than a few hundred dollars, and so do we. Please tell me about the payments you have received from FBN."

**PT**: "Payments?"

**JG**: "Yes, payments."

**PT**: "Uh."

**JG**: "Peter, as I told you, we know a lot. It is important that you are truthful with us."

**PT**: "OK. Ray told me to sign the documents because he has an arrangement with a couple of contractors who do work for Nationwide. Money is deposited into the FBN bank account. Bob handles it all. Every so often Bob gives me a check."

(Note: Taylor is getting closer to the truth.)

**JG**: "How many checks have you received?"
**PT**: "I don't know maybe a dozen."

(Note: A dozen is a good start. There are 36 checks.)

**JG**: "How much money have you received from FBN?"
**PT**: "I don't' know, a few thousand dollars or so."
**JG**: "Peter, listen to me, there is no reason to not tell us the truth here. I already told you that we know a lot. Part of this process is to see if you are going to be completely honest with us. Just giving us a little bit is not going to work. Do you understand?"
**PT**: "I am not sure how much money I've received, maybe $50,000 or so, Okay. I need the money for my family. My oldest girl has special needs, and it costs a fortune for her care. My wife only works part time and has to stay home most of the time to take care of her. I don't make that much money here. I have been laid off three times. Burke told me he could help, so he arranged for me to be paid."

(Note: Taylor is closer to the truth. However, the review of FBN documents revealed that Taylor has received $260,500. Taylor is explaining his participation in the fraud by claiming he needs the money for his daughter. Maybe he does. Taylor is trying to distance himself from the fraud by implying that Burke is a great guy who knows that Taylor needs the money for his daughter and is there to help. Also, based on what Lanier stated about Taylor finding out what's going on, Burke did not just out of the goodness of his heart arrange for Taylor to be paid.)

**JG**: "Peter, why would Ray offer to help you to the tune of $50,000 or more?"
**PT**: "Like I said, Ray has this relationship with two contractors. Ray has something going on with that weasel Shelton, the contractors are paying Burke for the contracts. I saw what was going on. Ray always has a lot of cash, always drives expensive cars. He bought a million-dollar house. He is a braggart. I told Ray that I knew something was going on. He offered me an opportunity to make some money to take care of my girl. So, I did it."

(Note: Taylor has revealed the truth about how the arrangement occurred. The bottom-line of why he is involved.)

**JG**: "Okay Peter, thank you for telling us that. When did you tell Ray that you knew something was going on?"

**PT**: "Right before Bob and I formed FBN. He said I could use the money for my girl."

**JG**: "Okay. Who are the two contractors?"

**PT**: "Who else, Premiere and ABC."

**JG**: "Does Premier and ABC make payments to FBN?"

**PT**: "Yeah. But I don't handle the FBN money, Bob does."

**JG**: "How much money have they paid FBN?"

**PT**: "I have no idea."

**JG**: "You said you have received around $50,000. When we obtain the FBN documents from the bank, is it possible that we will see that you have received over $300,000?"

**PT**: "It can't be that much. I didn't keep track."

**JG**: "Could it be as much as $150,000?"

**PT**: "I don't know, it could be."

(That as far as that line of questioning needs to go. Taylor does not need to confess to the exact amount. Ever since FBN, was mentioned, Taylor is trying to figure out who talked. Could it be Burke, Lanier, or somebody or something else. Taylor cannot be told that Lanier supplied the bank documents. When the investigation progresses to the United States Attorney's Office, the FBI will obtain a subpoena for the FBN documents from the bank. At that time, Taylor will review the documents and acknowledge the actual amount.)

**JG**: "Okay. Let's move on. You said that Premier and ABC are paying Burke for contracts. Doesn't Gary Shelton approve and award the contracts?"

**PT**: "Ha-ha. Ray runs the show here. Shelton is just a pawn. Shelton just 'rubber stamps' anything Burke tells him to 'stamp'."

**JG**: "What does Shelton receive for rubber stamping everything Burke tells him to stamp?"

**PT**: "I don't know, I am sure Ray takes care of him."

**JG**: "Okay. Let me ask you this. What do you know about Premier?"

**PT**: "The owner, John Novak is some sort of organized crime figure. I heard he has people killed. There is some sort of Federal Grand Jury on him now. I am scared to death of him. Now I'm really cooked. I want protection for me and my family. The ABC guy, Roger, is mob connected too. Him and Novak run everything in this town."

**JG**: "OK Peter. What can you tell me about Jeffrey Freeman?"

**PT**: "Freeman is Novak's boy. He is slick. Novak had Ray get him the Contract Administrator's job so they can clean up on the change orders for the Distribution Center. They are making a killing."

(Note: "clean up" and "making a killing" are colloquialisms for making a lot of money.)

**JG**: "How do you know that?"

**PT**: "Ray told me that most of the change orders are false."

**WM**: "Excuse me. This is a little bit out of my league, shouldn't Peter have an attorney present?"

**JG**: "Bill, that would be Peter's choice. I will tell you this. As you can hear, what Peter is saying is serious. I am glad he is being honest with us today and he needs to continue to do so. If Peter wants an attorney, that is his choice."

**WM**: "Peter, I think you need to stop and talk to an attorney to protect your interest. This is beyond my ability. I will do the best I can for your job, but this is beyond my capability."

**PT**: "I can't believe this is happening. I need an attorney. Will Ray know I was in here?"

**JG**: "Listen, Bill, you cannot advise Peter to not answer questions. That is Peter's decision."

**PT**: "I want to stop and talk to an attorney. Will Ray know I'm here?"

**JG**: "We are not going to tell Ray that you were here. However, you should be aware that it is always a possibility that he will find out. What you need to decide is how you are going to move forward. Are you going to cooperate with us or not? This investigation will more than likely move out of our control and be handled by the United States Attorney's Office and the FBI. I suggest that you make a decision to cooperate with them when that time comes."

**PT**: "The Feds are already investigating Novak. I want an attorney."

(Note: Since Nationwide investigators are not government law enforcement, Taylor is not in custody. Taylor asking for an attorney does not trigger any required warnings. Miranda is not involved and does not prohibit continued questioning. However, Taylor has already confessed. His union representative is advising Taylor to talk to an attorney. It is prudent to stop asking Taylor questions at this time to avoid claims of coercion and false imprisonment.)

**JG**: "Ok Peter. We will stop the interview for now. Bill, I am cautioning you to not discuss what you heard here today with anybody. It is critical that you do not. In addition, you may be called to testify to what you heard today."

**WM**: "Oh Gosh."

**JG**: "Do either of you have any questions for me?"

**PT**: "What's going to happen to me?"

**JG**: "I cannot answer that. Just continue to be truthful and cooperate. That is your best course of action." "Anything else?"

**PT**: "No."

**WM**: "No."

**JG**: "The time is now 1:47 pm, the recorder is being turned off."

**End of Transcript**

After the recorder was turned off Grant asked Taylor and Menendez to sit tight for a few minutes. They agreed. Grant went to Duncan's Office and called Williams and briefed him on Taylor's interview.

Williams called the VP of Store Operations, Wilbur Gunn. Gunn made the decision that Taylor could not return to work and would be "taken out of service" pending a company hearing per the union rules.

> (Note: Union employees have due process contract considerations and cannot be disciplined without a formal hearing. Management/Non-Union employees, such as Burke, Shelton, and Freeman, can be fired "at will" without a hearing, unless they have an employment contract that states otherwise. Burke, Shelton, and Freeman do not have employment contracts.)

Burke, as Taylor's management supervisor, would normally be the one to take his subordinate out of service. Gunn decided that he would talk to Taylor. Gunn will also prepare and fax to the OI Chicago office a formal "Removal from Service" letter to be given to Taylor.

Fifteen minutes later, Grant returned to the interview room with two copies of the letter and called Gunn directly from his cell phone and handed the phone to Taylor. After Taylor spoke to Gunn, Grant handed the letter to Taylor and provided a copy to Menendez. Taylor began weeping and asked if he was going to lose his job. Grant told him that he could not answer that question and added that Taylor's best course of action was to be truthful and cooperate with the investigation. Grant provided Taylor and Menendez a business card and instructed them to call if anything happens. Grant also told Taylor that if he retains an attorney to have the attorney call. Duncan escorted Taylor and Menendez out of the office and again warned them to not discuss this with anybody.

## CASE STUDY—PART 5 EXERCISE

- Evaluate the Peter Taylor interview.
- Discuss Taylor's involvement in the fraud as it pertains to the Fraud Triangle and the 10-10-80 Rule.
- Prepare an ROI of the Taylor Interview.

# Case Study—Part 6

## PRELIMINARY MATTERS—JEFFREY FREEMAN INTERVIEW

On Friday, May 9 at 9:05 am, Jeffrey Freeman arrived with an attorney, identified as George Hutchinson from the law firm of Hutchinson, Dickens, and Fenster. Hutchinson provided his business card. Grant introduced himself and Duncan and asked to be referred to by first names. Freeman and Hutchinson did not reciprocate. Refreshments and use of the restroom were offered and declined.

Hutchinson stated that Freeman resigned his employment with Nationwide that morning and is only appearing as a courtesy to Nationwide. Grant informed Hutchinson and Freeman that the interview would be recorded to ensure that everything was captured accurately. Hutchinson also wanted to record the interview; however, Grant informed him that Office of Investigation policy does not allow their interviews to be recorded by interviewees or their representatives. Hutchinson balked at this policy. Grant informed Hutchinson that there could come a time when a copy of the recording would be made available. Hutchinson still balked and Grant suggested that the interview not take place. Hutchinson conceded and agreed to commence with the interview.

## JEFFREY FREEMAN INTERVIEW TRANSCRIPT

**JG**: "Mr. Freeman, thank you for coming in today. Today is Monday, May 9, and the time is 9:17 am. As discussed, this interview is being recorded and you agreed to this. Is that correct?

**JF**: "I guess."

**JG**: "Mr. Hutchinson?"

**GH**: "Yes, however I must object to your policy that does not allow me to also record the interview."

**JG**: "So noted. Okay. I am investigator Jack Grant. Also present is Nationwide Investigator Mary Duncan, Jeffrey Freeman, and his attorney, George Hutchinson. We are in interview room number 2 at the Office of Investigation Chicago office. Mr. Freeman, your presence here is voluntary and you are free to leave at any time. Do you understand?"

**GH**: "I already informed you that my client appearing here today is a courtesy. Of course he can leave at any time."

**JG**: "Yes, I am repeating this for the recorder. Do you understand that your presence here is voluntary and you are free to leave at any time?"

**JF**: "Yeah."

**JG**: "Mr. Freeman, why did you resign this morning?"

**JF**: "I don't like working here."

**JG**: "Okay. Do you know what our office does?"

**JF**: "I have no idea."

**JG**. "We look into matters that affect the efficiency of Nationwide's operations, including waste, misuse of assets, and fraud."

**JF**: "I thought you caught shoplifters."

**JG**: "Well, our office does investigate organized criminal shoplifting rings."

**JF**: "Wow."

**JG**: "Mr. Freeman, do you know why we need to speak with you today."

**JF**: "I have no idea. Only what you told me on the phone. That you are looking into something."

**JG**: "Yes. We are examining a Contract Administrator's duties."

**JF**: "The duties are published. You can find them there."

**JG**: "That's true; however, like I said, our office looks into the efficiency of Nationwide's operations. We would like to see if there are any deviations from the procedures. Before we start, I would like to obtain some background information. Okay?"

**JF**: "What do you want to know?".

**JG**: "Please tell us where you reside."

**JF**: "I reside at 11021 Lakeside Drive, Chicago, Illinois, 60692, my phone is 312-555-6432; my cell phone is 312-555-9876."

**JG**: "Thanks. Please tell us about your employment here at Nationwide."
**JF**: "You want to know about my employment here at Nationwide?"
**JG**: "Yes, please."
**JF**: "What exactly do you want to know?"
**JG**: "How long had you worked for Nationwide before you resigned this morning?"
**JF**: "I am sure you know exactly how long I worked for Nationwide."
**JG**: "I do. Can you tell me?
**JF**: "I can, …three years."
**JG**: "Thank you. Please tell me where you worked prior to your employment with Nationwide."
**GH**: "I am sure you have that information in Mr. Freeman's personnel records. I am advising Mr. Freeman not to answer any questions regarding his past employment. It has nothing to do with Nationwide. Please move on."
**JG**: "Mr. Hutchinson, it is normal to inquire about an employee's previous employment."
**GH**: "Mr. Freeman is no longer an employee. I am advising Mr. Freeman to not answer questions regarding past employment."
**JG**: "Okay. Mr. Freeman, could you please tell me about your duties as a Contract Administrator with Nationwide."
**JF**: "I administered contracts."
**JG**: "What does that entail?"
**JF**: "Do I really need to sit here and tell you what my job entailed. Can we get to the point of this interrogation?"
**JG**: "Mr. Freeman, Mr. Hutchinson, this is not an interrogation, I am merely asking you questions."
**JF**: "I'm sorry, I don't see the point in this. Read the procedures."
**JG**: "Mr. Freeman, is there a reason you do not want to answer our questions?"
**JF**: "I just don't like wasting my time."
**JG**: "Okay, let me ask you this. In the past three years while working at Nationwide, were you simultaneously employed somewhere else?... Let the record show that Mr. Freeman is consulting with his attorney."
**JF**: "No."
**JG**: "Okay, other than your salary from Nationwide, what other source of income do you have?"

**JF**: "That is not your business."
**GH**: "I am advising my client not to answer questions regarding his income. Can we get to the point of this...these questions?"
**JG**: "As I said, we are examining a Contract Administrator's duties."
**GH**: "I am sure my client was not asked to appear to talk about Contract Administrator's duties when you can look those up in the manual."
**JG**: "What was your client expecting to discuss?"
**GH**: "Listen, I think we are done here. Jeff, let's go."
**JG**: "Okay, gentleman, I appreciate you taking the time to come in. The time is 9:39 am. The interview is ended, and the recorder is being turned off."

**End of Transcript**

Hutchinson and Freeman rose from their chairs, Grant heard Hutchinson whisper to Freeman, "This was a big waste of time." Grant ushered Hutchinson and Freeman out of the offices.

**Instructor's Note:**

The Freeman Interview Objective should be based on Knowledge and Theory, which includes:

- Associated with an organized crime figure, Novak.
- Nationwide Contract Administrator for 3 years.
- Previously worked for Premier Construction for 10 years.
- Lanier stated that Freeman was put in place to facilitate false change orders for the Distribution Center. Taylor stated the same.

  The Theory should be that Freeman, an associate of Novak is probably involved in the scheme to defraud Nationwide by facilitating false change orders under Novak and Burke's instruction. So, the interview objective should be to have Freeman acknowledge his involvement, if it is true. However, based on what is known, it is important to not ask questions that would provide Novak information about the investigation. Additionally, it is critical that questions do not jeopardize Lanier and Taylor. So, the objective should be to have Freeman answer questions regarding his duties and practices as a Contract Administrator.

  An experienced investigator, or a new investigator being coached by the supervisor, would know that when an attorney is present, the tone of the interview changes. It is difficult to build rapport. The interview almost did not occur; however, it was worth the attempt in the off-chance that Freeman and Hutchinson would come in and disclose the scheme in return for some leniency. However, keep in mind that Nationwide Retail Company investigators are in no position to offer leniency. Freeman and Hutchinson realize this.

So, since Freeman and Hutchinson did not come in with "their hat in hand" and disclose the scheme, it should be apparent that they were there to learn about the investigation with no intention to cooperate. So, what could have been done differently? Could there have been a better attempt to build rapport? Maybe. However, Freeman's attitude was one of total uncooperativeness. He did not want to answer simple questions.

Asking Freeman about his prior and simultaneous employment, as well as other sources of income were good questions. The fact that Hutchinson did not want Freeman to discuss his prior employment is very telling. Hutchinson wanted Grant to bring up Premier and Novak.

Grant asked Freeman if he knew why he needed to talk to him. Freeman said he had no idea. If he would have said that he was there to talk about a kickback scheme, then that would have been Grant's opportunity to ask an open question: "Please tell me what you know about a kickback scheme." However, since Freeman said he had no idea, it was better not to mention the scheme. Freeman did not want to talk about Contract Administrators duties and Hutchinson tipped his hand by saying he is sure that is not why his client was there. In addition, Hutchinson would not divulge what Freeman expected to discuss, and ended the interview.

- After Freeman's interview, Grant called Williams and updated him on Freeman's resignation and the interview. Grant opined that Freeman and Hutchinson were fishing for information so they could inform Novak. Grant agreed.
- Grant contacted the AVP Contract Administration, Henry Ernst. Ernst told Grant that he did in fact receive Freeman's resignation that morning. Ernst was surprised that Freeman left so abruptly. Ernst added that Freeman did a good job.
- Grant and Duncan then went to Freeman's recently vacated Nationwide Office. A search revealed that Freeman must have

removed all personal items. Files from a four-drawer cabinet were seized for later examination. A monitor and keyboard were on the desk; however, there was no computer.

- Grant called Ernst who stated Contract Administrators are issued a company laptop that they utilize at their office, in the field, or at home. Ernst said he will contact Freeman and have him return it. Grant informed Ernst that the files in Freeman's office are being seized in furtherance of an investigation.
- Williams called Grant and discussed interviewing Burke, Novak, and Billings. Grant and Williams opined that more than likely the three are aware of the investigation. It was decided to interview Burke, since he is an employee and obligated to appear and cooperate.
- Grant contacted Burke and asked him to appear that day at noon. As expected, Burke asked the reason. Grant responded and Burke agreed to appear.
- Prior to Burke's expected arrival, Grant and Duncan prepared a KTOT for Burke.
- By 12:30 pm, Burke had not arrived. Grant called his office phone and left a voicemail. At 1:00 pm, Duncan called AVP Wilbur Gunn and learned that Burke injured his back earlier at the Distribution Center job site and was taken to the hospital.
- Grant called Williams and provided an update. Williams informed Grant that it is time to brief Nationwide's General Counsel and CEO. At 3:00 pm Grant, Duncan, Williams, the General Counsel, and the CEO participated in a Zoom Meeting. The General Counsel gave the go-ahead to contact the United States Attorney's Office.

## CASE STUDY—PART 6 EXERCISE

- Discuss Freeman's attitude.
- Evaluate the interview.
- Prepare an ROI of the Freeman interview
- Prepare a KTOT for Burke. After the Interview Preliminary Topics Section include an appropriate Opening Statement.

## CASE RESOLUTION

The United States Attorney's Office accepted the Nationwide. All of the individuals and entities involved were criminally and/or civilly prosecuted. All individuals who were criminally prosecuted pleaded guilty and received prison sentences and restitution orders. All entities who were civilly prosecuted acknowledged responsibility and paid restitution and penalties.

# APPENDIX A
## *KTOT Example*

Following is a KTOT example involving an allegation that contractor John Simpson (Simpson), President of Camden Contractors (Camden), is paying the tuition at Granger University for XYZ Procurement Officer Fred Thompson's (Thompson) daughter Anne in return for Thompson awarding Camden a $20 million contract to build three stores. Albert Murray (Murray), CFO of Camden, made the allegation. Murray provided documentation supporting the allegation.

The preliminary investigation revealed that Thompson did award a contract to Camden for $20 million to build three stores. Granger University provided that Anne Simpson's tuition was paid via an anonymous benefactor.

### KTOT—FRED THOMPSON

**Knowledge**

- Thompson has been employed at XYZ for 10 years.
- Thompson has been a procurement officer for 6 years.
- Thompson's daughter, Anne, recently was accepted as a freshman at Granger University.
- Anne's tuition was paid by an anonymous benefactor.
- Whistleblower Albert Murray, CFO of Camden Contractors, alleged that Simpson, with Camden funds, is paying for Anne's college tuition and expenses for 4 years in return for Thompson awarding Camden a $20 million contract to build three stores.
- Murray provided supporting documents to support his allegation.
- Thompson did award a $20 million contract to Camden to build three stores.

## THEORY

- Thompson accepted a kickback of college tuition for his daughter Anne to award a $20 million contract to Camden Contractors for the construction of three stores

## INTERVIEW OBJECTIVE

- To have Thompson acknowledge/confess to accepting the college tuition and expenses from Simpson/Camden in return for awarding the contract to Camden if it is true.

(**Note**: It is important to add, "if it is true" to this objective. KTOTs could be discoverable, and the correct Forensic Mindset should be presented. If the allegation is not true, your objective should not be to have Thompson confess.)

(**Note**: If Thompson confesses, have him relate the details. If Thompson denies the accusation, reveal some evidence. If he continues to deny the accusation, have Thompson explain the evidence. If he provides an alternate explanation that raises doubt of your clear and convincing evidence, retreat from the accusation and move to the Key Topics.)

## KEY TOPICS

- Job duties
- Contract award to Camden for three stores
- Other bidders
- Meeting with bidders
- Choosing Camden
- Conversations with Simpson
- Meetings with Simpson
- Socializing with Simpson
- Simpson offering anything of value
- Thompson accepting anything of value
- Anne's tuition
- The anonymous benefactor
- What will Simpson say

# APPENDIX B
## *Interview Example*

In the following interview example, ABC Retail Company (ABC) Investigator Jack Grant (Grant) required information about ABC's cleaning supply procurement process pursuant to an allegation of vendor kickbacks to an ABC buyer. To accomplish this, Grant interviewed ABC Vice President of Procurement Harold Smith (Smith). The interview took place in Smith's office. The interview was recorded and transcribed. First read the transcript of the interview, then read the Report of Interview (ROI) that effectively captures the interview.

### INTERVIEW TRANSCRIPT

**JG**: "Good afternoon Mr. Smith. I am Jack Grant. I spoke to you on the phone earlier. I appreciate you taking the time for me. I am brand new here and am getting the lay of the land."

**HS**: "No Problem, Glad to Assist. It gives me a chance to stop reading all of these spreadsheets. And please call me Harold"

**JG**: "Thank you. And call please call me Jack. As I mentioned, I am recording this interview with your permission."

**HS**: "No problem."

**JG**: "Great. Thanks. Harold, as I told you on the phone, I would like to gain an understanding of the procurement process as it pertains to purchasing cleaning supplies. Okay?"

**HS**: "Sure."

**JG**: "Before we get started with the main questions, could you please provide me with a little background on your employment with ABC?"

**HS**: "Sure. I started here about 13 years ago. I was hired as a procurement manager. I was then promoted to Director of Procurement. When the former Vice President of Procurement left, I was considered the most qualified among the 3 Directors, so I was given the job."

**JG**: "How long were you in each position?"

**HS**: "Let's see, I was the manager for about 3 or 4 years. I can't quite recall. I can have my secretary provide that information to you if it is important."

**JG**: "No that is not necessary, thanks. Go on."

**HS**: "Okay, let me see. I was the Director for about 3 years. Hold on let me check something. Yes, 3 years."

**JG**: "So, you have been the VP for how long?"

**HS**: "About 6 years, give or take a couple of months."

**JG**: "Thank you. Please explain how ABC purchases cleaning supplies."

**HS**: "Sure, ABC has one designated buyer who handles all procurement of cleaning supplies for all ABC stores and offices throughout the United States.

**JG**: "Who is the buyer?"

**HG**: "Ross Weaver."

**JG**: "Where is Weaver Located?"

**HS**: "He is located here in ABC Headquarters."

**JG**: "Thank you, go on."

**HS**: "Weaver has established a network of cleaning supply vendors throughout the United States. Weaver issues Purchase Orders to the vendors annually. Each ABC store and office requests supplies that they anticipate are needed for a 3-month period. Weaver will then contact the vendor in the specific region to deliver the supplies to the stores and offices in that region."

**JG**: "When do the vendors get paid?"

**HS**: "When the supplies are delivered, the store or office management sends Weaver the delivery manifest and Weaver authorizes payment through Accounts Payable."

**JG**: "Does Weaver ever solicit new cleaning supply vendors?"

**HS**: "Near the end of every year, Weaver should seek out other vendors and send them, as well as the established vendors, a Request for Proposal to provide cleaning supplies for the following year. Weaver should review the proposals and select the most responsive bidder to receive the Purchase Orders."

**JG**: "Please tell me what you mean by responsive bidder?"

**HS**: "A responsive bidder is one which has the ability to meet ABC's needs and has offered the lowest price for like products."

**JG**: "Harold, thank you for your time, I appreciate it. It was a pleasure meeting you. Please do not discuss the fact you were interviewed today with anyone, including Weaver."

**HS**: "Okay. It was a pleasure meeting you. Good luck here at ABC."
**JG**: "Thanks. If I have additional questions may I give you a call?"
**HS**: "Absolutely."

**End of Transcript**
**See the ROI below**

**Report of Interview**

**ABC RETAIL COMPANY—OFFICE OF INVESTIGATIONS**

**ROI**

| Case # | 13-0512 |
|---|---|
| Interviewee | Harold Smith,<br>ABC VP of Procurement |
| Interviewers | Primary: Jack Grant<br>Second: N/A |
| Location | Office of Harold Smith<br>ABC HQ 5th Floor |
| Day and Date of Interview | Thursday, May 9, 2013 |
| Start Time | 2:30 pm (approx.) |
| End Time | 3:00 pm (approx.) |
| Date of Report | May 10, 2013 |

---

On Thursday, May 9, 2013, I interviewed Harold Smith (Smith), Vice President of Procurement for ABC Retail Co. (ABC). The interview was conducted in Smith's office on the fifth floor of ABC Headquarters. The interview commenced at approximately 2:30 pm and concluded at approximately 3:00 pm.

Smith **stated** that he understood the purpose of the interview, which was for him to provide information regarding the procurement process involving cleaning supplies. Smith **provided** that he has been employed at ABC for 13 years. He began his career at ABC as a Procurement Manager. After several years, he was promoted to Director of Procurement. He held that position for 3 years and was then promoted to Vice President of Procurement, a position he has held for approximately 6 years.

Smith **explained** that ABC has one designated buyer, Ross Weaver (Weaver) who handles all procurement of cleaning supplies for all ABC stores and offices throughout the United States. Weaver's office is located in ABC Headquarters. Smith further **explained** that Weaver has established a network of cleaning supply vendors throughout the United States. Weaver issues Purchase Orders (POs) to the vendors annually. Each ABC store and office requests through Weaver supplies that are anticipated for a 3-month period. Weaver will then contact the vendor in the specific region to deliver the supplies to the stores and offices in that region. When the supplies are delivered, the store or office management sends Weaver the delivery manifest and Weaver authorizes payment through the Accounts Payable section of the Finance Department.

Smith **added** that near the end of every year, Weaver should seek out other vendors and send them, as well as the established vendors, a Request for Proposal (RFP) to provide cleaning supplies for the following year. Weaver should review the proposals and select the most responsive bidder to receive the POs. Smith **explained** that a responsive bidder is one which has the ability to meet ABC's needs and has offered the lowest price for like products.

Upon conclusion of the interview, I **asked** Smith not to discuss the interview with anyone including Weaver. Smith **agreed** to do so. Additionally, I **received** a commitment from Smith that if I had additional questions, I could contact him.

ROI prepared by
(Signature) ________________________________ Date __________
Supervisor Approval
(Signature) ________________________________ Date __________

**Note: The bolded action verbs are for instructional use. Do not bolden your words in the ROI.**

The ROI certainly captured the pertinent information found in the Question-and-Answer transcript and is much easier to read. This interview was a short simple interview that lasted approximately 30 minutes with just a little over two pages of questions and answers.

# INDEX

Note: **Bold** page numbers refer to tables and *Italic* page numbers refer to figures.

For Product Safety Concerns and Information please contact our EU
representative GPSR@taylorandfrancis.com
Taylor & Francis Verlag GmbH, Kaufingerstraße 24, 80331 München, Germany

www.ingramcontent.com/pod-product-compliance
Ingram Content Group UK Ltd.
Pitfield, Milton Keynes, MK11 3LW, UK
UKHW022317250926
475702UK00046B/899
* 9 7 8 0 3 6 7 7 7 1 4 6 1 *